HAYDEN

HAYDEN

John Stubbs

William Heinemann Australia

Published 1989 by
William Heinemann Australia
a division of the Octopus Publishing Group
Cnr Salmon and Plummer Streets, Port Melbourne, Victoria 3207

Edited by Venetia Nelson
Designed by R.T.J. Klinkhamer

Typeset in Australia by Southern Cross Typesetting, Keysborough
Printed in Australia by Australian Print Group, Maryborough

National Library of Australia
cataloguing-in-publication data:

Stubbs, John (John N.).
  Hayden

  Bibliography.
  Includes index.
  ISBN 0 85561 339 4.

  1. Hayden, Bill, 1933-   . 2. Politicians –
  Australia – Biography. 3. Australia –
  Governors-General – Biography. 4. Australia
  – Politics and government – 1965-
  I. Title

994.06092

The author and publisher thank the following for permission to reprint copyright material:
Angus and Robertson Publishers for extracts from *The Hawke Ascendancy* by Paul Kelly, 1984, and
Hayden: a political biography by D. J. Murphy, 1980; Allen and Unwin Australia for extracts from
Machine Politics in the Australian Labor Party by Andrew Parkin and John Warhurst (eds), 1983, and
Wran: an unauthorised biography, by Michael Steketee and Milton Cockburn, 1986; Blanche d'Alpuget
for extracts from *Robert J. Hawke: a biography* by Blanche d'Alpuget, Penguin Australia/Schwartz
Publishing Group, 1984; and Graham Freudenberg for extracts from *A Certain Grandeur: Gough
Whitlam in politics*, Sun Books, 1978. Permission has been sought to reproduce extracts from *A Bunch
of Amateurs* by J. A. Cumes published by Sun Books/Macmillan in 1988.
Every effort has been made to trace and acknowledge copyright material, but should an infringement
or incorrect acknowledgement have occured, the author and publisher tender their apologies.

Contents

For Romey, Will, Susie and Sasha

ACKNOWLEDGEMENTS

On the long journey from the cottage at the dusty end of Mabel Street to the manicured lawns of Yarralumla, Bill Hayden has been associated with people through the full range of humanity, from crooked Queensland coppers to British Royalty. I am grateful to those who have known him who have taken time to talk to me about this complex, admirable and difficult man.

It is one of the conundrums that are common in Bill Hayden's life that he has been fiercely protective of the privacy of his family while pursuing a career that makes trespass by outsiders inevitable. It has, in the large part, been a penalty he has reluctantly accepted as the cost of attempting to further the cause of social justice and reform in this nation. A book of this sort — over which he did not have, and did not seek, any control or influence — must come close to the ultimate intrusion. I am particularly grateful to him and to Dallas Hayden for the good grace with which they accepted my endeavours, and for the time he made available for interviews during a particularly busy and stressful period in his life.

My perspective on Bill Hayden's life is slightly different from most of the political commentators I have known over more than twenty-five years spent writing about Australian politics or working for politicians. My father was born opposite the Palms chutney factory in East Brisbane, a few streets from where Bill Hayden spent his childhood, and later I was subject to a cheerless educational experience while growing up in Cunnamulla in far west Queensland. As a result I have a keener admiration for Hayden's achievements, and an appreciation of the difficulties he has faced in dealing with the powerful forces based in Sydney and Melbourne that shape Australian society.

It is not possible to understand Bill Hayden without some knowledge of the social, religious and political conflicts and changes that have taken place in his lifetime and in which he has often been a passionate participant. Australia has been well served by the quality of the accounts of these turbulent years written by people including Gough Whitlam, Graham Freudenberg, Paul Kelly, Blanche d'Alpuget, Laurie Oakes, Robert Murray and Clem Lloyd. Tragically, Denis Murphy, who wrote a biography of Hayden which was published in 1980, died soon after being elected as a Labor member of the Queensland House of Assembly in 1983 before he had an opportunity to fulfil his promise as an historian and reforming politican. I have drawn on the work of these and other writers and journalists, including John Edwards, Alan Ramsey, Michelle Grattan, Janet Hawley, Sally Loane, Brian Toohey, Peter Bowers, Geoff Kitney, Barry Cohen and Jim McClelland, and would like to express my gratitude as well as my admiration for their work. Australia's political cartoonists are unmatched and I thank Bruce Petty, Alan Moir and John Spooner for permission to reproduce examples of their work.

I extent particular thanks to my friend and former boss Clyde Cameron and his wide Doris who provided much encouragement, as well as accommodation, information and fine red wine.

Others to whom I am grateful for assistance, which was often exceptionally generous, include: Gough Whitlam, Cathi Collier, Sir James Killen, Chris Hurford, Caroline Wilson, Ruth Gardiner, Tom Burns, Brian Sweeney, Eric Walsh, Norm Harriden, Di Fingleton, Betty Surmon, Mr and Mrs Ron Baynes, Natalie Funell, Wayne Swan, Kim Swan, Ann Warner, Deane Wells, Bob Gibbs, Norm Gulbransen, Joan Hipkins, Ed Casey, Greg Crafter, Di Gayler, Neil Collins, Dick Klugman, Graham Richardson, Peter Walsh, John Dawkins, Tom Uren, Richard Farmer, Ken Davidson, Gay Davidson, John Black, Mick Young, Harpoon Harry, Harry and Terri Williamson, Louise Holgate, John Orr, Tony Koch, Peter Bowers, Ian Collier, Don Henderson, Edgar Waters, Yvonne Miller, Quentin Dempster, Steve Bishop, Paul Keating and Bill Glasson. Christian Kemp of Skiptrace in Brisbane and Mrs E.E. Tucker, historian of Lismore, who are still searching for George Hayden, assisted with research. Thanks also to Sasha Stubbs, tape transcriber, whose unsolicited interpolations on John Dawkins' graduate tax have been omitted, Susie Stubbs, roving red-haired graphic designer, for international intelligence, and Will Stubbs who discovered that fish rained on Ipswich when Bill Hayden became Governor-General.

I have had help and understanding too from those professionally involved, including two of my editors at the Sunday Sun, Bill Murray and Steve Fox, and the paper's owner, Frank Moore, as well as Teresa Pitt, Louise Adler and Maryann Ballantyne who have been involved in publishing the book and Venetia Nelson who edited it with an unusual blend of firmness and sensitivity.

The people who are responsible for the project being started and finished are, in reverse order, my wife Romey, and John Timlin who runs an outfit in Melbourne called The Almost Managing Co., a title that is more fitting for the author.

Part I

The Boy from Mabel Street

ONE

Before the
dew is off
the grass

*It showed there was a lot of free thinking in
the family.*

Bill Hayden

ON 16 February 1933, in Brisbane's Fortitude Valley in the
depths of the Great Depression a tattooed middle-aged
American piano-tuner married a young widowed Queensland
barmaid. On the same date fifty-six years later their eldest son, Bill
Hayden, who was a month old when his parents were married, was
sworn in as Australia's Head of State, 'an event so improbable to many
of those who thought they knew him that they resolved to witness the
ceremony in the flesh, if only to satisfy themselves it really happened'.[1]

The mystery of Bill Hayden, the policeman who became a radical, the
atheist and reputed republican who became Governor-General, began
with the circumstances of his birth, and was reinforced by his upbringing.
He had a difficult childhood: both his parents had experienced hardship
and tragedy before they met. Their wedding took place in the most
difficult of circumstances, but they had decided to stick together in those
times that held little hope for a better future. The day after their wedding
they registered the birth of their son.

But the Depression went on too long for George Hayden, and by the time his eldest son Bill Hayden reached adolescence the marriage was scarred by poverty and ill health and the erratic and sometimes violent temper of an alcoholic and ageing father who earned little and spent much of it on drink. The family's problems were compounded by a significant age difference between Hayden's parents; his father was fifty-one and his mother twenty-seven on their wedding day.

Both parents were secretive: his father was evasive about his past, both with authorities and his family, and his mother constantly advised her family against confiding in friends. Bill Hayden, an attractive man who inspired loyalty but seldom felt confident enough to return it in full measure, was in a way following in a sad family tradition. He seldom formed or maintained close friendships, or confided in associates. It was a handicap in political life that sprang from the roots of his childhood. 'I think you a little unfair wanting fairly personal details of my younger years,' Hayden wrote to journalist John Edwards in 1972. 'I say that kindly, not nastily or resentfully ... I would be fearful that they would appear in print. I have a brother, two sisters and a mother who could be considerably hurt if some aspects of our childhood were to become public knowledge.'[2]

There are mysteries unresolved even to Hayden in the background and almost bizarre life story of his father. Only one photograph of him is known to exist and in 1988 Bill Hayden did not have a copy of it. He has no photographs of himself as a baby or small child; it is an index of his early deprivation. Both parents had a powerful influence in moulding traits that shaped his life and his political career, but many of those influences were negative; in a real sense Bill Hayden is his own creation, a late developer who drove himself to the limit of his endurance and abilities and devoted those efforts to the improvement of the underprivileged. His strengths and weaknesses combined on 3 February 1983, at a turning point in Australia's political history when, in an unprecedented act of personal sacrifice that stemmed in part from a characteristic lack of self-confidence, he relinquished the leadership of the Australian Labor Party on the day a national election was called. The capricious fate that determined he would be denied the nation's most powerful office also, by guaranteeing the defeat of Malcolm Fraser and victory for his party under the leadership of his rival Bob Hawke, established the circumstances for his appointment to its highest, yet potentially most pompous and impotent, position.

At the time Hayden was born his father was a raffish drunk whose best friend was a Maori wrestler. His only attempt at establishing a business had been ruined by the Depression, but he had nevertheless married the barmaid who had borne his son despite the fact that they were forced to live on meagre rations. But at the time Hayden was becoming aware of his family's place in the world George Hayden was tiring of the struggle, and his mother, while caring for four young children, faced constant financial worries. Later, even while exercising significant political power, Bill Hayden retained powerful feelings of insecurity, forever fearful that his children would slip back into the restrictive depressing surroundings from which he had broken free. He actively sought and then accepted the post as Governor-General in the hope that someday his children and their children might be proud of the 'old chap' from the wrong side of the river who had risen so far. The same Bill Hayden had himself been among the most effectively scornful critics of the office, saying at one time that the Governor-General should be put in his proper place — as a character on leave from *The Merry Widow*. He also dismissed a former Liberal politician, Sir Paul Hasluck, who went on to occupy the post with some distinction, as 'a bumptious little bastard who is really only good for a future Governor-General'. Two of the key mysteries surrounding Hayden's life will long be argued but never resolved: if he had remained leader of the Labor Party for just a few more hours in 1983, could he have led it to victory in the election he said a drover's dog could win? and what sort of Prime Minister would he have made?

At the time of his becoming Governor-General there was a softening in Hayden's memories of his father that had not been apparent earlier in his life, but it is plain he grew up in a disadvantaged and troubled family. His first memory is of being woken by his father crashing dead drunk on the narrow verandah of their tiny Brisbane home. Yet his father's radical background and distrust of authority shaped the son's early political views; his mother imbued him with her emotional sympathy for the underdog.

Both Hayden's parents had been married and widowed before they met. His mother's family was Irish; her great grandfather, James Dawson Newbury from County Tyrone, married Mary Brown in St James, Sydney, in 1855. Neither could write their names and their wedding certificate records the fact that they both 'made their mark', a common practice then for those who were illiterate. Violet Hayden's father was born John Newbury at Kempsey on the Macleay River in New South Wales, but took the name John Brown. Hayden believes that he may have done this in an attempt to disguise his Irish origins. John Brown moved to Queensland and went broke attempting to grow sugar cane in the early days of that industry. He had set himself up as a blacksmith when Violet was born at Brandon, near Ayr, in north Queensland on 24 March 1905. Her mother, Kathleen Mary Byrnes, known as Kate, was born in Casino, New South Wales, and her family, who were rural workers, were also of Irish descent. There are, as was common in those days, some variations in ages and details on various surviving official certificates and records, but it appears that Bill Hayden's mother, Violet, was still only nineteen when, in 1924, she was married for the first time at Longreach in central western Queensland to Cornelius Claude Quinn, a twenty-seven-year-old shearer. The following year they had a son, Colin. On 31 January 1926, her husband drowned while swimming in Con Hole on the Boulia Road near Winton, another remote hard little town further along the trail.[3] The young widow Violet became a barmaid in Rockhampton on the Queensland coast.

George Hayden, according to entries on his death certificate and some other documents, was born at Oakland, California, in 1881. A check of official records in Oakland in 1988 showed no trace of him. The family tradition as recorded by Bill Hayden's friend Denis Murphy is that George Hayden was the son of a Californian contractor and a product of a strong Catholic family who wanted him to become a priest. Bill Hayden's mother Violet told Murphy that George had spent some time in a Catholic seminary before fleeing, around the turn of the century, to join the American merchant navy in which he endured extraordinary hardships as a deckhand on old cargo boats and became involved in radical industrial activities. 'Hayden senior himself was something of a radical who was opposed to the economic system which had all but destroyed his livelihood and he was vocal in his support for the ideas of the Industrial Workers of the World, a militant American revolutionary organisation that Billy Hughes had outlawed in Australia in 1916.'[4]

Bill Hayden can remember his father, a short, wiry man, who habitually wore a dust coat and a felt hat, often, when drunk, singing a rowdy radical song that started something like: 'Early in the morning before the sparrow farts, the hobo rises from his nest ...' He could not clearly remember more of the verses. Historian Edgar Waters and folklorist Don Henderson have traced several versions of this song, including one that was collected by Banjo Paterson around the turn of the century, and which appears in *Old Bush Songs*, edited by A.B. Paterson, under the title 'Hang The Man Who Works'. The polite version collected by Paterson contains the lines:

> We rise up in the morning, we rise up from our doss,
> We rise up in the morning, before the dew is off the grass;
> From The Harp [Hotel] into The Shamrock we fly like birds of the air,
> And never cry a go, my boys, till bottled up with beer.

All the versions of the verse are tales of a professional bum, or hobo, wandering the country cadging provisions, preferring that than to 'work upon the harvest and let the cocky [farmer] starve us'. The common refrain is 'humming our chuck wherever we go, and hang the man who works,' or 'And if we've luck, we'll hum our cheques and shoot the man who works.'[5] Waters and Henderson say the version sung by George Hayden was one of many variations of a song that was popular with members of the Industrial Workers of the World.

Bill Hayden remembers his father's recitals often being followed by a stirring harangue on the evils of capitalism and the promise of revolution. An Industrial Workers of the World membership ticket shown to me in 1989 by Pat Mackie who was, like George Hayden, once a merchant seaman on ships operating out of the west coast of North America, carries a statement of the organisation's philosophy which matches the sort of views Bill Hayden remembers his father expressing. Under the heading Preamble, it says:

> The working class and the employing class have nothing in common. There can be no peace so long as hunger and want are found among millions of the working people and the few who make up the employing class have all the good things in life. Between these two classes a struggle must go on until the workers of the world organise as a class, take possession of the earth and the machinery of production, and abolish the wage system.

Mackie, who played a prominent and radical role in one of the major Australian industrial disputes in Australian history at Mt Isa in Queensland in the 1960s, has pointed out to me that the IWW regarded political parties and unions as no better than bosses or Communists. The Preamble on the membership ticket also says: 'The trade unions foster a state of affairs which allows one set of workers to be pitted against another set of workers in the same industry, thereby helping to defeat one another in wage wars ... We are forming the structure of the new society within the shell of the old.'

Sometime before World War I, a few years before Prime Minister Billy Hughes banned the IWW in Australia, George Hayden jumped ship, probably in Sydney. Somewhere, possibly in the seminary, he had learnt the art of piano tuning and he followed that occupation for most of the rest of his life. During World War I he became manager of a music store at Lismore in northern New South Wales. There, on 23 December 1916, aged 35, he married Jean Anderson, a 25-year-old described on the wedding certificate as a tailoress. Unlike his second marriage, that wedding did not take place in a Catholic church, but in the local Presbyterian manse. On that wedding certificate George Hayden gave his birthplace as San Francisco, his father's name as John Hayden and his mother's maiden name as Margaret Richardson.

In the early 1920s he moved to Rockhampton on the central Queensland coast and established his own business selling and tuning pianos, and there his first wife, Jean, died slowly of tuberculosis. It was in Rockhampton that George Hayden met Violet who was working as a barmaid in the pub where he drank each day. Soon after she had become pregnant, George's business collapsed; it was not a good time to be selling musical instruments or tuning pianos. George and Violet decided to move south to the anonymity and hope of employment that Brisbane offered. These were hard times. Violet's young son from her first marriage, Colin, was sent to live with the family of her sister who was married to Tommy Millward, a shearer at Longreach. Violet also had a brother who lived in Longreach where he worked as a street sweeper.

There was little sympathy for the unemployed in rural Queensland and particular antagonism to those with radical ideas. 'The inability to find employment appeared to have produced a feeling that, in some way, the individual was responsible for being unemployed rather than being a victim of conditions of the economic system,' C.G. Law said, discussing the situation then in Queensland.[6]

In country centres, the unemployed became targets for public hostility. The most serious disturbance was the Cairns riot of Sunday 17 July, 1932. Citizens, wanting to ensure that the annual show would be held on time, sought to evict local unemployed camped in showground buildings. When the 'squatters' resisted an ugly brawl broke out in which cane knives, iron bars, fence posts and clubs were used ... Four thousand townspeople forcibly evicted up to 170 unemployed ... one hundred people were injured ... The 'nomadic unemployed' were escorted out of town and the show took place as scheduled.[7]

At that time, in a similar Queensland coastal town between Cairns and Brisbane, Violet Quinn was two months pregnant and George Hayden was bankrupt.

Things weren't much better in Brisbane, where authorities feared civil disorder among the destitute. When an Unemployed Workers' Movement was established, the Brisbane City Council, at the direction of the State Government, closed camps that had been established for the unemployed. Hayden later heard a story of how his father had been a victim of the almost sadistic humiliation to which the unemployed were sometimes subjected. His parents when living in Fortitude Valley at the time of Bill's birth were forced to live on rations that were provided to the unemployed who were on the road looking for work. Bill Hayden's recollection of the family folk memory goes like this: 'The old man had a good friend who was a Maori guy. He was a wrestler, and they used to be thick as thieves; you used to always hear stories about them. My mother and father had the deepest affection for him; he was one of those generous, knockabout people who stuck by his mates during the Depression.

'I am pretty sure this story is correct: you had to go thirty miles, I think it was, during the Depression to collect your rations. Him and the old man got as far as the old Booval police station, and the sergeant there was a tough old bugger with a German background, a big fellow. I ran into him much later, but I never let on I knew the story. A lot of the unemployed had managed to get a lift up to Booval on the back of a truck, and the sergeant, sounding sympathetic, said: "Jesus, some of you are lucky, you got a lift up here on the back of a truck from Brisbane," and asked which ones they were. A number were foolish enough to indicate it was them. The sergeant then said: "The law says you have to walk thirty miles, not ride," and refused them the rations. This Maori guy and the old man were two of the fellows who got caught out. They got nothing.'

Hayden's parents were renting a room in a boarding house at 127 Gotha Street, not far from the heart of Fortitude Valley, a racy near-city area of itinerants, brothels, illegal bookmaking joints, Chinese restaurants and working-class families, when their son Bill, named William George after his father, was born on 23 January 1933, on the fringe of Brisbane's central business district at the Lady Bowen Lying-in Hospital in Wickham Terrace, a relic of colonial times that was demolished in 1938. The witness named on his birth certificate was Sister Heaven. When, on 16 February 1933, George Hayden and Violet Quinn were married at St Patrick's Church in Fortitude Valley according to the rites of the Roman Catholic Church, George described himself on the marriage certificate as a salesman; when, on the following day, they registered their son's birth, he put himself down as a piano-tuner.

'In those days, of course, it was not an acceptable thing to do to have a child out of wedlock,' Bill Hayden said. 'It showed there was a lot of free-thinking in the family. There was a lot of social duress around in those days. God! it was narrow minded and intolerant; really, the change that has taken place in quite a short time is revolutionary in a social evolutionary sense.'

The following year, in the winter of 1934, with Mrs Hayden pregnant again with her second child, George and Violet rented a cottage at the bottom of Mabel Street across the river from Brisbane's city centre in the then working-class suburb of Highgate Hill. Bill was nearly eighteen months old, and still in nappies, when his parents walked down the street where he was to grow up. They had the choice of two tiny weatherboard houses that were for rent, and selected number 48 because it had a small enclosed verandah on the back which Mrs Hayden told neighbours would be ideal for George to use for his piano-tuning work.

Mabel Street is a narrow pinchbacked street that arcs across a steep hill and down to a deadend on the edge of a gully. In those days it was just a dirt track and the houses, in common with most of Brisbane, were not sewered. A more substantial thoroughfare, Gloucester Street, follows the crest of the ridge which Mabel Street spans, and a tramline used to run along it. At the intersection with Mabel Street, above the Hayden cottage, the tram drivers would jump from the moving tram to punch a time clock, and there was a working-class pub, the Gloucester Hotel, where George was to spend an increasing amount of his time and money. Bill Hayden grew up a couple of doors up from the gully where Mabel Street ends outside a house that, at the time he became Governor-General, still had an ancient chook-shed in its front yard under a huge Moreton Bay figtree.

Ten days after the Haydens shifted to Mabel Street, Ernie Surmon with his wife, son and five daughters moved into the other vacant house, across the street at number 51, and one daughter, Betty, still lives there.

'All the people in the street were working people,' she says. 'There was only the taxation bloke who had a better than average job. In later years I used to play with Bill's sister, but Bill kept to himself; there were only one or two boys his age in the street. We kept to our own houses in those days. The Haydens didn't entertain or have visitors. Sometimes a relative would visit us. Nobody had much money. My father's boss would go to the market and get a case of fruit or vegetables, and we would share them around. We would work out the cost of each item and then I would go and tell Mrs Hayden we had some oranges or a lettuce for so much, and we would share them around. Later when Bill's brother John was sick, Mrs Hayden would come over and buy pawpaws from our backyard trees, and she said that helped him through his illness.'[8]

Betty Surmon recalls George Hayden as a small man who Bill Hayden has come to resemble more closely as he grows older. Violet Hayden wore her hair in what was called an Eton cut, and was believed by the neighbours to have been a former nurse. Betty Surmon remembers sitting on the verandah one afternoon watching as George Hayden, struggling to open the front gate of his cottage, lost control of a watermelon he had carried all the way home from the Red Brick Hotel. It rolled at increasing speed down the steep little street, smashing into pieces when it hit George Peters' fence at the bottom of the road.

Hayden remembers his mother's views as being strongly influenced by the working people who lived around them and those she had known through her brief marriage to Quinn the shearer and her sister's marriage into another shearing family. 'I was brought up in a home in a poor working-class area. The aristocrats there were wharfies and meatworkers; not only because they got good money, but they were regarded as a good cut of person. I had my teeth ground on the bit about the bush worker, the shearer in particular, and how important they were for my mother, how important the union was: the Australian Workers' Union took up a lot of her life, that was pretty obvious. It was apparently pretty important to western people in those days. The union people ended up in Parliament: I used to hear all these names, like Clarrie Fallon; they were literally household names.' Fallon was State secretary of the AWU and Federal president of the Labor Party.

George Hayden was a hard man who had had a hard life, while Violet was more sentimental, yet in many ways more practical. George would sometimes, in those Depression days, be paid with vegetables or a chicken. Betty Surmon, the neighbour who was about Bill's age says: 'I remember Mrs Hayden saying; "That's all very well, but it doesn't pay the rent." '

'My father was radical in his political values; my mother was too in quite a different way,' Hayden says. 'He was intellectually radical in a way that the anarcho-syndicalists of the Industrial Workers of the World movement were, and they did have strong suspicions about the Communists, and probably saw through them much earlier than most others as inevitably being centralising and authoritarian. My mother was much more sentimental about her radicalness, and was about giving people a fair go, much in the Australian-Irish tradition. She had strong views about women's rights, about a fair go for battlers, a fair go for blacks. She could always come up with a saying or an anecdote. Her favourite saying was, "There are no boys born bad, it is their experiences with the system that has made them bad." I tend to think she got the expression from the founder of a boys' home, and obviously it had had a profound impact on her. She wasn't that hostile to law enforcement authorities, by the way, although she had that Irish chip on her shoulder generally about authority.'

Violet Hayden put her name on the State electoral role on 29 March 1935. George Hayden did not. As well as being an atheist, he had structured ideological views. 'He absolutely hated police and thought of them as instruments of class repression,' Hayden says. George Hayden was sensitive about a tattoo he bore on the inside of his arm which depicted a horseshoe and the hands of friendship. There is a suggestion it may have had some connection with a political or industrial organisation. Bill Hayden has said: 'The old man used to say: "Never get a tattoo, the police can identify you from it." He would wear his shirt sleeves rolled down to cover it; there is absolutely no evidence he had been guilty of any wrongdoing, but I gathered from the things he said that he had been an active unionist at a time when that wasn't popular.' Pat Mackie was unable to trace any connection between the horseshoe and hands of friendship tattoo design and the IWW. A Special Branch detective in Brisbane assured me there was, but was unable to produce evidence.

George Hayden occasionally referred to incidents in his life that reflected some of the hardships he had suffered and some of the radical views that had been forged by them. 'You know, seamen had an awful life in the days he was in the merchant marine,' Bill Hayden says. 'They would take a cargo to Europe as deckhands, and then be paid off: that was it, no holiday pay, no severance pay; they got nothing until they found another ship. He used to make one exception in his condemnation of police, and that was his opinion that the police of Hamburg in Germany were gentlemen because they didn't beat up unemployed seamen, who often had to sleep in public conveniences in inclement weather.' He told young Hayden angrily many times of a sign on the bund in Shanghai that said dogs and Chinese were not allowed and of signs in trams in California that designated a section for blacks. 'My home had radical values; there were strong humanistic influences. On my father's side they were intellectual and ideological; on my mother's, sentiment and emotion, which is just as important, about rights and fair play, and really about the inherent goodness of human beings if they are properly handled. I think that is a Catholic social philosophy and a sense of tolerance about people's rights.'

There was also a dark underside to Hayden's family life as drink and age made life more difficult for George Hayden and he found it increasingly hard to get work. 'He was a remote father who spent most of his money on drink, then took out his frustrations on his family with a rubber tube from his piano-repair kit,' Janet Hawley wrote after a rare intimate interview with Bill Hayden in a Sydney coffee shop in 1980.[9] During that interview Hayden told Hawley the story of his earliest memory, his father crashing dead drunk on the wooden front verandah.

> The revelling Hayden senior had brought the meat from the butcher's shop, and dropped it all down the street to their house.
> Young Bill had to go out and pick up the trail of lamb chops, while all the kids in Mabel Street yelled at him: 'Ah ha, your father's drunk again!' He didn't throw the chops at them — he couldn't. The family was too poor, and it wasn't in his nature to hit out. Very early he'd surmised the way to survive was to keep a poker face and mask his true emotions when he saw his family shunned, and was exposed to some of life's more brutal lessons. The masking is still an instinctive habit he finds difficult to shake off, that is why so little is known about his background or private life.

George Hayden turned sixty-five when Bill was fourteen, but could not afford to retire and in fact was still seeking work when he was past seventy. By this time Bill had a brother John and two sisters, Pat and Joan. Bill Hayden told John Edwards in 1972 of the difficulties that had confronted his father:

> He was busted in the Depression, and I have a vivid recollection of him heading off early in the morning with his kit, chasing a bit of work door-to-door, and bringing the piano frames home on the old drop centre trams; the trammie would be abusing him, and he'd be abusing the trammie. Everyone was struggling to exist in those days. Often as not he wouldn't get paid. So it was a pretty tough existence.[10]

The Depression ended, at least briefly, for the Haydens and many other Australians with the outbreak of war. George Hayden enlisted in 1941, at the age of sixty, after putting back his age and giving his birthplace as Cork in Ireland so as to have British citizenship. He served within Australia and was promoted to the rank of sergeant. 'He joined the Army, not because he thought he was going to be a hero but because he thought it would be an opportunity to earn a regular income for a change,' Bill Hayden told Edwards. Towards the end of the war, Bill met his half-brother Colin Quinn. Quinn had come in from Longreach to stay in Mabel Street while waiting until the day he was old enough to enlist in the Air Force. Bill was later to attempt to follow his choice of service.

After the war there were brief periods when George Hayden seemed to be succeeding, and over a period he bought two cars. 'He started off with a big old Essex with louvres on the motor and a canvas hood,' Bill Hayden recalls. 'It was like an old draughthorse that had come home so often it knew the way by instinct. He'd get pissed at the Gloucester Hotel. He used to wear an old grey dust jacket and felt hat, or his old Army great coat in winter, and he'd pile into this bloody car and I'm sure it used to drive him home itself. Then he thought he'd step up market and got a little Ford Prefect utility.'

About this time the Haydens were told their cottage was to be sold and they would have to move out, so they decided to buy it. 'I don't know why, I think they could have done a bit better with half a go, but the old man didn't have any great aspirations about that,' Hayden says.

TWO

Out of tune

Fear thrust through every part of my being
to lay its dreadful grasp upon my very soul.

Bill Hayden

T HE NUNS in charge of St Ita's modest little Catholic primary
school in South Brisbane made a small administrative decision in
September 1939 that was to have a lasting effect on Bill Hayden's
life. According to family legend, referred to several times over the years
by Hayden, they took away the contract for tuning the school pianos
from his struggling and irascible father and gave it to the major city firm,
B.B. Whitehouse. George Hayden reacted with his own decision: young
Bill was promptly taken out of St Ita's and sent to nearby Dutton Park
State School, nicely situated between a maximum security jail, a venereal
diseases clinic for women and a railway line.

It was the month that the Second World War began; there wasn't a
great demand for piano-tuners, and these were increasingly strained and
worrying times for the Hayden family. They would not improve until
1941 when George worked out a way to enlist in the Australian Army.
An abrupt change of schools is always difficult for children and the
disruption in this case was increased by the circumstances. Bill Hayden
was then seven years old, and had been at St Ita's for almost two years,

having started school in February 1938. The nuns may not have had him for long, but they made an indelible impression on him. In an essay written many years later, he gave a view of how he had seen Heaven and Hell when he was a devout Catholic kid in South Brisbane.

Most of the families I knew were working class and of Irish Catholic extraction. One father was a villain — we all knew it at school; the nuns would sometimes mutter their despair about his neglect of his family, and we mostly knew that he boozed too much, often left home and sometimes even had the police looking for him. We also knew that he swore a lot, but as most of us boys were trying to develop not only an adequate swear-word vocabulary, but also an effective use of that vocabulary, we tended to give him credit for that. One day, while still relatively young, he died quite unexpectedly, leaving a wife and a large brood of youngsters to fend for themselves in a rather inhospitable world. One of the bereaved children invited a friend and me to the family home, near the convent, to see the father's encoffined body. I guess it might have been some sort of wake arrangement. The sunlight filtered in a dusky way through the drawn curtains of the tiny loungeroom in the small timber-worker's cottage. The widow stood near one wall in the sparse room; a thin grey person who'd suffered too much already in her bondage of misery, and now with nothing but gloomy prospects and the thin soup of the poor to sustain her and her brood in the immediate future.

I had never seen a dead person before and I was terrified. I left quickly and silently. Fear thrust through every part of my being to lay its dreadful grasp upon my very soul. My meekness, the product of terror I suspect, was mistaken for due reverence and sorrowful concern. We walked away, my friend and I, at a smart pace with lips sealed by fear until we were far enough from the home not to be seen, and then ran — and how we ran.

The dead man had been a bad man and I was terrified that the Devil himself would lunge out of the flaming, boiled bowels of the earth and snatch me away forever for having come so close to one of his own. Next day I was still hostage to terror when school fell in, but miraculously I was saved. Instead of going straight to Hell and condign punishment, the dead man's soul was to spend some time in purgatory, drying out as it were; a sort of sinners' anonymous, I expect, and then go to Heaven.[1]

Young Bill Hayden, it seemed, did a lot of running away in those days — an activity that was not to be a feature of either his police or political career. He told Janet Hawley of two incidents: one evening he had been hanging around the schoolyard with a friend when they spied an American soldier and his girlfriend climbing into a trench dug in the schoolyard for use in case of air raids. The boys crawled up and kicked dirt on top of the lovers. 'It was a mean thing to do, a sentiment the soldier wholeheartedly shared. He rose with a flood of abuses and tried to chase us with his pants around his knees. But he was a good soldier, we noted as he gave chase; he hadn't taken his boots off.' His mother had enrolled young Bill in the Scouts and he went on a camp beside a creek bank when a big red-bellied black snake crawled into view. 'The scout-master yelled, "Quick boys, get back!" I ran a full mile before I stopped.'[2]

Hayden recalls his State primary school days with a combination of nostalgia, always expressed in tones of mocking irony, and bitterness at wasted years. When one compares today's schools with the educational opportunities that were in his day only available to a privileged number of his contemporaries, there is some justification for his sense of deprivation. The kids in Mabel Street walked to school through the backyard of a neighbour and up a steep gully to the dusty, dreary weatherboard school in the shadow of Boggo Road prison where they baked in summer and froze in winter. But if Hayden's education was little different from that of hundreds of thousands of other Queenslanders who attended State schools at that time, his attitude to it was: he has continually given the impression of savage regret that he was denied proper educational opportunities and stimulus in his earlier years. The depth of his feeling is sometimes questioned by his colleagues and contemporaries: when in Canberra years later he once made some reference to going to school in bare feet, a senior journalist who had attended the same school was moved to say: 'Come on, Bill, none of us wore shoes in those days.'[3]

He can be lyrically inspired in his condemnation of his school experience at Dutton Park:

> I loathed school. Setting off each day was like leaving for prison, where the daily punishment was the dread of dull repetition. A like apple, B like bat ... sonorous incantations from a silly litany, the only conceivable purpose of which was to guarantee the educational experience would be as boring, irrelevant and heartily disliked as human ingenuity could make it. Educational primitiveness, a forced march through a dreary parched land where neither joy nor happy challenges were allowed to take root, let alone flourish.[4]

Memory, however, can soften the harshness of the past, and present well-being tends to obliterate old traumas. In September 1984 Dutton Park State School celebrated its anniversary with a reunion and Hayden was invited as a guest of honour. He was about to leave for Central America and sent a message to be relayed by Sir James Killen, another past student:

'I look back with the fondest nostalgia on those important formative years which I spent at Dutton Park. I can still remember the lovely blue and gold days of Spring and Autumn, the metrical cadences of fondly remembered teachers like the late Joe Hines, Miss Hogan, Mrs Green, to mention quickly a few names that come to mind, and of course I shall never forget the splendid playing fields distinctively carpeted in what I seem to recall was quarry gravel, or at least that's how it always felt on bare feet. Dutton Park State School, of course, must be a uniquely remarkable institution for it to have accommodated people like Jim Killen and me in roughly the same period without collapsing in a huge convulsion of shock and horror. I suppose the simplest thing I can say is that the influence of Dutton Park State School has been responsible for so many of the things which Jim Killen and I did to Australia subsequently in the national parliament. I leave you to interpret that comment at your will.'[5] Hayden's cheerful comments, composed for the official ceremony, could have had in mind the audience gathered there that night; they also reflected his ambivalence in remembering his schooldays. Dutton Park left an indelible mark on him. In March 1989, on his first official visit to Queensland after becoming Governor-General, Hayden, in an arrangement made months earlier, swept up to the Dutton Park State School escorted by a phalanx of police motorbikes.

Like many Hayden gestures, the visit was subject to conflicting interpretations. His intention, he had told friends, was to demonstrate to the deprived children of his old school, and similar schools across the nation who were likely to see glimpses of the visit on television, that they could rise from such a humble beginning to high office as he had: it was the glory and the hope of the Australian way of life that one of the young Aboriginal girls attending Dutton Park State School in 1989 could some day be Australia's Governor-General. There is little doubt that the symbolism wasn't meant to end there: the visit was also intended to illustrate to a wider audience Hayden's own humble origins in contrast with the pomp and ceremony and apparent importance with which he was now surrounded; he had come a long way, along a very hard road. To some it was seen as an attempt to romanticise his past. But the sadness of the occasion to many who had worked with him over the years in the Labor movement was that his lifetime struggle and achievements were much greater and socially important than his appointment as Governor-General. His life had, in their view, been diminished not only by the fact that he had accepted such a ceremonial role, but that he regarded it as of such importance.

In later years Hayden has said that he now realises that some of his trouble at school may have been caused by hearing difficulties. His partial deafness is in some measure congenital, although he believes it may have been exacerbated by two incidents in his childhood. While doing a tightrope act on the railing of the front verandah in Mabel Street he fell and was badly concussed. Later he began to suffer fainting spells. After many visits to doctors and hospitals he was eventually diagnosed as having lead poisoning which it was thought had been caused by his habit of licking raindrops from the decorative railings on the verandah which had been painted with lead-based paint.

Hayden always had a great appetite for learning. It was frustrated by a cluster of circumstances, including his problem family, a poor school and the handicap of his partial deafness. It was school, not books or learning, that he loathed. 'I hated school and I think a lot of my teachers didn't like their job either. But when I look back I think a lot of my troubles may have been caused by this hearing problem; even then I was having trouble keeping up with what was happening because of that. I would read the history book voraciously before school started. I just loved it. And I did well at subjects like arithmetic.' When he was twelve, Hayden went to the South Brisbane Intermediate School which drew its pupils from a slightly wider, but socially similar, area. Its curriculum included classes in domestic science for the girls and wood and metalwork for the boys. Young Bill showed some enthusiasm and ability, and after school began making toys for his brother and sisters at a little bench under the house.

Bill Hayden's serious education started later in life, and in a real sense has never stopped. But there are indications that he always took education seriously, though by his early academic records he was never much more than an average student, and that he remembered and was influenced by the attitude of his teachers. After he lost the leadership of the Labor Party to Bob Hawke in 1983, he replied seriously and at length to a sympathetic letter from Ron Baynes, who had taught him at South Brisbane Intermediate School.

'There is no doubt at all in my mind that one of the important formative experiences of my life was being a pupil in your class. I guess mature-age schoolteachers have so many experiences in the course of a day, let alone a year, and more especially over several years, that small things go unnoticed in spite of their importance to the immature young student.

'Do you recall disagreeing rather vigorously once in class when you asked the question: "What did Hitler and Napoleon have in common?".

'I responded with my normal enthusiasm, "Too much ambition". Of course you were referring to the breakdown of both their armies on the Eastern Front.

'I think my point then was substantial and I still think so. I think Hitler was a dreadful bastard, but Napoleon an impressive character. They both had the fatal flaw though and were trying to achieve too much too quickly.'

Hayden told Baynes that he still held warm and affectionate memories of him that had not diminished over the years.

'You were an important creative influence on my life. In those dingy classrooms at the old South Brisbane Intermediate in your own influential way you did much to formulate the mind and values of someone who was subsequently a Minister for Social Security, who in that term [of office], I suppose immodestly, believed I achieved much; then became Treasurer of this country in a very difficult period, and showed, I hope, that he had enough toughness to stick with unpleasant decisions in the interests of the national good, and subsequently went on to be Leader of the Opposition, nearly Prime Minister, and certainly Minister for Foreign Affairs.'[6]

Written at a time of great stress, it is, nevertheless in many ways a strange letter to have written to a man who had taught him forty years before, and whom he had not seen since, although they had exchanged letters from time to time when Baynes wrote to him at important points in Hayden's career. Ron Baynes had just returned from the war when he taught Hayden, and for that reason was something of a romantic figure to the students. He remembers Hayden as 'one of the boys', and one not particularly keen on study. Baynes did not put forward political views, and takes satisfaction in having numbered Don Cameron, the Liberal MHR, among his past pupils.[7]

Natalie Funnell, who was in Hayden's class at the intermediate school, and whose brother was dux of the school, has two outstanding memories of Bill Hayden then: he was brilliant at mathematics, and was very fair and good looking and blushed madly if a girl looked at him. 'He was quite stocky and was into football. He was normally gregarious, except with girls: we all thought he was lovely. He was always neat and his clothes were well cared for.'

She remembers the school as being a particularly happy one, and says she has later been at a loss when reading comments Hayden has made about his schooldays and environment. 'Men led their own lives in those days. Shakespeare didn't lie around on the coffee table, it was lower middle class and working class, but it wasn't a slum; it wasn't tacky. Bill sometimes sounds a bit bitter and twisted.'[8] Ms Funnell's brother, Air Chief Marshal Ray Funnell, as the senior officer in the Royal Australian Air Force in 1989, played a prominent role in the ceremonies surrounding Bill Hayden's transformation to office as Governor-General.

Hayden passed the State Scholarship exam in 1947, and went on to Brisbane State High School the following year. These were bitterly difficult days for the family, and particularly for Violet Hayden. George Hayden had reached the normal retiring age of sixty-five in 1946. Hayden's mother was still only forty-two, while Joan, the youngest of the four Hayden children living at home in Mabel Street, was just two. The family simply could not manage to live on a single old-age pension and George, who was often sick and drinking more heavily, was forced to continue seeking work as a piano-tuner and repairer.

'I was always a very poor reader,' Hayden told John Edwards during the 1972 election year.

> I was a typical product of the deprived socio-economic background that I understand now but didn't then. There weren't many books in our home — we couldn't afford them. It was poor, that was all. Bloody poor. But you've got to realise you're poor, and we didn't. We seemed to be happy, and it wasn't until much later in life that I realised just how deprived the area was in those days. When I go back down there sometimes I nostalgically drive back down the street, and it's a real slum area, and all the old residents have left. Migrants have moved in.[9]

At the time Edwards was writing this profile, the first significant piece about Hayden and still perhaps the most perceptive and revealing, Hayden wrote to him expressing concern about the responses he had given to Edwards' questions on a number of topics. Edwards returned Hayden's letter to him sixteen years later, in 1988, when they met in Teheran. In the letter, written on 10 February 1972, Hayden had said: 'In stressing my desire to obtain a better education etc. for my kids, I do not want to be misinterpreted as aiming at having them become neat, well programmed, conventional middle class adults who will duly and dutifully settle uncritically into "ticky tacky boxes" in the suburbs. I hope they are concerned about and involved in society and feel some commitment to their fellow man, and his rights.

'My stress on education is that I found it opens up wider, more interesting and satisfying horizons. I guess I would say the biggest benefit to me was that it allowed me to escape from ignorance and prejudice, at least in some worthwhile degree.'

Hayden said in 1988: 'Having the letter returned and reading it again gave me a surprise, but if you look at it, I think you'll find I stuck pretty much to what I said to John Edwards when the children were very small. What I had hoped for from life was that they would succeed in education, and that they would carve out a decent niche for themselves. Our kids have been told that making a lot of money wasn't the important thing in life: satisfaction from what you are doing, and having an interesting job, which, by definition, means having educational qualifications, in my view, is important.

'I think the kids are fitting into that mould, and I was rather pleased to see the letter because I had forgotten all about it.

'One of the pressures on me to see the kids succeed was, of course, coming from a rather poor background and not having a lot of education and not having gone as far as one should have gone: I don't want to see the kids slide back into that. I don't think I harangue them about it — I hope I don't anyway.'

Thinking back to his own childhood in 1988, Hayden added: 'I've never said to my kids, "I had to work a bloody sight harder around the yard and around the house". I had all sorts of odd jobs. I used to do a paper delivery. Working for the butcher, I remember getting the sack once because I had made the deliveries all upside down; there was a bit of trouble at home which had me a bit worried, and I remember going around the delivery and I just couldn't get the orders straight. When I say trouble at home, it was between mother and father.'

When he was sixteen, at the end of 1949, Hayden passed the junior public examination with his results reflecting Natalie Funnell's assessment of his ability at mathematics and his own view of his reading skills: he scored an A in arithmetic, B passes in history, geography, geometry, chemistry and physics, and C passes in algebra and English.

His move from St Ita's took Hayden out of the mainstream of a Catholic upbringing and education, but did not remove him entirely from its influence: 'We were taken away from St Ita's in high dudgeon. It had been my mother's influence that got us there. Afterwards I used to go to Mass with faulty discipline: I'd go for a while, and not for a while. There were two nice young women who lived near us in Mabel Street who used to chide me, especially if they saw me playing around the streets on Sunday morning, asking why I wasn't at Mass, and I'd go again for a while and [then] drop out. I always think that they always thought I was heading in the wrong direction, but that there was still some hope for me: they spent a bit of time on me, they were good Catholics.'

Hayden still has an uncomfortable relationship with organised religion. Although he was the first Australian Governor-General to make an affirmation, rather than an oath on the Bible at his swearing-in ceremony, he admires many clergy, and follows with close interest, and sometimes regret, changes in the rituals of the Catholic Church. 'When I was in early adolescence I had a fond thought that I might even become a priest; I am not sure why. I used to even go to benediction on Sunday afternoon for some time, but that came and went. A lot of young people have that sort of influence on them,' he said in 1988. 'I didn't have a clue what was happening in the Latin Mass, but it did seem to be awfully close to Jesus Christ and God for a young person whose emotions were easily moved: the Celtic part of the family background, I expect. I find even at this stage of my life I like the company of priests and nuns. I like the ritual of the church, there is a richness about it, and there's a formality about it which I still find attractive, a reverence, all these things.'

Hayden's attitude to religion was, like some of his other views, influenced in a complex way by the extreme opinions of his father George, who had never softened in his bitterness towards the Catholic Church. But for all his radical background and sentiments, George Hayden did not want his son to follow a life similar to his own. 'He didn't have much respect for education being a guarantee for a job because he'd seen what happened in the depression,' Bill Hayden said in 1980. 'Go into the public service or become a salesman and you'd be right for life — that's what he taught us.'[10] And that's what Hayden did: as soon as he left school he became a junior clerk in the State Government Stores. People who worked with him there say that as a junior he was given the worst and most boring jobs. But they remember him as a lively lad. Chris Bennett, who still has a faded snapshot of Hayden on a State Stores picnic surrounded by six girls, says: 'If he hadn't joined the police force, I think he could have easily finished up on the other side of the law.'[11] Hayden says: 'It was an awful bloody job. I hated that. They had me doing the invoices: you had to put them in order, and punch holes in them and put them in a book cover and screw the thing up. And I thought: Jesus Christ, is this what life's all about?'

THREE

A force divided

If we are prepared to tolerate a second rate
police force, we will end up with a
second rate democracy.

Bill Hayden

B ILL HAYDEN was, for an important part of his life, exposed to the full range of human experience that a policeman encounters — from seductive bribery to life-threatening violence. It was his first adult job, the result of his own deliberate decision: a career choice that shapes the destiny of many people. Hayden survived without visible scars, but emerged with a typically contradictory, and, in many ways, admirable, response: he had sympathy for the victims and the law enforcers, and wondered whether there was not a better way.

He saw the darker side of human nature, and did his share of coping with horrific accidents and, as an outsider now, revisited desperate, depressing scenes of domestic violence. Yet, years later, he retained some nostalgia for his younger days as a single policeman, as he revealed in a story that he did not intend to be recorded:

> I was a young copper up north. I had just started and I went into the pub, and there was this barmaid. Coppers seem to have a thing with barmaids and she took to me. Anyway, she says would I like to go for a picnic on Saturday afternoon, just the two of us down by the river. I had nothing

to lose so off I went with her to the bank of the river for the picnic on Saturday afternoon. Every Saturday it becomes a regular thing. Lunch, then nature takes its course beside the river. Suddenly being a cop wasn't all that bad. It was some time before I found out that the local SP bookie was paying for her to have lunch with me to keep me out of the pub so he could run his book every Saturday.[1]

Although he seldom tells them, Hayden has a fund of colourful stories about some of his minor adventures during the eight years he spent in the Queensland Police Force. They nearly all reflect the ambivalence of his attitude to the experience: he enjoyed much of his life as a country cop and he appreciates fully what a difficult lot the policeman has in his working life; yet he knows that there is a powerful authoritarian and anti-intellectual strain in the Queensland force, and that it has long been tainted with corruption. Hayden told the story of the barmaid to *Penthouse* writer Owen Thomson while they were walking round his garden in Ipswich before they started a formal interview in the lead-up to the 1980 election campaign. He did not expect it to be written, although he apparently did not say specifically that it was not for publication. The day after it was published he was going to a Labor Party Parliamentary Executive meeting in Melbourne and he asked his press secretary Alan Ramsey to telephone *Penthouse* and complain. Ramsey did nothing. Several of Hayden's male political colleagues enjoyed the story, as they indicated with a few nudges and winks at the Melbourne meeting. Ramsey heard no more about the need for a complaint.

Hayden acknowledges that his decision to join the force, in 1953 at the age of twenty, at the time of his father's death, was influenced by the conflict between them: 'My father absolutely hated the police; he thought of them as instruments of class repression. Consciously or unconsciously my joining the police might well have had something to do with the fact that we didn't get on too well together.'

George Hayden died suddenly on 28 April 1953, at home in Mabel Street, aged seventy-two. The causes of death were given as coronary occlusion, coronary disease and arteriosclerosis. On his death certificate his doctor noted: 'sick for years'.

Bill Hayden's experience in the police force, which he left only when he won a seat in Parliament in 1961, shaped many of his attitudes, and, in the view of a number of his political colleagues, reinforced the suspicious and distrustful side of his nature, while also giving him a useful instinct for the deceit he was often to encounter, as well as to suspect wrongly, in his political life.

He was a conscientious, straight — but not overly ambitious — policeman, who had several brushes with authority in the force. His decision to join was also prompted by the fact that on his father's death he was the family's main support; at the age of twenty he was still being paid as a junior in the Public Service, whereas in the police, after an initial twelve-week training period, he was entitled to adult wage rates. It is also notable, though, that he showed no aversion to institutional life: he had tried to enlist in the RAAF air crew two months before his eighteenth birthday, but had been rejected. He enjoyed life in the Navy when he was called up in the first national service intake, not only as an escape for the first time from a difficult home life, but for the male comradeship. He had found such team spirit the main attraction of rugby football and rowing, the sports he enjoyed. Although part of the reason he never played tennis or golf was the fact that they were for the rich kids, he was not attracted to them.

While he became increasingly a loner in his later political life, as a young man he was comfortable in the institutional life of the service. Much later, as Opposition leader, he astounded his staff advisers when, immediately after supporting a proposal for the formation of a volunteer corps of unemployed people to engage in community work he asked: 'What sort of uniforms will we put them in?'

In his first few months in the police Hayden lived at home, and with his first adult pay packets bought a dictionary and then material to paint the tiny house and enclose the front verandah, giving himself at the age of twenty his own bedroom for the first time. Betty Surmon remembers him walking down Mabel Street in his police uniform, and her father commenting that he didn't have a copper's walk; but she recalls that when a car ran away in their steep little street one day and crashed into a tree, a few weeks after he had joined up, he emerged from the house and dutifully took charge, assisting an injured man and taking down the details in his notebook.[2] A friend who had been at school with him, and who had recognised his academic ability, was surprised to see him one day directing traffic outside the Brisbane GPO, but she didn't talk to him.

In 1954, after he had been in the force little more than a year, he was transferred to Mackay, a cane and cattle centre on the subtropical Queensland coast, and for some months relieved at Calen, a small town just north of Mackay. Later he was stationed at Sarina, another quiet little town down the road to the south, where he went to live cheaply in the back of the courthouse. Ed Casey, who later became leader of the Labor Party in Queensland, was secretary and then president of the party in the region as his father had been before him, says: 'The only contact I ever heard of that he had with our most prominent supporter in the area was when he approached him for a job driving trucks in his spare time. He told Hayden that if he had any extra work he would give it to his own men that worked for him during the week'.[3] Hayden says he made casual enquiries about joining the Labor Party at that time but had not been welcomed.

Owen Thomson, the *Penthouse* writer who talked to Hayden in 1980, enjoyed another of his police anecdotes about those days in the north, and the way Hayden told it:

He laughs in a way nobody has ever seen him laugh on television — animated, his hands gesticulating, his face beaming. The joking Bill Hayden seems to have little in common with the man Australians have heard or seen a thousand times complaining his way, point by tedious point, through a statement from Malcolm Fraser. This is a man any person of goodwill would like. Some of the Hayden jokes are long and have the air of a folk legend with little moral asides, flashes of local colour, and a point that becomes lost in the characters. Like The Man Who Didn't Get Away, another of Bill Hayden's stories about a blind cop in the cane fields:

Horses are a nuisance up there. They get into the crop and eat the cane, so whenever a horse was caught the owner would deny he owned it because the damages bill would be more than the horse was worth. One time this bloke picked up a horse and thought, well, bugger it, and slapped a brand on it and put it to work. Then a young fellow turned up and claimed it was his horse. It was a thoroughbred and it was worth an extraordinary amount of money. He had lodged a complaint so I had to go down and get the man who had the horse. It was at a place called Flaggy Rock, and I had to go by steam train and thumb a ride out to see him. So I picked this bloke up and I had to borrow his utility to take him in. We finally got to the station and I had to arrange a court, which meant two local JPs. Such is the supreme independent and impartial quality of justice that I got out the criminal code and showed one of the JPs the section the bloke had been charged under, and I said: 'Look, it's a pretty trivial thing, you just give him a lecture and put him on a bond and tell him if he does this sort of thing again he'll be in real trouble.' The independence of the court had to be preserved so we held it underneath the police station, which was a house up on stumps. I went up to the cell to get this bloke and he's white and languid and wide-eyed, a real mess. It turns out a big snake had crawled through his cell and he'd been screaming and we hadn't heard him. I got him to court but he was not in good shape. Then the silly old JP read the wrong section of the Act and told the bloke he was liable for fourteen years' imprisonment. It was too much for him, and he fainted on the floor.[4]

A horse features in another of Hayden's north Queensland cases, a saga that acquired some notoriety. Ted Loane, then the clerk of petty sessions at Sarina and now a retired magistrate living in Rockhampton, tells the story: 'Bill Hayden was custodian of a horse that was involved in an alleged attempted carnal knowledge case. It involved a man named Edwards who had been arrested standing naked on a 44-gallon drum outside the post office facing the back of the bay mare.

'Bill moved into the back of the Sarina courthouse, and had responsibility for making sure the horse stayed in the paddock there. Later I remarked to the other constable there, Dave Richards, that I hadn't seen the horse for about six weeks. Dave said: "Bill's the only bugger in town who doesn't know it's gone — he hasn't had time to go and have a look." A month or so later the Mackay police came down for the horse. Luckily someone found her in a paddock about sixteen kilometres away, and Bill was sent to catch her and ride her back. He didn't have a saddle, and she was a poor skinny old thing. It must have been like riding a hat rack. He came back very sore.'[5]

One of the reasons Bill Hayden hadn't missed the horse was that in his time at Sarina he was holding down two full-time jobs. He was still the main breadwinner for his family. His mother had no qualifications, but had gone back to work: 'She was scrubbing floors and polishing floors in the days when a lot of people didn't have floor polishers,' Hayden recalls. 'She found it pretty hard because some of the people who employed her were fairly brutal in the way they would treat her. I presume at that level they wouldn't have been too well off themselves, and she often got gypped in the amount of pay she got, and she would come home quite upset.'

Ted Loane says, 'He did a lot of work around the place. He drove a milk truck owned by a bloke named Kev Campion up over the top of the Sarina Range with another constable named Geoff Holloway. They would take it in turns to drive this truck, visit all the dairy farms and pick up the cream. They'd be down before daybreak, around three or four o'clock every morning. They'd be back before lunch and then they'd do general carrying around the township.' Holloway was a giant of a man, and Hayden still keeps a faded, out-of-focus, Box Brownie photograph of them together in uniform leaning on a utility. 'That was just one job Bill had,' says Ted Loane. 'He'd also harvest cane, he'd plant cane, he'd cut cane for planting, he sank dams, and when he finished one job he'd be looking for the next. He was a strong young fellow in those days, a good style of lad, good looking, always immaculately dressed; he did his own washing and ironing. He was a bit lonely then.' Hayden spent his twenty-first birthday at the Loane home, where they had made a cake for him, and about that time he told Ted Loane he wouldn't always be a policeman. Hayden still recalls the Loanes' hospitality. 'That was the first birthday party I ever had,' he said. 'My family never had enough money.'

In 1956 he was transferred from north Queensland back to Brisbane, where he worked as a plain-clothes constable with Detective Sergeant Norm Gulbransen at the CIB in the city. Gulbransen who later became assistant commissioner and a close associate of Commissioner Ray Whitrod in the heroic but unsuccessful attempts to clean up the force in Queensland, describes Hayden as one of the best young policemen he ever encountered.

'He had a particulary great ability to talk to people. We had a few good cases. One was a murder case; a Maltese fellow named Charles Plum had belted another fellow and he died. Bill and I were working on the early shift, starting at 6 a.m. There was always a lot of competition in those days between various detectives. The city fellows got all the promising leads, and we were given very little. But Bill had worked in one of the suburban stations at Rosalie, and we went out and talked to the local fellows and they were able to give us some idea of where to look for him, and we found him. We had quite a talk to him before we took him in: there was method in that because we knew once we got him into town, the big nobs would take him over and we'd be left out. I can still remember Bill giving evidence because he had to corroborate me. I wondered how he would be, him being at that stage quite inexperienced. I can still picture him sitting in the witness box in the Supreme Court, with one leg up over the knee, and as calmly and as naturally as could be he answered questions and so on. He was a very good witness.'[6]

Gulbransen, who is now retired, said that he had recognised that Hayden had the ability 'to work himself up intellectually to match anyone. But after a time, I don't know what happened, he fell foul of one of the inspectors, he was sent over to Roma Street to the uniformed section. I never found out what had happened, I think it was something that arose from a suburban station. But Bill wasn't right for it anyway, and he stood up for his rights. Well he put his head down and did some very good detective work. He had a couple of cases in the plain-clothes branch that he had to complete, but by the time he had finished those he had picked up such an amount of information about a number of other things that he had to stay on a bit longer.'

Hayden eventually moved to Roma Street station in central Brisbane from which police were rostered on guard duty at Government House, the residence of Queensland's Governor, in Fernberg Road just a few kilometres away. There was an office in a small gatehouse near the entrance to Government House where the police, who seldom had any work to do while on guard duty, passed their time; and it is now accepted legend in the Queensland police force that Bill Hayden did some of the study that put him on the road to Yarralumla while guarding the Queensland Governor. Hayden says he did, in fact, do guard duty but at that stage had not yet begun studying again. Gulbransen says: 'I always found him mild mannered — but he was always prepared to take anyone on. We had a common interest in wood-chopping. I had competed at the Brisbane Exhibition in 1938. At the time I knew him, he was still helping to support his mother, and there was an extra allowance for men at two-man stations, and he managed to get transferred to Redbank.'

Hayden says: 'Norm Gulbransen was good to work with. One night we got a call to Lennons, then Brisbane's most exclusive hotel. There were two women who were staying there and were in trouble. They had come down from some country place where Norm had served — and he knew them — one was the wife of a professional man and one was the wife of a businessman. They had been having a night out on the town and someone had knocked off their jewellery; it wasn't very hard to put it all together, what had been going on. Anyway they were able to give Norm a bit of a guide on it, and we went over and grabbed the guy and Norm had a long heart-to-heart talk with him, a pretty tough one; he asked me to step outside the room where he was interviewing him. He got the jewellery back and took it back to the hotel and gave it to the women, and there was nothing on the books about it. His line simply was: "There is no point in it — we got the jewellery back and it would bust up two marriages." There were lots of cases like that when I worked with him. Norm was an active Mason. We got a young bloke who was in trouble, and it turned out the kid had a sister who was a nun, and it was a good Catholic family and Norm said: "This is going to be fine, isn't it: bust up a family like this." So we never charged him.

'I understand cops aren't supposed to make those judgments: but you do a hell of a lot. I always felt I was lucky working with Norm Gulbransen. There were quite a lot of humane guys who joined the police force during the Depression. That was one of the few jobs they could get into.' Hayden can't recall the incident that led to his transfer out of the plain-clothes branch, but says he didn't regret the move.

'Quite frankly I could see I wasn't cut out for the police force once I left north Queensland and came back to the city. It wasn't the same. I enjoyed it out at Redbank, but I could see there was just no future. The things about it I didn't like — I know it sounds fastidious, but there is nothing more gruesome than having to empty the bloody pockets of a street drunk. And just locking them up, it seemed to me, was a hopeless sort of exercise.

'Promotion was awfully slow so there didn't seem to be much of an opportunity for challenge or personal satisfaction, and, frankly, I wasn't impressed intellectually by many of my superiors: at times of crisis, major accidents for instance, I could sort out very quickly in my own mind what should be done to keep things moving, while a lot of them would be running round with their heads up their bums.'

The Queensland police force during those years was not infected to the degree it was later with the twin evils of systematic graft organised at the highest levels and massive political manipulation and corruption. Hayden did, however, maintain a long-term interest in the problems of the force and its members, and when Sir Joh Bjelke-Petersen began using the force for political purposes through the Vietnam War demonstrations and against other manifestations of social change in the late 1960s he took a public stance.

In 1970, when he had been a politician for about the same time as he had been a policeman, the Labor Party journal *Trend* published a substantial article in which Hayden reviewed the standing of the Queensland force, then shown by an opinion poll to have the poorest public reputation of any in the Commonwealth, and made recommendations for reform that suggest either some cynicism or a touchingly naive view of the responsiveness of the force to fundamental change. Hayden's article showed both the qualities of a concerned former policeman and the objectivity of a radical against whose new associates the force had been directed.

> Mainly the reputation of the force will be determined by the deportment of a police officer in his dealings with the public. But a good deportment — that is, an alert, courteous and able response to the needs of the public — must spring from a well-established base. Three months instruction, as at present, covering physical training and dreary lectures on powers of arrest and the essential ingredients which make an offence convictable, are scarcely the stuff from which a well-informed mind, freed of prejudices, can be developed and later applied to the wide range of social problems with which a police officer comes in contact in the course of his duty.[7]

Hayden's 1970 recommendations for reform of the Queensland Police training course very much suggest the regimen he had privately set for himself: 'There would be no great difficulty in developing a course taking in a broad span of education on social behaviour which could help towards the development of a tolerant, informed mind, better able to handle the task of protecting a democratic system and preserving the right of dissent and conformity within that system.' He recorded gravely an enduring truth: important conclusions reflecting policemen's attitudes were affected by superficialities and emotional impressions; long hair and beards were marked as evidence of deviation from the norm.

The enduring tenor of the Queensland police force is captured in Hayden's essay: 'Recently a colleague of mine sought a permit from a commissioned police officer to conduct a protest march on the Vietnam war. With Olympian disdain his application was arbitrarily refused and, to boot, he was treated to a lengthy and aggressive dissertation by this officer on the disloyalties of such a protest.' This was the professional milieu from which Hayden had, almost by accident, escaped into reformist politics eight years earlier. His article continued with detailed and practical proposals including the abandonment of kill sheets, which he explained were offensively named lists displayed for plain-clothes staff which showed the number of arrests and convictions each had recorded, and called for the scrapping of the system of promotion by seniority which destroyed the enthusiasm and dedication of many young police officers.

In his efforts to improve the standards and performance of the Queensland Police, Hayden unwittingly became involved in an incident that was used to great effect by corrupt officers in Queensland. Hayden had discovered that Gough Whitlam was keen to encourage greater cooperation between the Federal and State law enforcement authorities. Hayden knew the reformist Queensland Commissioner, Ray Whitrod, who had previously been a senior officer in the Australian Security Intelligence Organisation, senior security officer on two royal tours and head of the Commonwealth Police from 1960 to 1969 and the Papua New Guinea force in 1969 and 1970.

Hayden arranged a meeting between Whitrod and Whitlam. Hayden later recalled that at the end of that meeting Whitrod had, 'in his usual hospitable way' invited Hayden and Whitlam to lunch. Evidence was given to the Fitzgerald Inquiry into police corruption in 1988 that Whitrod's enemy and rival, Terence Lewis, reported the fact that Whitrod had social contacts with Whitlam to the Queensland Premier, Sir Joh Bjelke-Petersen, a man who had vowed to destroy the Whitlam Government. Bjelke-Petersen engineered Whitrod's resignation and Lewis became Police Commissioner. Lewis was later sacked by Mike Ahern who succeeded Bjelke-Petersen as Queensland Premier.

Hayden's sympathy for the lot of the ordinary policeman in the Queensland of his time is understood by many honest cops of his generation who have followed his career with interest, and even promised violence against those who may consider writing unfavourably about him. It is well expressed in the conclusion of his 1970 article:

> We even foist upon him the unwanted role of literary and artistic censor without in any way training him for the highly technical and demanding job, and, when he makes a botch of it, as he most likely will if he has not been trained to appreciate the implications and purpose of these forms of cultural expression, we tend to sneer instead of being alarmed that we should so poorly treat a man occupying such an important role as to ill-equip him to do his job.[8]

Hayden's final words proved prophetic nearly twenty years later as the Fitzgerald Inquiry exposed the links between corrupt police and politicians in Queensland. In 1970 Hayden wrote: 'If we are prepared to tolerate a second rate police force then we will end up with a second rate democracy.'

FOUR

Finding
a home

*There suddenly came an awareness that I
had to make a bit more out of my life.*

Bill Hayden

A S A YOUNG MAN Bill Hayden played hard and enjoyed hard physical work, yet there was a hollowness in his life and he was becoming naggingly aware of it. He did not have a place to live that he could call home. He was not getting professional or intellectual satisfaction from his job and he had little chance of giving expression to his growing compassionate and radical views. He was unhappy with the limited prospects for promotion or challenge within the force, and at the same time he was having to cope with sordid situations, with drunks, domestic violence, and the misery of the homeless, and he increasingly believed there needed to be political rather than policing solutions. Then, within a comparatively brief period, a series of random events gave him opportunities which he seized, and his life began to take focus and shape. At the beginning of 1957, as a twenty-four-year-old police constable, he was transferred to the two-man police station at Redbank, west of Brisbane on the outskirts of Ipswich. In terms of Brisbane police force priorities, Redbank was a backwater on the fringe of another, though larger, backwater, Ipswich. Within five years Hayden was married, had begun serious academic studies, and been elected to Federal Parliament.

The direction of his life had been fashioned in the fibro and galvanised-iron setting of police barracks and railway refreshment rooms and the political ethos of a small inland Queensland industrial city that relied for its living on hard industries that were, even then, outdated: rusting factories, underground coalmines, railway workshops, a woollen mill and the Dinmore factory that made pedestals for lavatories.

Hayden's preparation had been slow and random, yet he had shown himself open and sympathetic to influence. Apart from the inheritance of his parents, a number of specific experiences had made a political imprint on the young and emotionally vulnerable Hayden that lasts to this day. 'One morning when I was a young cop on the beat I was sitting in a Brisbane Tramway signal box near Petrie Bight talking radical political values to the operator,' Hayden wrote to John Edwards in 1972. 'He was an old chap who had been through the depression, and had been knocked about by police in the great tramway strike. He urged me to read and recommended Upton Sinclair's *The Jungle*. That was my introduction to radical reading. I guess people like Sinclair, Jack London and even Steinbeck (who was warmly human and compassionate) were considerable influences at that stage. The defect was the reading was undisciplined, undirected, and lacked a framework of intent and purpose. This came when I commenced study and learned how to use library resources, how to read critically, and to develop goals and so on.'[1]

When he was in his first stultifying job filing invoices in State Stores, Hayden had long discussions with a fellow worker, Merv Young, who was a member of the Communist Party. 'He was a very fine and impressive man. I was very friendly with him, and he used to talk about the coming revolution and how things would be different; it would be a working man's Utopia and deserts would be turned into fertile fields; the existing state of affairs was all the result of a capitalist plot. Well, it made a lot of sense to me,' Hayden reflected in 1988. 'It wasn't my fault that our family was battling at the margin. I blamed it on the system, when, of course, a lot of it was our fault because of my father's drinking problem. It seemed unfair to be left out when you are young. But when I look back it was a strong incentive to improve, though, of course, a lot of people just can't break out.'

About the time he turned eighteen in 1951, Hayden was profoundly affected, in a complex and contradictory way, by the introduction of conscription by the Menzies Government at the time of the Korean War: he was so fiercely opposed to the concept that he almost joined the Communist Party, then spent six of the most enjoyable months of his life to that time in the Navy as a conscript.

'When Menzies brought in conscription it was a political stunt, and seen as such,' Hayden says. 'I objected very strongly to conscription, to being told I had to do something: it's the Irish pig-headedness coming out. There is particularly strong evidence of this on my mother's side; she would dig her toes in if anyone started pushing her around or bullying her. I rebelled. I went to a rally at the Brisbane Trades Hall which was organised by the Communist Party — I was really fired up. There were about twenty people in the small upstairs function room, and I was sitting on a chair and nobody came near me. I was a reasonably shy sort of person, but I was trying to get near these people to try to talk to them. I was prepared to join; I was that furious about being told I had to do something I didn't want to do, and these were the only people opposed to it. I could see a number of people eyeing me off and muttering to one another. One was a guy I didn't know then, but he is such a distinctive character, and I got to know him well later when he was president of the miners' union in Ipswich; his name is Bluey Millar, a lovely bloke, one of those Communists you had to respect because of the standards he applied in his own personal conduct. Looking back on it, I think they thought I was a young police plant trying to get among them. They wouldn't have a bar of me, so I was saved from a fate that would probably have destroyed all sorts of opportunities that opened up for me subsequently.'

Some months after Hayden had told me this story I came across a picture of him and Mr Millar taken by security police during a peace march after Hayden had become a member of Parliament. One of Hayden's former staff members claims that Hayden once told her a story about how he had been sent as a policeman, on duty, to keep order at a Communist rally, and had been so affected by the rousing speeches that he had decided to join the party. 'You will know the story is true when you hear the end,' she added, 'He found he didn't have enough money in his pocket to join.'

'The irony of my passionate opposition to conscription,' Hayden said much later, 'is that I went into the Navy and I really loved it. I loved every minute of it; I was sorry it was not for six years instead of six months. But right up to the end there was still this resentment at being told I had to do it; that is a common characteristic among Australians if they are told they have got to do something without someone explaining to them why it is desirable and persuading them. They get their back up very quickly.'

Hayden's move to Redbank came in the year of the Queensland Labor Party's greatest crisis and the Split that was to deny it power at the State level for more than three decades. The years between 1953 and 1957 were a particularly bitter and messy period in Labor and industrial politics across Australia, and no less in Queensland than elsewhere, as industrial grievances and religion became enmeshed in the deadly struggle between predominantly Catholic members of the anti-Communist Industrial Groups, or Groupers, and their opponents. At the Labor Party Federal Conference in Hobart in March 1955, delegates representing the Industrial Groups were refused admittance and in the following month the Victorian branch of the party expelled those Federal and State parliamentarians associated with the Industrial Groups, who then formed a separate political party which later became the Democratic Labor Party.

This division and struggle had been going on for several years within the party before it came to the pitch of public war that was reached at Hobart. According to Denis Murphy, Hayden had earlier tried to join the ALP in Vince Gair's stronghold of South Brisbane in 1953 [when he was twenty] but, in the intense power struggle then going on in the Queensland branch of the Labor Party and which permeated down to branch level, Hayden's father's reputation as a left-winger was probably the factor that kept young Hayden out.[2]

Vincent Clair Gair, a short, neckless, dumpling-shaped figure with brutal pudgy fingers and a political instinct to match, was a staunch Catholic married to a former trainee nun who he had met when he was the postman delivering mail to the convent. He won the seat of South Brisbane, which enveloped Mabel Street, in 1932. Gair's entry into Parliament took place a year before Bill Hayden was born and nearly three years before the Haydens moved into the heart of his electorate. Gair became Premier in 1952, and in the following year George Hayden died and Bill joined the police force.

At the time the teenage Bill Hayden became interested in politics,

SUNSILK CONDITIONER
                      X
FIESTA   WHITE MAGIC
              BLEACH CLEANER.

                  X

KITTEN   GLO-WASH (CAR)

              X

PICALLILLI
           X

the Labor Party across Australia was in the grip of a ruinous brawl between the predominantly Irish-Catholic Right and the Left which was supposedly soft on Godless communism. At the level that affected Hayden the conflict took the form of a battle for numbers and control of party units, down to suburban and village branch level. In the electorate of Gair, who was later to be a significant figure in the breakaway Democratic Labor Party (DLP), and later in the fall of the Whitlam Government, Hayden would have been viewed with suspicion as a potential left-winger, the son of a drunk and dying radical. He was not the sort of member Gair's stalwarts wanted.

Hayden says: 'People living close to us in Mabel Street were members of the Labor Party, and I asked them about the party. I said I'd like to be involved. I never got a firm answer. I got to know another ALP member who used to visit his sister at State Stores and I asked him about it but he kept fobbing me off.'

When Hayden moved to Redbank what had been a disadvantage now counted in his favour. 'I was lined up,' Hayden says simply. 'The Split [between those who formed the DLP and those who remained in what was left of the party] was coming up and they were looking for bodies. There was a branch in Redbank that was going to stick with the party and not go with the DLP. It is funny when I look at it. It was not done with great subtlety; people would pull me up in the street and start talking to me, seeking my views. It was known I had strong Labor views. They must have had a council of war and decided I had enough political purity from their point of view to be trusted into the party.'

Murphy records Hayden's initial contact with the party:

> When he first arrived at Redbank Hayden asked a local, Jack Eustace, where the police station was. Eustace, who worked in the laundry at Wolston Park Hospital, was one of those Labor stalwarts who either belonged to or held office in almost every organisation in and around Redbank. Hayden struck up a friendship with him and his wife Vera and soon joined the Redbank branch of the ALP of which Eustace was president.[3]

The feud of the 1950s involving the Catholic Grouper elements in the Queensland Labor Party and their opponents was inextricably entwined with another struggle which, in the words of Robert Murray in his definitive book *The Split*, was 'almost as old as organised Labor in Queensland.'[4] This was the struggle for control of the ALP in Queensland between the two big union battalions: those unions affiliated with the

Trades and Labor Council on one side, and, on the other, the State's biggest union, the Australian Workers' Union. The AWU had traditionally been aggressive in recruiting members, not limiting itself to particular trades or industries, and at the same time politically and industrially conservative. The chief obstacle to the AWU, Jack Egerton, who was to dominate the Queensland ALP during much of Hayden's political career and later achieve notoriety by accepting a knighthood from Malcolm Fraser, was then secretary of the Boilermakers' Society and a key organiser of the Trades Hall group. He detested what he saw as the AWU's arrogance, tame-cat industrial tactics, and extraordinary rapport with employers' organisations. He also detested Gair.[5]

Egerton was suddenly able to realise his ambition to form a coalition to get rid of Gair when, in 1957, the Premier bucked the AWU by refusing to implement party policy and grant three weeks' annual leave to workers under State awards. For once, and briefly, the Trades Hall and the AWU had an objective in common. On 25 April Gair was expelled and, with his breakaway supporters, including most of his ministers, soon afterwards formed the Queensland ALP which later merged into the DLP.

On 3 August a conservative Country and Liberal Party coalition government was elected in Queensland. It was Australia's McCarthyist period of Cold War paranoia in the aftermath of the Korean War and the Petrov Affair; sectarian and political feeling ran high throughout the community and was heightened among those involved in Labor politics by the formation of the DLP.[6]

'It was a pretty awful time,' Hayden recalled more than thirty years later while talking of the man who had introduced him to the ALP. 'It took a lot of courage to stick with the party, and Jack Eustace was a good Catholic; he had seven kids. He'd go down to Mass on Sunday morning and he'd hear the most fire-and-brimstone denunciation of the Labor Party. He'd be ostracised at church; nobody would speak to him. He had a hard time. Those people really were heroes of the Labor movement.'

Another breakthrough in Hayden's personal development came when he decided to sit for an exam to gain promotion to the rank of first-class constable; he discovered he had more potential academic ability than he had realised, and became determined to use it. 'For the first time in donkey's years I sat down and really studied. I had never pushed myself at school, or even taken much interest; I really got through on what I casually caught up with in class or casually read. When I was doing this police exam I really got stuck into it. For some reason, I don't know how, there suddenly came an awareness that I had to make a bit more out of my life. I got a very good mark, and I thought: "Gee, that went all right, I can do it after all," and I thought I would like to study more, but I didn't know how to go on. I had been up the bush for years, and it has a sort of country village effect on you.'

The opportunity for further study presented itself by chance within weeks of his success in this exam. 'I was in Ipswich and had to take the police motorbike into the police depot in Brisbane to be fixed up. I had time on my hands waiting for it, and while I was wandering around I saw a display on education by correspondence in the window of the *Courier Mail* in Queen Street.' Hayden had at this time also just read an article by the rocket scientist Werner von Braun who said he had been a dunce at mathematics as a kid and had decided that if he was going to get anywhere he'd have to sit down and go over it until he did understand it.[7] Hayden determined to emulate him.

'I took myself in hand and started to drive myself harder and tried to make something out of my life,' Hayden told me. 'Until then I had just been prepared to drift along and take the chances as they came, trying to enjoy life, in a rather pointless way in many respects, but a way which was not uncommon in the sort of community in which I had grown up — we didn't have high expectations; the horizons around where we lived were not particularly high either.'

In 1958, in police uniform, Bill Hayden walked into Badke's barber shop and casket agency in Ipswich for a haircut, and there behind the counter was Dallas Broadfoot, a quiet young woman with sparkling eyes and long dark hair, then twenty-two years old. For months afterwards friends often noticed Bill in uniform leaning against the counter talking to her, and soon they were going out.

In the division and attrition that followed the Split, Hayden had become an active and energetic party worker, closely aligned with the left-wing Trades Hall faction that now controlled the Queensland ALP. He was soon secretary of the Bremer State electoral executive committee and spent much of his free time with Labor and trades union activists and supporters. Dallas, who was a miner's daughter, was soon introduced to the social life of Labor Party functions. 'They went to lots of balls and

Dallas always looked exquisite; she wore dresses her mother made for her; she had long hair and a beautiful figure. Bill was very proud of her,' recalls Joy St John-Hort, a Labor Party member at that time.[8]

Early in 1959 Bill and Dallas decided they would marry in the following year. Nineteen sixty was to be a furiously active and critical year, the turning point in Hayden's life. At the start of the year he enrolled in adult matriculation classes, taking four subjects including economics and logic, and began attending political science lectures at a new Labor college established at the Brisbane Trades Hall by Dr Max Poulter who was senior lecturer in education at the University of Queensland. Hayden found Poulter an attractive figure because he was down to earth and 'not at all sissy' as he had expected academics to be. Poulter was elected as a senator in 1961 but died the following year.

In May 1960, Bill and Dallas were married in the Central Methodist Church at Ipswich. Their first home was a rented cottage with no curtains or hot water, a tin bath and a wood stove, in the semi-industrial Ipswich suburb of Dinmore. In the same month a State election was held and Hayden, by now also president of the Oxley Federal divisional executive of the Labor Party, was among the more energetic and effective of the campaign workers. A carefully prepared speech he made in Ipswich during the campaign attacking the economic policies of the Menzies Government came to the attention of the heavies at Trades Hall, Jack Egerton and Frank Waters, who arranged for it to be published in the official ALP journal, *The New Age*.[9]

Besides his political activities, Hayden was finding study hard work although he had taken to it with dedication approaching fervour.

> I used to get up at five in the morning and go late at night, and when I was on duty I used to work away at it when I was in the station; if I was on the beat I'd sneak into the men's meal room at the railway station and pore over these bloody trigonometry problems and calculus. I could sometimes spend a long time on a problem because there was nobody to ask. It used to be awfully hard at first, and then something happened; there was a breakthrough and I got it.[10]

The brief alliance between the AWU faction and the Trades Hall group in the Queensland Labor Party did not last once it had served its purpose of dumping Gair. When the division was reopened within what remained of the Labor Party after the Split, Hayden suddenly found himself in a position of prominence. A leading Labor figure in the ALP in his local electorate, Bert Warren, a sawmill owner who had been the party's candidate in Oxley at the previous Federal election, was regarded as an AWU man. The Trades Hall group didn't want Warren, and its members encouraged Hayden to contest the party's preselection for Oxley against him. October 1960 was the deadline for selection of the Labor candidate.

Oxley was not seen as a likely Labor gain, but Hayden was aware, as he had shown by his active criticism of the economic policies of Menzies and his Treasurer, Harold Holt, that the Federal Government's credit squeeze was hurting in Queensland: unemployment had risen to the then alarming levels of 2.4 per cent. Ipswich as an industrial city was vulnerable to the chilly economic winds, and so, thought Hayden, was the Liberal Party's grip on its electorate.

Warren, who had stuck with the party through the Split, would not give in without a fight and the preselection plebiscite in which he and Hayden competed for the votes of rank-and-file party members was described by Denis Murphy as 'pretty rough' even by Labor Party standards. The fact that Hayden had married a miner's daughter overcame resistance to him as a newcomer, while his youth, energy and obvious competence were decisive in his victory by 393 votes to 133. At Blackstone, where most members were miners, he scored 170 votes to Warren's two.[11]

The seat of Oxley was held for the Liberal Party by Dr Donald Cameron, a lugubrious though well-liked local doctor who sat between two equally saturnine members of the Government in a section of Parliament that Eddie Ward used to refer to as Sunshine Alley. Cameron had delivered Dallas as a baby; he had won the seat in 1949 and had been Health Minister from 1956 when he succeeded Sir Earle Page.

Hayden later suggested that he had contested the election almost as an academic exercise: 'When I did stand for Oxley, we didn't think we'd win; the Labor Party wasn't meant to win on the area that had been taken into Oxley. I did it because I had commenced studying and one of the subjects I wanted to do was political science at university, and I thought if one contests an election one would know a damn sight more about it. It didn't look much of a chance.' Labor's vote had averaged between 40 and 42 per cent in Oxley over all the years Cameron had represented it, but Hayden threw himself into the campaign from the time of his preselection.

At the end of 1960 he matriculated and although he had decided to study law and was eager to take up the challenge of university studies he wouldn't start at university until the election was out of the way. There was an element of frustration in this decision: 'When I was younger, my mother was always telling me that one day I would go to university. She knew that.' Hayden did have one bit of unfinished academic business, however. At State High School he had taken German as a subject, but had never studied it: 'one of the problems was that I was just bone lazy and I didn't like school, and the grammatical structure is just far more complicated than in English. For some reason I had this feeling I had failed there and really should try to remedy that failure. When I was in the police in Calen I was talking to a schoolteacher one day and told him I would like to learn a foreign language, and he lent me some books. He had been a prisoner of war in Germany and his family had sent him some books to help him learn the language of his captors. He gave me three books, which I still have. I looked at them in Calen and they just didn't make sense to me. I never got under way. In 1961 I managed to complete four years of German by correspondence.'

Hayden carefully analysed previous election results and, although he decided to concentrate most of his effort in and around Ipswich where Labor's vote had been consistently higher in State than in Federal polls, he also worked out an exhaustive itinerary that would take him in his old Holden to every corner of an electorate of 11 000 square kilometres. In many of the small rural communities Labor branches had simply ceased to exist after the Split. Early in the election year of 1961 Hayden and Tom Burns, then a new State ALP organiser who was later to become the party's Federal president, spent two weeks on the road visiting every township, reviving or establishing party branches in many of them. Hayden carefully prepared his speeches for the smallest gatherings and branch meetings, often practising them alone in the bush around Ipswich. Usually they contrasted the performance of the Menzies regime with the achievements of the Curtin and Chifley governments more than a decade earlier.[12]

He visited factories and workshops, spoke on street corners, and with Dallas, who became pregnant with their first child in March, attended community functions. On 28 July 1961, Hayden had his first, notably inauspicious, meeting with Gough Whitlam, then deputy leader of the Opposition, who was on the final leg of a two-week, 5000 kilometre trip around Queensland; a crusade that was credited with contributing significantly to the gains Labor made in the State at that election.

Hayden, a fresh-faced twenty-eight-year-old constable, had the task of meeting Whitlam at the prearranged venue for the election rally to tell him that there had been a mix-up with the bookings and they could not have the hall they had wanted. 'As he leant into the car window, a tired Gough Whitlam told him what he thought of him and his hall ... and though this was only a tiny incident it set the scene for the Whitlam–Hayden relationship for many years,' according to an article by the political correspondent of the *Australian*.[13]

During the election campaign Norm Gulbransen went in plain clothes on police duty to a country show at Kilcoy and ran into Hayden: 'I had a drink with him, and he was called away to meet somebody. His campaign manager said to me, "He's going to win". I laughed. In my opinion he had no hope. His manager said: "I've never seen a bloke work like it. By the time the election comes around he will have been in practically every house in the electorate."'

The election was held on 9 December, six weeks before Hayden's twenty-ninth birthday, and a few weeks after the birth of his first child, Michaela. On that morning, as Denis Murphy records, he sat on the edge of his bed and thought: 'This sort of thing isn't for you. Working class policemen don't defeat Liberal cabinet ministers. You've made a mistake in all of this. You've got yourself into debt thinking you can toss a cabinet minister.'[14]

There was a landslide to Labor in Queensland, with a swing of 10.5 per cent across the State. Hayden polled slightly better than the average to score 52.6 per cent of the vote, a gain of nearly 11 per cent.

FIVE

'The boy delinquent from Queensland'

*The men, who through their sweat and back-
breaking toil at the coal face, have created
the profits...should not be callously cast into
the slaughteryard of unemployment...*

Bill Hayden

IN CANBERRA, Hayden quickly earned something of a reputation in Parliament as a brash and cheeky upstart. The truth was more complex: he was an intense and serious young man, flushed with reforming zeal, on a crusade to correct the obvious injustices of society, but he had arrived in the national capital only to find that the country was being run by a plump and pompous old man who, Hayden felt, had no interest in these injustices. What was even worse, he soon discovered, was that many Labor figures he had admired from afar — because of their reputation as radical firebrands — were cowed by Menzies' domineering presence, and fearful of his barbed tongue. Hayden was even critical of Menzies' appearance.

On the day he first attended Parliament, Hayden had his picture taken standing beside the front steps in dark blue suit, white shirt, and a soberly dark, but trendily thin, tie. He was in square-shouldered, statesmanlike pose: like a treasurer about to deliver a budget, he was carrying a large and shiny briefcase. It had been bought for him after a whiparound among Ipswich policemen, and presented to him at his send-off by

Sub-Inspector G.W. Allen who said, as he handed it over: 'Irrespective of matters of politics, Bill's election has brought honour to the force. He is a young man with a stable mind who could eventually become Prime Minister if he has the success to match his ability.'[1]

Journalists and parliamentarians noted, within a remarkably short time, that Hayden was one of the very few Labor members who could get under the skin of the Prime Minister. Menzies was then, despite his narrow 1961 election victory, still near the height of his powers, and increasingly cultivating a lofty, statesmanlike persona, seldom deigning to notice the gnats that attempted to discomfort him. Menzies had become Prime Minister for the first time in March 1939, six months before George Hayden had taken his bare-footed son out of St Ita's Convent and enrolled him in the Dutton Park State School. When Hayden entered Parliament, Menzies had, in his second term, been Prime Minister for twelve years. Yet, to the surprise of observers, Menzies could seldom resist responding to Hayden's provocations, describing him once as 'the boy delinquent from Queensland,' and later as a 'poor little ignoramus'.

Hayden, although twenty-nine years old, was the youngest member of that Parliament, and had much of the awkwardness characteristic of the short-back-and-sides Queensland copper he had so recently been. But from the start he made plain the trait that remained always an essential part of his nature: despite frequent private feelings of inadequacy, he simply would not be bullied or stood over. Ramrod-straight, with his arms crossed defiantly and protectively across his chest as he spoke, he would confront the Government from a position halfway round the Opposition benches towards the Kings Hall exit from the House of Representatives. From there he could face both the Speaker and Menzies, a big man with black, landscaped eyebrows, distinguished silvery hair and handsome jowly face. Peter Bowers, veteran *Sydney Morning Herald* political correspondent, recalls: 'Hayden used to stand up with his arms folded and deliver these serious economic critiques on the Government, and I used to think "Who is this cheeky bastard? Who is he?" and someone said: "He's an ex-copper," and I thought, "An ex-copper lecturing the Government on its economic performance? from Brisbane?" I got a bit interested in him right from the outset; he was different. And I liked his sort of quirky ways: of course, they all said we were a quirky pair.'[2]

Hayden, for his part, was in no way overawed in his first impressions of the giants of Australian politics, Prime Minister Robert Menzies and Country Party leader Jack McEwen. 'The biggest shock I got when I came down here was when I saw Menzies and McEwen: what an untidy, undignified pair they looked,' he said[3]. Hayden's first parliamentary baiting of Menzies came within the first minute of his maiden speech, responding to a reference that had been made to him by another newcomer, Liberal backbencher Don Chipp, later to become a minister, and then resign from his party and become a founder of the Australian Democrats. 'Although I did not notice him,' said Hayden, referring to Chipp, 'he could quite easily have been a casualty, as were a couple of the rebel members of the Liberal Party who were seen to be asleep during the Prime Minister's address — no doubt seduced to sleep by the deep, sonorous tones in which he said much, but conveyed little.'[4]

He then turned on the Treasurer, Harold Holt, who had, in a speech in the same debate on the Government's economic policies which Hayden had chosen for his first performance, referred to ghosts walking in the chamber. 'I can believe him because of his nervous manner and jerky delivery. He has been placed somewhat in the position of the Dickensian character Scrooge who saw three apparitions, representing his past, present and future. Scrooge was fortunate ... he had an alternative future which he could choose if he mended his ways.' The Government, Hayden said, had no future; its members were condemned by their past economic failure.

The speech, which he began at 9.44 on the night of 1 March 1962, attracted no great attention, but was above average for a newcomer. He strayed well from the convention, more widely observed in those days, that people making their first speech in Parliament don't make personal or provocative remarks, and in return are not rattled by interjections. Most of Hayden's maiden speech had been rehearsed, and the ringing sentences tested in lonely audition before the drooping stringy-barks on the rocky hills of Redbank in the summer since his election. It was roughly embroidered with good old-fashioned class rhetoric, balanced with a sensible approach to coping with changing times. The times were changing at a slower pace then, but the consequences were as disturbing for those affected by them. The debate wasn't about nuclear energy or computerised robots, but about coping with bigger machines. Hayden told the Parliament that the miners of Ipswich, who were being laid off through increasing automation, welcomed progress.

> But at the same time, the men, who through their sweat and back-breaking toil at the coal face created the huge profits which enabled the coal owners to purchase the extremely expensive equipment for automation and placed them in the position they are today, are entitled to some consideration and should not be callously cast into the slaughter yard of unemployment which the Federal Government has created.

As recently as 1986, while Foreign Minister, Hayden was continuing to make calls to journalists, making a case for assistance to the West Moreton coalfields. From time to time he would telephone me at the *Sunday Sun* in Brisbane urging me to push a line that had both merit and complications: the coalmines in his electorate are underground, and, compared with the huge open-cut mines in central Queensland where large parts of Australia can be quickly loaded onto ships bound for Japan, do not meet tests of efficiency demanded by free-market economics. But, as Hayden would point out a quarter of a century after he made his first speech in Parliament, they maintain a traditional community who could not move to the new mines. To close them would mean unemployment and despair, the disruption of families, the closure of schools, and the end of useful life for men, around his age in their early fifties, who had spent their lives underground working bloody hard to pay off their houses and educate their kids.

In his first speech in Parliament in 1962 there were a number of clear signposts to the Hayden of the future: some positive proposals, including suggestions for the establishment of new industries in his electorate based on local resources to compensate for the decline in its traditional base of railway workshops and mining; and solid evidence of hard work and genuine concern for those who had been hurt by the unemployment resulting from Menzies' credit squeeze. He then revealed some of the contents of the briefcase: 'I have here two notebooks,' he told his small audience,

> one completely full and the other half-full, of names of people seeking work; youngsters who have just completed their schooling and have gone out into the world to seek their destiny, bright eyed and eager-faced, many of them with excellent junior passes and a number of them with first-class senior passes. Their lot at the present is the dole and the soup kitchen line.

The rural industry in his electorate was not forgotten, including the struggling farmer who was supplied with poor-quality materials for top prices and was being ripped off by the 'exploitative, plundering interests and motives of the middle-man'. 'He gets barbed wire that is scarcely strong enough to tickle the hides of the beasts that brush past it,' the recently resigned Ipswich policeman informed the bemused representatives of the Country Party. There was something of the essence of Hayden in that line. It has a graphic quality and he had obviously worked on it. Later when he was Opposition leader and had speech writers he would demand that they include jokes in his addresses, and would invariably lose the thread and mess them up. He admired and envied, as did the humourless Bob Hawke, the quick and natural Irish wit of people they both knew like Mick Young and Eric Walsh. Yet Hayden had from the start his own sensitive and painful sense of observation and a way of expressing it, though he never fully trusted it. His most memorable expressions never came from speeches prepared for him by professionals.

Hayden lived something of a political double life in his early years. In Oxley he was the hard-working, parochial local member; in Canberra he was a doctrinaire acolyte of the Left. Double standards are less common in politics than most outsiders suppose, and Hayden has never been comfortable with them; at that time he had a youthful certainty that radical solutions were needed to heal the sorrows and inequalities he had seen on the beat and in his travels around Oxley. 'I came to Canberra burning with some sort of zeal; things must change, all the injustices that I knew were rampant in our society just had to change, and somehow we had to do it. But it seemed the system was built against you doing this,' he said in 1972.[5]

After winning the election in 1961 Hayden wasted no time in beginning work in his electorate; he was resolved from the start not to be that saddest of political figures, a 'oncer' who enters Parliament for only one term at an early age and faces problems of adjustment ever afterwards.

'Hayden carried with him then, and for a further decade, an air of uncertainty. However, this seeming lack of confidence masked not only a capacity for hard work but also a dogged determination to succeed,' Denis Murphy later wrote.[6] Early in January 1962 he began arranging a meeting of leaders of business, industry and trade unions in and around Ipswich, a sort of provincial summit, with the aim of developing plans to 'avert economic stagnation settling on the city' and made submissions and led delegations himself to the State and Federal governments for funds to generate and safeguard employment. He made other proposals for the establishment of a steel industry in the city and for protection for the timber industry and subsidies to primary producers. He continued to tour the twenty Labor Party branches that had now been formed across his electorate. As he drove around he would call in on farmers and attend stock sales and other rural gatherings.

In Canberra he moved in more radical company. Tom Uren, jut-jawed veteran of the Left, recalls: 'At the first Caucus meeting he attended, Bill came up to me and asked for the Left ticket, which he followed in the balloting for positions.' The 'ticket', prepared by faction leaders, was, like a party how-to-vote card, followed by faction members without deviation or question. Uren said: 'Bill stayed very close to Jim Cairns and me; wherever we'd go he'd kind of trot along. I learnt years later I'd hurt his feelings. Although I hadn't meant it in a derogatory way, I had said to him: "Bill, if you are going to stick around with us you're not going to get any dividends from it." I advised him to try to tone down some of his left-wing attitudes in his first few years. He was a very courageous young bloke, and was so far ahead of the Labor Party on things like homosexuality and social attitudes, and the old hardcore didn't understand those types of things. I thought he was good, regardless, but I just didn't think it was electorally wonderful, particularly in his type of electorate. But he knew better it seems, because as I understand it he used to go down to the saleyards and mix with the farmers in those early years, and he built great respect at the grassroots level.'[7]

Uren's relationship with Hayden over the years, one which straddled factional divisions, was one of the constant and complex facts of Australian politics. Hayden outgrew his early benefactor in some ways, while Uren retained an affection that was sometimes patronising towards his young friend and follower of those early days. Uren said in 1988: 'He drifted away from the Left over the years. He was never part of what you call the collective Left. Of course, we were a very informal Left in those days. Although he always asserted his independence he always voted for the Left and voted for Cairns against Whitlam in the 1968 leadership spill.'

Hayden has over the years become more radical on some issues while taking a more conservative approach on others, with his stance reflecting experience, thoughtful consideration, and, occasionally, political expedience or necessity. In 1977 he acknowledged: 'My old certainties have given way to an appreciation of the complexity and pluralistic nature of our society to a degree I wouldn't have thought possible.'[8]

One of Hayden's old certainties in his first years in Canberra was the need for high tariff protection, which he believed was necessary not only for secondary industry, and in particular the large Morris Woollen Mills in his electorate, but also for primary producers. Hayden was later to become an admirer of one of Australia's more eccentric, single-minded and far-seeing politicians, Bert Kelly, the Liberal member of the House of Representatives for the rural electorate of Wakefield in South Australia.

Kelly spent his political life crusading for a reduction of Australian tariffs. He was, in the early 1960s, about as far away from Hayden in background and attitudes as it is possible to get in the Australian class structure. With an outback suntan and a well-worn but well-made tweed suit and a faraway look in his eye, appearing as if he had just helped crutch a prize merino ram, which, as a wealthy grazier, he probably had, Kelly would launch into a discussion on economics with casual acquaintances. He carried on his crusade in Parliament and in articles and books, often writing under the pseudonym 'The Modest Member'. His line was simple: he sold his wool overseas for whatever price anybody was prepared to pay for it, and he bought imported machinery at prices excessive because of tariffs imposed on it designed to save Australian manufacturers of similar products from overseas competition. He then argued that because Australian manufacturers were protected in this way they had no interest in improving their efficiency or the quality of their goods. As long as this situation continued Australian manufacturers would never be able to compete on international markets and create significant employment opportunities for an expanding population.

The argument between free traders and protectionists was a debate that began before the federation of Australian States, and which still continues. Hayden had agonies of conscience over it, but the way in which he grappled with the issue played an important part in his political development. Kelly had already spoken in the debate when Hayden rose to make his first speech on tariffs in his first year in Parliament, and he began by berating the Liberal tariff reformer, characterising his views as epitomising the 'narrow, insular and parochial bigotry which is exhibited far too often by members of the Government'. Hayden said:

> They do not take an expansive view of the needs of the national economy or make an overall assessment of what Australia needs in order to develop. We of the Opposition take a more balanced view of these matters; we realise that tariffs are necessary. This cry of free trade and laissez faire has been

discredited during the past century of world history. We, on this side of the chamber, realise that we have to protect secondary industries, because while workers in those industries are earning their pay they spend it. They constitute the consumer market. They are the people who buy the products of primary industry.[9]

Hayden's arguments, as well as being passionately expressed, had a neat circularity that reflected his confidence in radical theoretical solutions which would benefit all in his electorate: workers, farmers and manufacturers.

In the following year, 1963, Hayden finally began his university course. In the time between his matriculation and starting university he decided to study economics rather than law. Murphy said Hayden changed his mind about what to study largely because he had been struck by the lack of knowledge of economics he had found among members on both sides of the House of Representatives, and because nobody in Parliament had been able to give him credible answers to his questions about why there had been a recession in 1961.[10] If nobody in Canberra could tell him, he was going to find out for himself. In retrospect, the fact that he felt such a decision necessary at that time provides something of an index to the changes that have taken place in the composition of the Parliament since he entered it. At the time he became Governor-General at a relatively early age, the Parliament he left was well furnished with people possessing formal economic qualifications and tertiary degrees; among Labor ministers those with tertiary educational qualifications were the norm rather than the exception. The changes in Labor's representation had outpaced even the changes in Hayden.

When he later recalled, with something of a cringe, his early speeches on economic matters, Hayden said:

If you want a condensation of why some of my opinions have changed in the time I have been in Parliament I'd say it was the result of the study of economics. It was just a gradual realisation that I'd been completely wrong. I had, you know, quite conventional views. I have a clear recollection of having made a speech on the timber industry in which I supported tariffs simply because the idea was to employ Australians. I look back on that and shudder. Somewhere along the line when I was studying I had considerable discomfort when I realised the problems of the dairy industry were not a simple result of conspiracy, but the result of economic forces.[11]

At home in his electorate, Hayden did not spend all his time at the saleyards and Labor Party branch meetings; he established close relations with the miners and worked hard on their behalf, in individual social service cases and on broader issues including a proposal for a levy on coal to improve their pension scheme. The miners showed their appreciation by making him the first non-miner to be granted honorary membership of the Queensland Colliery Employees' Union.

In the 1961 election, at which Hayden was elected to Parliament, Menzies had been given the fright of his political career. He survived by only one seat, with the critical victory coming in the Queensland electorate of Moreton that abutted on the eastern boundary of Oxley. Jim Killen held the seat by a margin of 110 votes only with the benefit of ninety-five Communist preferences after first receiving more than 80 per cent of the preferences of Gair's Queensland Labor Party.[12]

The composition of the first Parliament of which Hayden was a member created a situation fraught with possibilities for his future. In the early days of the Parliament Labor was keen to force Menzies to the polls, but with the passage of time enthusiasm waned and Menzies, while surviving on his knife-edge margin, began seeking justification for an early election. From the prospect of an early opportunity for his party to win government, Hayden now faced the possibility that he would not even serve a full term. Menzies was provided with the issue he needed by the response of the Labor Party, at the behest of Arthur Calwell, to the proposal to establish a United States naval communications base at North-West Cape in Western Australia. Despite the entreaties of Whitlam to have Labor's policy decided by the parliamentarians, Calwell referred a decision to the Labor Party's Federal Conference which met in Canberra on 18 March 1963. The canny and conspiratorial journalist Alan Reid saw Whitlam and Calwell, who were, under the party rules of the time, not entitled to attend the Conference, waiting outside while ALP officials, who had not been elected by the people, debated the issue behind closed doors. Reid slipped away and phoned a photographer.

When the photograph was splashed across newspapers, Menzies tagged the conference delegates the 'thirty-six faceless men' who directed Labor's elected representatives.[13] He exploited that issue relentlessly, and was given further assistance in October when the ALP's Federal Executive meeting in Adelaide gave instructions to all parliamentary parties, including the Labor Government of New South Wales, on the proper party attitude they should adopt to state aid for private schools, a bitterly divisive issue that had gained even greater political significance following the formation of the Democratic Labor Party. Despite its name and the fact that its leaders were all prominent former members of the Labor Party, the DLP was effectively, through the disciplined way in which its followers delivered their preferences, in an electoral alliance with the conservative Liberal and Country parties.[14]

The climate was right, the Labor Party was in confusion, and Menzies had issues he could exploit: he called the election for 30 November 1963. Just a week before polling day, on 23 November, the President of the United States, John Kennedy, was assassinated. If Labor had ever had a chance of victory it disappeared then; in a time of international uncertainty the electors of Australia were unlikely to change governments, and greater relevance and emotive power had been given to Menzies' central election theme: that the Labor Party, by its equivocal response to the proposed US nuclear submarine communications base in Western Australia, had jeopardised the ANZUS alliance. Labor lost twenty seats at the election, including three Brisbane metropolitan seats that it had gained two years previously.

Hayden's vote, however rose by almost 5 per cent. The Ipswich newspaper, the Queensland Times, said his greatly increased majority in the circumstances 'must be considered as a personal triumph and recognition that he has served the area well in the comparatively brief period since he captured the seat from the Government'.[15]

When Labor parliamentarians gathered again in Canberra in February 1964, Hayden nominated in the ballot for the parliamentary Executive, but was eliminated in the final round. He enrolled in an additional economics subject at Queensland University and intensified his study of literature to compensate for what he regarded as an inadequacy in his upbringing and education. He was a poor reader who had never mastered the art of reading aloud, a boy from a home without books. In his typical, methodical, manner he began with the Penguin classics and developed the habit, which was to last for years, of referring to the latest novel or play he had read in his speeches and, disconcertingly, in casual conversations with bemused colleagues and staff.[16]

'I am very conscious of the fact that I don't have middle-class values,' Hayden said as late as 1972. 'I'm much closer to working-class values. I'm quite conscious of the fact that there are serious defects in my education that would have come through a middle-class home, like my lack of acquaintance with literature, arts and music, and my limited ability to discuss these things. I've tried to plug up these defects in more recent times by reading and listening to records, more in the hope that my kids will benefit.'[17]

The intensity with which Hayden worked to transform himself from country police constable to serious political figure with a broad education in the arts and humanities took a deep personal toll on his family life that he was later to regret with bitterness and self-blame. 'I would be away all week and Dallas would be there by herself with the kids, and instead of having a normal domestic relationship, it would be just another normal day for her, with me locked up and poring over all this stuff. It says a lot about how she supported me, and the understanding she had; there was never any tension. It was pretty awful, looking back on it, for Dallas.'

Hayden was a loner on an all-consuming quest, faced with a daunting range of competing demands which he attacked with a single-minded passion: he continued to court the dairy farmers, the potato growers, the sawmillers and the coalminers; he became one of the party's leading spokesmen on economics, developing close contacts with academic advisers such as Bruce McFarlane and George Palmer, and making an impressive speech on the Vernon Report; he became a leading advocate of women's rights and initiated moves for married women to have the right to permanent employment in the Public Service; he took public stances on issues then regarded as so sensitive as to be politically dangerous: abortion, censorship, the peace movement and nuclear testing. In his politically bold opposition to censorship Hayden could not resist giving the wider world the benefit of his newly formed literary opinions of recently banned books; *Lolita* he thought was 'glossy, superficial and slick', while *Lady Chatterley's Lover* was 'a grossly over-rated work'.

He was a sponsor of the Australian Congress for International Co-operation and Disarmament in Sydney in early 1964 and in March 1966 took part in an Ipswich-to-Brisbane peace march during which he was secretly photographed by security police. I obtained copies of some of these secret photographs while researching this book. Hayden is shown standing beside identified Communist union officials. I have been unable to identify those responsible for the covert operation, but have confirmed that copies of them were later supplied to senior officials of the Queensland Government and the Federal Liberal Party.

From the cottage at Dinmore where he worked long hours reading and poring over Reserve Bank Reports and weekly editions of *The New*

York Times he would emerge for a peace rally or a cattle sale or a foray to Canberra to deliver sweeping indictments of Treasury officials who, he asserted, had 'become trapped in a web of ideological nonsense about the evils of planning they had spun themselves'.[18]

'Why does young Hayden keep raising the problem of the balance of payments? Why doesn't he just be like a normal politician and worry about his electorate?' Arthur Calwell asked Frank Waters, State secretary of the Australian Postal Workers' Union in 1965.[19] In that same year, Hayden came to prominence as a national figure in the decision-making forums of the Labor Party after Waters and Jack Egerton, who had been impressed with his left-wing views and his close links with the unions, arranged for his election to the Queensland Central Executive and from there to the Federal Conference of the party held in August 1965.

At that time Hayden, a political product of the Split, suspicious and critical of the role some Catholic activists had played in Labor Party affairs, was a caustic critic of state aid to non-government schools, and, although he did not share the anti-Catholic bigotry of some of his colleagues, notable among whom were influential members of the Queensland delegation, he voted in support of them. One Queenslander, Ernie Adsett, a Storeman and Packers' Union official, moved at the 1965 conference that '... the Australian Labor Party is unequivocally opposed to state aid in any form. Furthermore, all references to state aid be struck from the books of the party'.[20] Hayden did, however, speak in opposition to a further amendment proposed by his leader, Arthur Calwell, that there should be a constitutional referendum to let the Australian people decide whether Federal governments should have the power to provide financial aid to non-government schools. In a forceful speech he said he could imagine nothing more frightening than the consequences for the community and the Labor Party if such a referendum were held; both would be fragmented on sectarian lines. He said that if it endorsed a referendum Labor would be trying to avoid its responsibilities as a party and as an alternative government.

The state aid issue remained unresolved as the election year of 1966 began: a sour and painful year for the Labor Party; a year of deep and indelible tragedy for Hayden.

SIX

A personal
tragedy

*The government is bidding on the
international stock exchange of power where
deals are made with human lives.*

Bill Hayden, 19 August 1965

A
T THE START of 1966 the Haydens were settling into their
dream home, a modest ranch-style house they had built on a
double block of land under the brow of a hill covered with native
scrub on the western fringe of Ipswich. Dallas was helping cart rough
bush rock in a wheelbarrow to help make a semicircular driveway to their
fly-screened front door. Shared physical work on their house and in the
garden was a part of the pattern of their lives in the rare periods Hayden
spent at home, a traditional relaxation in times of stress; three days before
they flew to Canberra twenty-three years later for Hayden's swearing in
as Governor-General Bill and Dallas were laying paving stones that had
been delivered that morning. In 1966 the Haydens had four young
children: three daughters, Michaela, Georgina and Ingrid, and a baby son,
Kirk. They had also bought a new car, and were in considerable debt.

Politically, the year had begun promisingly for the Labor Party: Sir
Robert Menzies, the man who had dominated Australian politics for a
generation, resigned, at last, on 26 January. He had been Prime Minister
continuously since December 1949. He had been as ruthless about

potential challengers from within his own ranks as he had been to rivals in opposing parties: some who had challenged him had been made ambassadors, and others judges. Richard Casey had been made Governor-General. Within the parliamentary Liberal Party that had lived beneath his oppressive shadow, much of the growth was pale and weedy. With dignified fanfare Menzies handed Australia's political leadership to his chosen successor, Harold Holt, a handsome and amiable silver-haired political veteran who however simply didn't have Menzies' formidable abilities or his stature and authority. But Menzies' legacy to Holt, to national politics and to Australian society, included two historic decisions that proved, in the short term, to be time bombs for the Opposition.

The Menzies initiatives, one of which committed Australian troops to Vietnam, and the other which bound the Federal Government to provide aid to private schools, brought grievous divisions within the Labor Party into sharp focus. Their painful resolution provoked a leadership crisis in the ALP which brought Gough Whitlam to the brink of expulsion from the party. Bill Hayden resisted the introduction of state aid to private schools, while at the same time he was the earliest of the Labor Party parliamentarians to oppose American involvement in Vietnam and one of the best informed and most passionate opponents of Australian involvement.

The healing process of time has washed away with unusual speed the acrimony of the division within Australia over state aid: it was, in the words of Whitlam's biographer Graham Freudenberg, 'the oldest, deepest, most poisonous debate in Australian history ... The mystic incantation "state aid" has broken governors, governments, parties, families and friendships throughout our history.'[1]

In 1963 the Federal Executive of the Labor Party under the dominant guidance of its left-wing secretary, F. E. ('Joe') Chamberlain, a tough and devious man, had bullied the New South Wales Labor Government into withdrawing a promise made in its September Budget to provide a means-tested allowance of £2 a week to parents of children attending private secondary schools. Chamberlain was a clean-cut, lean and leftish West Australian type who made it clear to other Labor people that it was a traitorous act to talk to representatives of the capitalist press. But brown-paper envelopes with secret records of internal Labor Party discussions would arrive regularly on the desk of Alan Reid, the brilliant right-wing journalist and confidant of conservative prime ministers. The envelopes bore Perth postmarks.

Soon after Menzies heard, in 1963, that the New South Wales Labor Government had been forced to renege on providing state aid, he called a Federal election, and, with his usual destructive subtlety, gave a clear but limited commitment: his Government would subsidise the construction of science buildings at private schools. In the context of those times it was a bold move; Menzies had never had a Catholic in a senior position in his Cabinet and there had been very few Catholics in the parliamentary Liberal Party. Australian Catholics of Irish and Italian descent had, like Hayden, grown up regarding sympathy with the Labor Party as part of their heritage. Many senior Liberals had warned Menzies that there would be an electoral backlash against him by his Protestant followers. It did not occur, but, after his victory even Menzies conceded that he had been amazed at the new political reality which he described in memorable words as 'the impotence of bigotry'. The fact that influential non-Catholic private schools were to benefit from the policy reduced opposition to it.

Menzies had broken the mould: the New South Wales Government was turfed out in May 1965 and by the end of that year state aid legislation had been introduced in each of Australia's seven parliaments. The ancient debate was over, except in the Labor Party. On 8 February 1966, with Chamberlain again playing puppet master, the ALP Federal Executive carried a number of resolutions denouncing state aid. The clincher among them, which precipitated the party crisis, was a motion commanding Labor's legal and constitutional committee to take an appeal to the High Court challenging the constitutional validity of Menzies' grants for science blocks at private schools.

Whitlam, outraged, threw down the gauntlet in perhaps the most decisive and spectacular of his crash through or crash performances. He first wrote to the new Federal secretary of the party, Cyril Wyndham, informing him that he would refuse to serve on the committee that was to organise the legal challenge. Whitlam's first objection was a simple practical one: he did not believe it would get off the ground legally. He went on to put forward forcefully his view that no socialist party should tolerate the inequality of opportunity that existed among Australian schoolchildren or tolerate the poor standards of many Australian schools.

His leader, Arthur Calwell, the man Hayden was backing against Whitlam, made a broadcast defending the Federal Executive decisions. Whitlam responded with what amounted to a public challenge to those who had seized control of the Executive and the party, a group which he said wanted to use the party as a vehicle for 'their own prejudice and vengeance'. 'It is neither representative nor responsible. It will and must be repudiated,' said Whitlam. Then he turned up the heat further in a television interview in Sydney when, in referring to the twelve members of the Federal Executive, he said: 'I can only say we've just got rid of the thirty-six faceless men stigma to be faced with the twelve witless men.'[2]

In one of those stange coincidences that shape the fate of nations, there was a significant national political counterpoint to this internal party power struggle. At the very time it was going on, Whitlam was playing the role of sponsor and leading campaigner in a bid by a recently resigned senior public servant and authority on northern development, Dr Rex Patterson, to win a by-election for the Federal seat of Dawson, based on Mackay on the Central Queensland coast.

Patterson was a rare character, an academic rural socialist who had an engaging manner, and was a great campaigner. Early one morning he walked Whitlam down the main street of Childers, the home town of Chad Morgan who wrote such immortal Australian ballads as 'The Sheik of Scrubby Creek' and 'Chasing Sorts in Childers', a town with wide streets lined by pubs with swinging doors opening from the bar onto the street outside where there were horses tied up. Patterson introduced Labor's deputy leader to a weatherbeaten retired canecutter sitting on his little verandah in his tattered shorts and faded navy-blue singlet watching the passing parade. 'Come here and have a drink, I want to talk to you,' said the old man to Whitlam. He went and got three glasses, a bottle of milk and a bottle of Bundaberg rum, and poured them all a drink. 'A little early for me,' said Whitlam. It was nine o'clock. Patterson handed Whitlam his glass, raised his own and downed it, saying to Whitlam, who had no option but to follow: 'When in Rome ...'[3]

In late February 1966, while the Dawson campaign was under way, Chamberlain, with Calwell's support and confident that he had the necessary numbers, decided to attempt to expel Whitlam from the Labor Party, and called a special Federal Executive meeting for early March for this purpose, though the conspirators disguised their true intent by suggesting in their public statements that they were aiming only to censure him. Whitlam was saved by the voters of Dawson who elected Rex Patterson on 26 February with a swing to Labor of 12 per cent. Patterson flew to Canberra to thank those who had assisted in his campaign and went to the office of Allan Fraser, a senior Labor MHR who had made a brief appearance in the Dawson campaign. Fraser would have got Whitlam's deputy leadership if Calwell and Chamberlain had succeeded. While Patterson was in Fraser's office, Calwell telephoned Fraser to give him a progress report, claiming Whitlam would be out by lunchtime.[4] Patterson, alerted in this accidental manner to the plot, immediately telephoned the Queensland ALP State secretary, Tom Burns. Burns enlisted the backing of Egerton and Queensland's delegates to the Federal Executive were instructed by the Queensland Central Executive, against their intentions, not to vote for expulsion. Whitlam narrowly survived the 3 March Executive meeting with a censure.

Through this turmoil and in two later special Federal Conferences that were called in the course of 1966 to try to resolve the issue, Hayden remained solidly in step with the Queensland branch in its distaste for state aid, its anti-Catholic bigotry and its suspicion that aid to private schools was simply a device for assisting the wealthy. At the March special conference he unsuccessfully opposed a motion that a special committee be established to make recommendations to a further conference later in the year, saying he did not see how it could, in such a brief time, address and deal with the complex issues involved. Among those issues he identified were 'whether [state aid] policies would prop up privilege in the community'.[5] At the second special conference at Surfers Paradise on 29 and 30 July, Hayden again voted with Queenslanders opposing state aid. They lost: Arthur Calwell defected from his Victorian colleagues and ensured the passage by nineteen votes to seventeen of a motion that allowed Labor politicians to support existing forms of state aid. Calwell was so diffident and circumspect about switching sides that Cyril Wyndham, then Federal secretary of the Labor Party and a man now forgotten but responsible for many of its structural reforms, had to ask him whether his hand was up or down when he was counting the vital vote.

On the participation of Australian troops in the Vietnam War, the second of the Menzies heritage issues that bedevilled the Australian Labor Party in its dog year of 1966, Hayden took a crisper, better informed and more consistent line than Whitlam. Hayden was in tune with the emotional mood of the ideological Left of the party, but his speeches at the time were based on quite independent research into the origins of the conflict and of Australia's involvement. Characteristically, Hayden was never totally comfortable with the positions adopted by extremists on either side, and he was later to clash with some of the hard-line opponents of Australian public demonstrations against the war — he thought they lost votes. But at that time Hayden was such a severe and unremitting opponent of America's role in Vietnam that Calwell advised him to consider getting out of the Labor Party, telling him that his anti-Americanism was not in the party tradition. Calwell had an American ancestor and was proud of his ability to recite the names of all the American presidents, a feat comparable with the recitation of all Melbourne Cup winners. Hayden pioneered the view of the conflict that was to become accepted, even fashionable as the war dragged on and defeat loomed: as a post-colonial civil war in which neither America or Australia had a legitimate or useful role. In 1966, however, such a view got nowhere.

Australia's involvement in the Vietnam conflict began as early as May 1962 in a trivial but typical manner. At the urging of America, but following a formal and orchestrated request from the president of South Vietnam, then Diem, Australia agreed to send thirty military instructors to assist the army of South Vietnam. In November 1964, the Menzies Government decided to reintroduce conscription for Australia's armed forces, with those to be called up decided by a lottery; but even then most Opposition members, including Calwell, accepted Menzies' assurances that the decision had been in response to the increased tension between Indonesia and Malaysia and the consequences of that confrontation for regional security. On 29 April 1965, Menzies announced that Australia would provide an infantry battalion for service to South Vietnam. At that time conscripts were not to be called on to serve there. Hayden had from the beginning regarded the war in Vietnam as immoral and saw Australia's decision to become involved simply as a sycophantic attempt to curry favour with the American administration.

On 19 August 1965, Hayden made a major speech in reply to an announcement the previous night by External Affairs Minister Paul Hasluck, later to become a Governor-General, that the Government was to increase its commitment of Australian regular troops to the war in Vietnam and also increase the number of 20-year-olds who were to be conscripted for military service. 'The minister delivered his speech like the flat pedantic dialogue of a bored conducted-tour guide who is tired of telling the same story often and who is doubtful anyway about whether all the virtues he acclaims do exist,' Hayden said. He said that both the proposed moves were momentous in themselves and that he would have expected Hasluck to explain the underlying rationale in some depth.

> When all is said and done, the lives of young Australians are involved. It may fairly be inferred from the statements already made by the Government that quite a number of our 20-year-old conscripts will lose their lives in the foetid jungles of Vietnam. Instead of listening to some momentous statement from the Minister about what the Government proposes for the future; instead of hearing an outline of the plan and the principles that the Government is pursuing in its approach to our commitment in Vietnam and what it hopes to achieve, all we got from the Minister was a vague assertion that the aim was to hold the Vietcong. After that there was a vacuum. The conceptions of our commitment, our strategy, in Vietnam do not extend beyond this point.[6]

Hayden went on to say that the only candid statement he had been able to find about the reasons for the commitment had been made by Senator McKellar who had recently been appointed as Minister for Repatriation. He quoted a report of McKellar's comments from the *Australian* of 11 August which said: 'Australia was in Vietnam to ensure American help in the future ... this is why we have had to face up to the position in Vietnam and give aid to our allies. If we did not agree to send our troops, what would happen in the years to come if we got into a pickle and appealed to our allies in the United States?'

Hayden was one of the very few politicians of substance in Australia at that time who had an appreciation that the conflict in Vietnam could develop into something more than an opportunity for Australia to take out insurance against getting into a pickle in the future. In his speech to Parliament he said:

> ... [McKellar] was saying that it comes down to this simple denominator: the Government is bidding on the international stock exchange of power where deals are made with human lives. It was not a matter of considering the virtues or the principles involved in the war in Vietnam; it was a plain straight out power deal as far as this Government was concerned without regard to social and economic problems. I have made it clear in the past that I believe this is a civil war.

Hayden ridiculed earlier praise of the former leader of South Vietnam, Diem, by Menzies:

> The Prime Minister lauds Diem ... and this is interesting. He refers to him as a brave and honest little man, and a patriot. This is quite interesting

because practically every writer I have read on the subject of the history of Vietnam regards Diem as a corrupt, nepotic, despotic administrator who was responsible for some of the worst forms of religious discrimination. Even today people are incarcerated in concentration camps into which they were thrown during the regime of Diem solely because they disagreed with the way he was administering the country.

Hayden recalled that he interrupted Hasluck the previous evening when the Foreign Minister referred to the appointment of governments in Vietnam, asking 'Who chose this Government?'

'It is a government which has been accepted by the people of South Vietnam,' Hasluck replied.

In his speech Hayden suggested that Hasluck had no justifiable grounds for maintaining that the governments of Vietnam derived their power or legitimacy from the approval of the people. 'The people of South Vietnam have never had a chance to decide which Government should be in power.' Hayden said. 'They have been left so spellbound and breathless by the rapidity with which governments move in and out that they would not know which government is administering their country.'

He recalled also that Hasluck had said: 'Every government that has come to power in South Vietnam and endured there has come there on the sole principle of resisting the Vietcong and continuing this struggle.' He went on:

Note that this is the sole principle. It does not matter if the government stands for corruption, oppression, cruel dictatorship and discrimination — all of which past governments of Vietnam have stood for. It does not matter if there is a perpetuation of vice, crime, poverty, suffering and want. It does not matter that the government maintains a feudalistic, exploiting land system within the country. None of these things matters so long as the government resists the Vietcong. Our Government is not interested in the social and economic considerations; all it wants is a government in Vietnam which will resist the Vietcong ... it does not matter that they are thugs, murderers, gangsters.

Hayden traversed the origins of Australia's commitment at the behest of America, and which had been undertaken without consultation with South Vietnam, and then turned on Menzies, reading again into the parliamentary record a quotation from the *Sydney Morning Herald* of 28 October 1938, a report of an address to the Constitutional Club about which the Prime Minister was particularly sensitive. Menzies had been reported as saying:

Why was Hitler able to tear up the Treaty of Versailles, absorb Austria and the Sudentenland without firing a shot? The dominating reason why he was able to do it all is that he gives the German people a leadership to which they render unquestioning obedience. If you and I were Germans sitting beside our own fires in Berlin, we would not be critical of the leadership of such results.

Hayden asked:

Can you not see the lingering longing for a similar chance to wield autocratic power? The noisy Jingoistic belligerence of the Prime Minister explains the authoritarianism which is part and parcel of the Government's foreign policy. There is another side that can be found in his history as an administrator. He was the reluctant dragoon of World War I, the party-less premier of World War II and he is the purposeless prime minister of the present.

Menzies' foreign policies, which he had exploited successfully at election after election, were based on twin foundations: support for his great and powerful allies, Britain and America; and the threat posed to Australia by communism in Asia, and, in particular, the supposed menace of an expansionist China which was seen as hovering expectantly above Australia on the globe, and ready to seize any opportunity to press downwards, almost as if assisted by gravity.

In the face of the Australian electorate's overwhelming support for these policies at that time, the Labor Party was divided both on attitudes to increasing Australian involvement in the war in support of America's growing commitment, and on the political strategy that should be adopted.

The wider political problem for the Labor Party in opposing Australian involvement in Vietnam was that its stance could easily be characterised as in direct conflict with both those accepted tenets: it was disloyal to our powerful ally, America, whose aim was to stop the downward spread of communism, and it would allow Menzies to again exploit his favoured tactic of suggesting that the Labor Party was sympathetic to communism which he was able to suggest appeared here in its most menacing Asian form. The internal problem for the Labor Party was that many of its traditional supporters and a substantial number of its parliamentary members shared Menzies' views, with Hayden and a small number of his close colleagues at that time in the formal Left of the party, including Dr Jim Cairns and Tom Uren, being notable exceptions. An added complication was that the South Vietnamese leadership and many of those most active in supporting involvement, were, like many members of the Labor Party, Catholic.

In the early days of Australia's involvement, Calwell himself faced something of a personal dilemma; he was extremely racist and had talked privately about the red lava of Chinese communism spilling down through Indo-China towards Australia; and he had long been an admirer of America. But Calwell had little choice: maintenance of his leadership in the face of a potential challenge from Whitlam made him entirely dependent on the support of the Left. Wholehearted opposition to the war was made easier for the Labor leader when, in 1966, Holt committed conscripts to the war: Calwell's first full-blooded political involvement had been in the battle against the use of conscripts overseas in the First World War, and he now renewed the battle with passion.

As a logical sequel to his battle with Calwell over state aid, Whitlam made a formal attempt to wrest the leadership from him, but failed when Calwell mustered sufficient supporters in the parliamentary party, including Hayden, to defeat his move to create a spill of leadership positions on 27 April 1966. Graham Freudenberg, as Calwell's speechwriter, had, in liaison with Dr Jim Cairns, written the speech of May 1965 that formed the basis of Labor's Vietnam policy.

The speech predicted, correctly, that it was only a matter of time before voteless, conscripted twenty-year-olds were committed to the war and the size of Australia's force greatly increased. Calwell told the fighting men that Labor's hearts and prayers were with them, but its minds and reason could not support those who had made the decision to send them. Speaking directly to Labor members he also accurately foresaw what lay ahead: 'I offer you the probability that you will be traduced, that your motives will be misrepresented, that your patriotism will be impugned, that your courage will be called into question.'[7]

A year later, Freudenberg, like many of ability in the party, had become increasingly uncomfortable with the ageing Calwell's leadership and attracted to the Whitlam cause. When, in April, Whitlam failed in his challenge, Freudenberg resigned to return to daily journalism in Melbourne on the understanding he would join Whitlam when he, inevitably, assumed the leadership. Several months elapsed before Calwell was able to engage a replacement for Freudenberg as his speech writer. The task was likened by the *Sydney Morning Herald*'s Ian Fitchett to that of Simon of Cyrene who volunteered to carry the Cross for the last hundred yards.

One Friday afternoon in the non-members bar I was called aside by a young Western Australian journalist named Mike Willesee whose father was a Labor senator. Jim Cairns had asked him to approach me to find out if I would become Calwell's press secretary. I agreed to help out until he could find a permanent replacement, and took on much of the task of writing Calwell's speeches for four or five months. Calwell insisted that I was paid and for that time I retained my position as a political journalist in the Press Gallery and was also being paid by the Public Service Board. Fiery speeches about the 'dirty unwinnable war' were hammered out with the assistance of notes from Jim Cairns, long letters from Jessie Street,[8] the anti-war newsletters of the American I.F. Stone, and contributions of some young academics and of journalists who had been in Vietnam.

Calwell was sitting in the passenger seat of his car after he had delivered one of these speeches at the Mosman Town Hall in Sydney on the night of 21 June 1966, when a disturbed youth named Peter Raymond Kocan fired a shot at him at close range. The shot shattered the car window, spraying Calwell's face with broken glass, but he was not seriously injured. There was no swelling of public sympathy for the old, embattled leader. Opposition to the Vietnam commitment was confined at that time to academics, the political Left and a relatively small proportion of potential conscripts; pop singers and cricket stars were photographed happily shouldering their rifles. Kocan recovered, won several literary awards and later had two of his works set as prescribed reading on the syllabus of the New South Wales education system.

Jim Cairns had taken leadership of the protest movement, while Calwell was largely a passive, almost captive figure of those who had enabled him to deny Whitlam the leadership. Hayden had been one of them, and was to vote for Cairns against Whitlam when Calwell departed, but he had drawn back from the leadership and organisational conflict then going on; he believed his hold on his electorate of Oxley, and as a consequence his political career and his income, was in jeopardy. His emotional involvement in the Vietnam tragedy did not decline; a journalist dropping into his office late one night found him holding a magazine picture of a dead Vietnamese woman with a crying baby huddled beside her. Hayden was writing a prose poem about the scene.

Harold Holt had been to America in July and had declared himself at a White House dinner to be 'All the way with LBJ'. The American

President, Lyndon Baines Johnson, more than returned Holt's favours by making a triumphal visit to Australia in October 1966, at the start of Holt's first election campaign as Prime Minister. In Melbourne anti-war demonstrators alienated many people when they broke through tight security to spray paint over the American President's car as he drove through cheering crowds. During another triumphant cavalcade through the centre of Sydney, demonstrators lay down on the road in front of a car carrying Johnson and Liberal Premier Robin Askin, who later was, after his death, revealed as profoundly corrupt, a creature of organised crime. Askin, showing off to Johnson, gestured towards the demonstrators and told his driver to 'run over the bastards'. He was proud of the statement, and he became a conservative hero.

Back in Ipswich, Bill Hayden was constantly on the road, doorknocking, addressing factory gate meetings, attending every local function he could manage across his sprawling electorate and at the same time studying for university exams.

In Brisbane something like mass hysteria gripped the crowds that lined the streets to farewell Johnson on 23 October on the final day of his conquest of Australia.

Sullen, bruise-grey skies hung over Ipswich that sleepy Sunday morning in Ipswich as Hayden left home to drive the fifty kilometres up the fertile Brisbane Valley to a Labor Party meeting in the conservative old farming town of Esk. The soft rain was falling as he joined the small gathering of party faithful who shared his fears about the coming election.

Every Sunday morning the Hayden's eldest child, five-year-old Michaela, would walk with a group of friends the short distance to the Sunday school at the local Congregational church. She had been sick with a cold for several days and Hayden asked her whether she would like to go with him for the drive, but she did not want to miss Sunday school. Because it was raining that morning and because she had been ill, a friendly neighbour offered to drive Michaela the short distance to the church, and was waiting in the car across the road when the children came out.

Michaela recognised the car and dashed across the road through the rain in front of a car she had not seen. She was knocked down and fatally injured. Hayden had to be traced and then had to be driven home by a friend. Michaela died soon after he returned.

It was, as his friend Denis Murphy recalled years later, 'a personal tragedy which struck deeply at the Hayden family and left Hayden sick at heart for years to come'.[9] Hayden still had to get through the election campaign. Dallas, recalls Mrs St John-Hort, was a rock during the tragedy: 'At the funeral Dallas had Kirk, then a tiny baby, in her arms. Bill broke down and sobbed in the car, and she put her arms around his shoulders. The strength of that woman is extraordinary.'[10]

Part II

The
Economist

SEVEN

The Implications
of Democratic
Socialism

*There is a moral obligation on all of us
to work for the good of society and our
fellow man.*

Bill Hayden

MEMORIES of that sour and tragic year of 1966 cause grief to
Bill and Dallas Hayden to this day. The lingering effects on
the family following the accidental death of their eldest child
were magnified by the circumstances surrounding it.

A belief, shared with other working-class people who have extended
their abilities and improved their position in life, that the next generation
can be raised on the shoulders of the present, had been and remains a
motivating spring of Bill Hayden's life. Echoes of that central theme
appear in comments he has made at intervals over the years, like: 'I want
my kids to have the experiences and do the things I missed out on', and
'I've tried to plug up these defects [in my education] by reading and
listening to records, more in the hope that my kids will benefit'.[1]

One of the motives for his efforts at education had been brutally
undermined by the death of his daughter. Fused with this was a sense
of guilt: Hayden felt that in his relentless pursuit of his studies and
political future he had neglected his family — that, if he had not been
away campaigning, somehow things might have been different.

Bill and Dallas Hayden still find it difficult to talk of the tragedy, even to each other. At the time Bill wrote poetry which he showed only to Dallas, and which she has told friends was sensitive and beautiful. She told a friend once years later that she and Bill had never really discussed the death of Michaela. In 1987 Hayden said: 'It was the lowest point, the greatest down moment. Losing our daughter was the most painful thing and still is.' Hayden had written poetry earlier in his parliamentary career, on the Vietnam War and other subjects, and often read his work privately to his close friend Tom Uren. There is a very Australian incongruity in this emotional intimacy between the Ipswich ex-copper and Uren, a former professional boxer who had been a genuine war hero while working as a prisoner of war on the Burma railway. Uren says Hayden was the second most sentimental member of Parliament in his thirty years there; he claims first position for himself.[2]

Hayden was undergoing a sea change, personally and politically, at the time of Michaela's death and the 1966 election. Although he won his seat with 57.2 per cent of the primary vote, Labor lost two Queensland seats and was spurned by the electorate across Australia, attracting a national vote of only 40 per cent. Hayden was distressed and disillusioned by the nature of the Vietnam debate, the enthusiastic response of the Australian people to what he regarded as the crude and shallow campaign of the Government, and the frustration Labor had experienced in communicating its policies to the public. At the declaration of the poll he blamed Labor's defeat on the problem it had had in 'getting its message to the public' and suggested the establishment of a National Newspaper Commission, something along the lines of the Australian Broadcasting Commission, which would publish independent national newspapers.

Hayden was also to suffer a further blow when the parliamentary Labor Party met early in 1967 to elect its Executive. In the opening ballot Hayden and Senator Jim Keeffe were the only two of nine surviving Queensland members to vote for Jim Cairns when he was beaten by Whitlam for the leadership:[3] in the following ballot for Executive positions Hayden was beaten by Rex Patterson, who had been in Parliament less than a year. Hayden was now no longer a rising star of the Queensland ALP on the Federal scene; that position had been taken by Patterson, an academic who wore an Akubra hat and elastic-sided boots, a burning-eyed rural crusader who had played a role in saving Whitlam from expulsion from the Labor Party, but had little interest in socialist theory.

Hayden was also finding at this time that his economic studies were leading him into deep waters where his increased understanding brought him into conflict with views he had earlier believed in deeply and expressed widely. It is characteristic of Hayden, though not common among politicians, that he is prepared to change his mind on issues once he has been converted by thought and study to a different point of view, and that he is prepared publicly to acknowledge the change. The combination of these factors in 1967 caused him seriously to consider abandoning politics.

> Somewhere along the line when I was studying I had considerable discomfort when I realised the problems of the dairy industry were not a simple result of conspiracy, but the result of economic forces. I came to the unfortunate conclusion that I couldn't continue to represent the electorate because I couldn't continue to put that point of view. This was getting towards 1967 and I discussed it with my wife. Fortunately a redistribution saved me from having to worry about it.[4]

Typically, Hayden didn't keep his conversion a secret. In a speech in Parliament on the second day of the first session in 1967 he aggressively made plain to his parliamentary colleagues his new attitude to excessive tariff protection of Australian industry:

> This encourages sloppiness, it encourages inefficiency, and it encourages the maintenance of industries which have far surpassed their economic contribution to the welfare of the country. If we have excessive tariffs we are asking people to forgo part of the living standards which they are achieving and which they would have if we got rid of this silly sort of sloppiness which is fostered by the tariff policies of the Federal Government.[5]

For the most part, however, Hayden shunned mainstream political life that year. He was for a time in deep shock and had lingering periods of black depression and spells of binge drinking. He began reading more complex and profound literature, and became immersed in the murky world of Kafka, as well as Sartre, Brecht and Moravia.[6]

But it has been a hallmark of Hayden's career that he has been productive in the face of adversity; when many would fade into sulky impotence he has, after periodic retreats into painful introspection, bounced back, worked relentlessly, and made significant contributions to Australian public life and political thought. Towards the end of 1967 he had begun work on setting down his political philosophy, an analysis and justification of his beliefs and an outline of his views on Labor's role in bringing about a fairer society. The 7500-word essay was published as a booklet by the Victorian Fabian Society in June 1968, under the title *The Implications of Democratic Socialism*.

According to an anonymous report in Brisbane's *Courier Mail* in July 1988, people who knew the Hayden family well at the time of Michaela's death believed its circumstances were responsible for Bill forsaking religion. The story is more complex than that; Hayden had, in fact, abandoned the formal practice of religion before the tragedy although he had, as a politician, attended religious gatherings. But he maintained, and still does, a sympathetic contact with members of the clergy of several religious denominations. Among them in his most difficult days was an older, gentle man whom Hayden found comfort in talking to. Their discussions inspired Hayden to commit himself to the recuperative task of analysing and expressing his political and social views in a major work.

'I was good friends with an old Presbyterian minister, George Johnstone, minister of St Stevens in Ipswich,' Hayden recalled more than twenty years later. 'These church people keep coming up when I reflect on my life. He got Aboriginal welfare going with a group here long before others showed any interest; he had a beautiful Scottish burr, and he was, as I understood him to be, a democratic socialist.

'He had to be discreet with his parish, of course, but he upheld the right values. He had me along several times when I got into Parliament to speak from the pulpit, which was really quite something: it's putting an imprimatur on you in a subtle way. He used to get me along now and then and we'd talk about socialism and democracy and liberalism and the rights of people and all of these things; it was always over a cup of tea, and the tea was served in a big china pot with a big hand-knitted cosy around it. Sometimes I'd lapse into a bit of moralising, and he was good, because he couldn't stand moralising, as distinct from being moral. He said to me one day: "Why don't you write something about democratic socialism?"

'He said: "What you've got to understand in politics is that it's one thing to woo a mass of people, but in the political system there are centres of political power: these are the influential people, and some of them are in business and some of them are in newspapers, and so on … other places. They are not numerous, but they can exert a lot of power at certain points. The Labor Party, somehow, has got to stop frightening these people. It's got a reasonable case to argue, it's a very moral position that it wants to take up, even when it is sometimes unwise in the way it puts these things forward. You have got to learn to present your case." ' Hayden paused, and added: 'And that's why I wrote it.'

The Implications of Democratic Socialism is a radical document. It burns with hurt at inequality and injustice; it is infused with the earnest striving of an idealistic person, a reformer, to come to terms with the real and cynical world he has experienced as a policeman and politician and to attempt to suggest a better way. Viewed through the reducing lens of time, looking back at it two decades later, some of its sentiments can be seen to be naive, but that is, perhaps, our loss. 'One must be inspired always by a socialist philosophy of equality, fraternity and liberty,' Hayden wrote (p. 26), but he was as critical of some aspects of traditional Labor politics as he was of those he identified as controlling 'the commanding heights of capital' (p. 4).

> The lack of socialist philosophy could easily lead to what has been termed laborism politics. In this the approach to social and economic issues is imprecise and piecemeal. Rather than trying to change the present socio-economic system through wide-ranging but dovetailed policies of radical reform, the existing social structure is accepted and efforts are made to outbid the government for support within the structure, for example, by offering 20 cents a week more for the pensioner than the government is prepared to offer. 'Jobs for the bhoys', [*sic*] featherbedding and raiding the 'pork barrel' in order to reward supporters are symptoms of this sort of outlook. This type of approach only adds to the inefficiency of the capitalist system without causing any diminution of the inequalities and injustices of the system. It is not remotely connected with socialism and, indeed, seems to be inspired more by some form of sentimentalism and personal advantage than it is by carefully thought out, rational socialist objectives. (p. 26)

Hayden clearly defined his standpoint: 'It is the belief of socialists that there is a moral obligation on all of us to work for the good of society and our fellow man instead of concentrating our efforts upon personal gain' (p. 4). He acknowledged, though, the difficulties in the task of explanation and clarification he had been set by the old clergyman. 'The lot of the democratic socialist would be so much easier if Democratic Socialism was the subject of a neat, comprehensive definition which eliminated all areas of doubt on what are the correct ways and means of achieving a democratic socialist society,' he said at the beginning of his essay.

> But socialism is concerned with a system of moral and political values and a single, narrow path, from which only the wilfully errant could wander, is out of the question. The simple reason is that Democratic Socialism, which is concerned with a system of human values and which is involved

in the creation of a new and improved society for mankind, cannot afford to be a rigid theory. Human life and the society it is continually developing are not rigid. They are richly varied and constantly evolving. (p. 3)

Hayden's expressions, like the words 'new and improved', have now been taken over by soap powder salesmen rather than social reformers; but Hayden was not shy about making quite specific and radical proposals, some of which were later implemented by Hayden himself during his term as Treasurer in the Whitlam Government, others by the Government headed by his successor as Labor leader, Bob Hawke, and others that both he and the Labor Party have subsequently abandoned. In his essay Hayden summarised research by Professor Ted Wheelwright and others which showed a concentration of economic power in the hands of a small number of decision-makers.

To effectively combat and reduce this sort of power, socialists in government would have to show a preparedness to engage in public enterprise, to impose a capital gains tax, to levy an excess profit charge, to redistribute the tax burden more equitably, to collect death duties in the form of property rather than cash, and to demand a public equity and voice in private enterprise in cases where that enterprise is financially assisted by the government. (p. 6)

At the time he became Governor-General the Hawke Government was moving towards divesting itself of involvement in public enterprise, but had introduced a capital gains tax; Hayden had, in 1975, with the support of Gough Whitlam, been responsible for the most significant reforms of taxation to meet the aims he had outlined ... and nobody was talking about collecting death duties in the form of property.

But Hayden's work went much further than slogans. It is clear that he was, even then, able to identify some of the shortcomings of the traditional Australian Treasury approach to management of the national economy: 'The present economic policies operate in terms of rather huge aggregates, and this is their great weakness,' he said. 'Stabilisation policies framed in terms of such aggregates, for example, investment totals, are too general and unselective to neutralise and smother really powerful destabilising influences at their source' (p. 8). He was also critical of the lack of constructiveness in traditional Treasury policy to deal with the economy overheating. The policy, he said,

seemed to be motivated by a general impulse to believe that the boom is caused by too much money chasing too few goods, that is buyers' inflation.

Always the emphasis is on cutting back the demand, that is holding wages down so that they don't start off the mythical wage-price spiral, cut back lending, reduce allocations from the budget to public works. Rarely is the emphasis on pushing ahead with the production side so that it can catch up with demand; hurrying and shortening the construction period of public works so that power, transport, etc. become quickly available; gearing wages sensibly to productivity and cost-of-living so that there is a real incentive to workers to improve productivity; increasing investment in raw materials to overcome shortages and bottlenecks. (p. 8)

The main thrust of the essay is to outline both a philosophy for approaching political and social problems and a strategy for an assault on inequality, through better education, health services and the development of other social services run by qualified social workers.

A social security system for socialists would not be hobbled to providing what is regarded as a marginal level of existence at best precariously balancing on a knife edge just above poverty. Life to be meaningful has to provide happiness, but there are no joys in the marginal and sub-marginal areas. Until a positive campaign to eliminate this poverty in our midst is waged, the children of poverty will beget children of poverty as their values are stunted and their sensitivity destroyed by the permanence of depressing squalor about them. (p. 14)

Hayden drew attention to the plight of part-Aboriginal fringe dwellers, a subject then not much discussed:

It would take a conscience of case hardened steel not to be moved by the sight of the deplorable conditions of those unfortunate part Aborigines who live in tin and hessian humpies congregated on the outskirts of some of our cities. Usually these little pieces of hell are considerably [sic] tucked away in the scrub where they will not offend the comfortable sensitivity of their 'better heeled' non-coloured brothers. The poverty of these people is probably the most appalling of that to be seen among any of our poverty dwellers. (p. 13)

Hayden says that only when discrimination and inequality are removed can the concept of freedom become a reality:

What sort of liberty is it to know that if you are poor then most likely your children will be poor, for you will not be able to afford the opportunities for them that will allow them to escape from this lot? It is a cramped sort of liberty which forces the working man's son to be less than he wishes and for which his abilities suit him vocationally merely because the father's income cannot afford extra education ... liberty is a much qualified concept in our society whilst choice is restricted so much by economic discrimination, social barriers and outmoded prejudices. (p. 16)

He argues for the adoption of a pragmatic approach to reform, in evolution rather than revolution, and says that those who want to make progress by 'Seven League boots or not at all' are acting against the interests of those who would benefit from socialist reforms. He is critical too of those who believe in the inevitable collapse of capitalism followed by the creation of a great new socialist era: 'While the holder waits for the inevitable, the capitalist is shoring up his system in an effort to push that day of inevitability further and further into the distance' (p. 20). But he also warns against opportunism in words similar to those now used by today's radicals against the approach of the Hawke Government:

> Just as rigid dogmatism is a fetter to progressive thought and action, so too is the too-flexible tactician whose grasping for consensus support leads into the realm of political opportunism. Implicit in this sort of approach is a desire to avoid controversial issues and a belief that success is achieved by an unprincipled courtship of popular support; an attitude that 'the boat must not be rocked' pervades. A party based on such an attitude is timid in Opposition, and it would be a weak Government. Such a set of false values would prevent progressive socio-economic reform of any worth, for a party so based would be too frightened to challenge the established power of the 'commanding heights' of capital and in turn would become the docile servant of that power. (p. 23)

In discussing wider social questions, Hayden said it was obvious that there was a need for new thought, and possibly new policies, on social problems such as abortion, prostitution, homosexuality and divorce. 'Certainly more effort is needed on the much neglected fields of prison reform and juvenile delinquency,' he said (p. 21), and concluded: 'The appeal of democratic socialism is compelling.'

> If there have been any shortcomings in its attraction to the electorate these shortcomings lay not in the intrinsic merits of democratic socialism but rather in the fact that it has not been explained properly. The challenge for democratic socialists then is to be positive and constructive. To think and talk in terms of issues and policy and to articulate the ideals and aims of democratic socialism and the path to be taken to achieve these things. The relevance of democratic socialism in our age is undeniable. Our task is to rationally and reasonably demonstrate this relevance to the electorate so that democratic socialist policies may be carried out in the federal administration of this nation. (pp. 26–27)

The cottage at 42 Mabel Street, Highgate Hill, Brisbane, where Bill Hayden grew up. This picture was taken after Hayden's father's death when, using money from his first pay as a policeman, he enclosed the front verandah to create his own bedroom. Until he was twenty he had slept in the living room.

The Hayden family in their back yard at Mabel Street, Highgate Hill, Brisbane. Left to right: John, Bill (wearing John's cubs' cap), Joan, Mrs Violet Hayden and Pat.

Bill Hayden, aged 20, poses proudly in his police uniform in the backyard at Mabel Street for a picture taken by his mother with a Box Brownie. The trousers were a little large for the slim and athletic Hayden who, according to a neighbour, didn't walk like a copper. The motor mower hadn't been invented. (Photo courtesy of Bill Hayden.)

Bill Hayden as a teenager at the front of a lineout playing club Rugby Union in Brisbane, at the time he was working in the State Public Service. He was a fine team player. He happened to play in the same club and the same position as a famous international and got limited opportunities at representative level. "It is the story of my life," he said once. A promising career came to an end when he joined the police force and was transferred to the country. (Photo courtesy of Bill Hayden.)

Bill and Dallas at an ALP social
function in Ipswich soon after they
were married in 1960. (Photo
courtesy of Bill Hayden.)

Taken by security services in 1964 when Hayden was regarded as an
extreme radical. Hayden is shown in the company of members of the
Communist Party playing a prominent role in an Ipswich to Brisbane
'Easter Aldermaston March' protesting against nuclear arms and French
atom bomb tests in the Pacific. The identifying details were: Front file;
J. Perrett (ALP Branch Official Ipswich), W. Llewellyn (Communist
retired miner in Ipswich), W. Hayden (Federal ALP Member of
Parliament for Oxley). Second file; C. McCarthy (president Cairns
branch of Peace Committee) and his son. Third file; carrying banner
Ivy Scott (Communist), Norma Chalmers (ALP Wynnum).

At home in Ipswich in June 1975
when Bill was appointed Treasurer.
From left Ingrid, 13, Bill, Kirk, 8,
Dallas and Georgina, 15.
(*Sunday Sun* photo.)

Opposite (top) A exchange with Sir James Killen across the floor of
parliament. At the time Killen was Defence Minister and a Labor
backbencher was claiming that the Defence Department was concealir
records of the sighting of an unidentified flying object. Killen sent
Hayden a note reading: 'If I can find the UFO I would be sorely
tempted to get on it, Killen.' Hayden returned it with the scribbled
addition: 'Your company would be neither stranger nor more
unbelievable than you have to bear with here, B.H.'

Opposite (bottom) Note sent to Killen by Hayden when Prime Minister
William McMahon was giving a less than moving oration on the deat
of his predecessor Sir Robert Menzies: 'Who are we burying? Menzie
or McMahon?'

Bill

If I can find
Re N. F. O. I would
be sorely tempted to get
on it.

Kellow

Your company would be
neither stranger nor more
unbelievable than you have to
bear with here BA.

PARLIAMENT OF AUSTRALIA
HOUSE OF REPRESENTATIVES

PARLIAMENT HOUSE
CANBERRA, A.C.T. 2600
TEL. 72 1211

Who are we burying?

Menzies or McMahon?

Dear Elector

On December 13th you will cast a vote which will be crucial
to the future stability of our country.

Australia has been plunged into an unprecedented crisis
which cannot be resolved unless and until the proper
functioning of our democratic system of government is
restored.

This crisis transcends party political affiliations.

The election of December 13th will determine whether or not
the possibility of Australia becoming ungovernable is endorsed.

A vote for the Liberal/National Country parties would condone
the thorough impropriety of their recent behaviour and
would establish a system whereby governments could be made
or unmade at the whim of the Senate, which is not the seat
of government. The seat of government has always been, is
and must continue to be, in the House of Representatives;
the popularly elected house of the Parliament.

To fail to endorse the legitimacy of the duly elected
Whitlam Labor Government on December 13th will mean that
new precedents, which will become conventions, will be
firmly implanted in our system of government. In the
words of the influential British magazine, "The Economist" -
"...if the precedent is followed, Australia could prove to
be ungovernable".

One man's ruthless determination to satisfy what is increasingly
apparent as an overwhelming ambition to grab power at any
cost must not be allowed to undermine the stability of our
democratic institutions and the smooth and stable functioning
of our parliamentary system of government.

The key issue for this forthcoming election is whether electors
will stand firm in their defence of democratic principles
and of their democratic institutions.

I submit that this can only be effectively displayed by their
voting for the Australian Labor Party; by their returning the
legitimate, elected government of Australia - the Whitlam
Labor Government.

Yours sincerely

Bill Hayden

(BILL HAYDEN)

Letter to electors after the dismissal
of the Whitlam Government in
1975.

John Spooner, the *National Times*,
1—6 August 1977

Neville Wran conceals his enthusiasm as Hayden launches Labor's 1980 election campaign in Brisbane on 5 October 1980. Dallas is sitting between Wran and Hayden's friend and biographer, the late Denis Murphy.

1980 Election advertisement, the *Queensland Times*, 8 October 1980.

MAKE THIS QUEENSLANDER A PRIME MINISTER

A.L.P.
OXLEY

BILL

HAYDEN M.P.

Postal Voting — Electoral Information

Phone

372 3207, 288 3737, 379 7104, 379 1137, 288 1222

The Implications of Democratic Socialism may not have fulfilled the old Presbyterian minister's advice that Labor should stop frightening the horses, but it did have a lasting political influence. When I discussed Hayden's career at length in 1988 with John Dawkins and Senator Peter Walsh, both ministers in the Hawke Government, both said the work had not only first brought Hayden to their attention but had played a significant part in shaping their political views. They were among many Labor figures of their generation who were similarly influenced. Hayden's work was, for its time, a pioneering effort for a practising politician.

Dawkins and Walsh had also been involved in the Western Australian Fabian Society which organised a seminar where an incident occurred that was to crystallise another transformation in Hayden's central political creed, causing him to become an open advocate of state aid. Hayden later recalled: 'Menzies was the person who introduced state aid to this country, and Whitlam came back with counterproposals in an effort to try to hold together the Catholic vote which had been badly broken up for us by the Split. But the extraordinary thing was that if you went around to Labor functions in that post-Split period you would still find your staunchest, your most reliable, cornerstones of party support would be active Catholics. A lot of them put up with an awful lot from other Catholics who had left the Labor Party.'

'I had taken up a radical position in opposition to state aid. All of a sudden it just hit me: we were getting into a mess. I had a hard electorate to handle, a big rural area, and I had a lot of faithful supporters in little Labor branches which I had formed up all over the place. There was a guy named Dal Ryan who worked in the butter and cheese factory at Laidley, and he was riding his pushbike down the street one day, and he saw me. I can still see it: he wheeled around and pulled me up outside the Railway Hotel, and he went for me about the way we were going on over state aid. He was a dedicated Catholic but he'd stuck with us, and he was faithful to some of the silliest decisions, in the way in which Labor Party people are: there are some very silly decisions at times. But it was just getting too much for him. The sixties wasn't a great period for the party in lots of ways.

'Dal said: "What do you guys down there think you are doing? I'm working in this factory on bugger-all a week, I'm having a hard time. It's run by Country Party people; they're all Country Party people around me, they never leave me alone. I go to church, I'm copping it. I don't have to do this; I'm a volunteer in this party, I just happen to believe in it. But I'm telling you I'm seriously thinking of getting out of it." '

Hayden said the heartfelt outburst by his friend and supporter had come at a time when he was particularly sensitive and receptive. 'I was going through this sort of audit or reassessment of my own position on a lot of things: I had been thrown into a different situation as a member of Parliament, my experiences were different, and I had begun to realise that things are not as simple as you think. You are working an electorate and you can't impose your ideas on the people, you must persuade them.

'There was a lot of anti-Catholic bitterness masquerading as radical thought in the party in the post-Split days. I think a lot of my hang-up was a chip-on-the-shoulder attitude to the church for reasons that came out of the family, I suppose, and the bitterness that came out of the Split which was ill-informed, highly subjective and personal ... with not a small amount of anti-Catholicism in it. I can carbon-date my final change: I attended a West Australian Fabian Society weekend seminar in a magnificent place called York as one of the guest speakers. Jim Cairns got a question on state aid, and he said: "I have been opposed to state aid but I have asked myself a question, and the question is simply this: 'Who suffers if there isn't state aid for poor Catholic schools?' The poor Catholic schools are, in many cases, in far worse condition than the poor state schools. It is children who suffer; children who have no influence over determining which school they are going to attend. We can't tolerate that as democratic socialists." '

Hayden said that Cairns' answer gave him an almost physical shock. 'I thought: "My God, that sums everything up that I have been trying to get together, and trying to understand." I suppose, if I'm honest, it provided the exculpation for my moving away from this earlier position I had ... which was held so fiercely. Later on, Cairns denied he had ever said it, yet it was one of the most influential things in my life at this time, pulling my position together.'

When, in 1988, Hayden had recalled the process of his conversion on state aid, he added, in a reflection that encapsulates his political style: 'That was the trade-off between principle and pragmatism, between what was right and what was practical. It was a very important debate in the Labor Party. The Labor Party, out of all of these sorts of debates on a whole range of things, has matured a hell of a lot.'

Hayden was still balancing his parliamentary political commitments with his university studies and the task of holding a difficult electorate. He was not a natural or relaxed student: 'When I was studying and had to meet deadlines like that I had a tendency to read too widely, actually, and I'd get by on only a few hours' sleep a night, until I'd get the assignments done. I'd sometimes do them two or three times or more. It wasn't easy, of course; we had a very marginal electorate in those days with a big rural area. When John Gorton was Prime Minister the word went around, in 1968, that there was going to be an election. Exams were coming up, but I thought, "Bugger the exams, I haven't been up the country much lately," so I piled into the old station wagon, and I'm driving around, and I was up the country for three or four days, and I was driving into the Linville timber mill up in the Brisbane Valley and the mid-day news came on: "Mr Gorton has ruled out an early election this year." I drove into the timber mill and said to the blokes: "Good-day, goodbye," and went home and sat down with the bloody books to make up for lost time.'

EIGHT

The striver

You would almost call him a slow learner.

Queensland Labor colleague,
(anonymously)

ONE DAY in the late 1960s while the Hayden family was visiting Canberra Dallas became ill, and Bill took charge of their youngest child, Kirk, who was still wearing nappies. The Federal parliamentary Labor Party was meeting the same day to debate an issue in which Hayden had a particular interest; by this time he had eased up on Kafka and the drinking, and was fully involved in politics again. Knowing the sensitivity of members and the strict rules about who was eligible to attend Caucus, he approached Whitlam, explained his dilemma, and asked whether it would be possible to take Kirk to the meeting. 'Yes, comrade; provided he doesn't leak,' boomed the leader and marched on.[1]

Hayden did not loom large in Whitlam's assessment of people of importance at that time, while Hayden regarded Whitlam as a potentially dangerous autocrat; yet both, from their different perspectives, had arrived at almost identical views on a wide range of policy issues, and both were dedicated with unusual fervour to similar ideals of justice and reform. The speeches of Whitlam and Hayden at that period are among the very few that had vision and that do not read now with a sad and dated air. Their curious relationship was to last for the rest of their political careers as they marched to a similar drum, but seldom quite in step.

Whitlam was never a snob, yet he was not one to find great qualities in those who opposed his aims or did not share his view of his own destiny and the importance of his mission to rescue Australia from the grip of two decades of philistine rule. In a delightful article in the *Canberra Times* in 1977 under the heading 'Scavenging in the rubbish tip of a politician's psyche', the paper's political writer, Ian Warden, took rapier and broadsword to the emerging popularity of psychohistory which he described as

> basically ... a technique by which historians, psychologists, political scientists, and sometimes journalists, rummage around in the known childhoods and pasts of famous men for clues which explain their adult behaviour ... I mention this now because it seems inevitable that Mr Bill Hayden, heir apparent to Mr Whitlam and a possible first citizen of this antipodean democracy, will be attracting the psychohistorians, professional and amateur, competent and incompetent, any day now. In fact this process may have already begun. Within the past week one newspaper has made a big thing of an altercation that Mr Whitlam and Mr Hayden had 16 years ago in Ipswich, Queensland.[2]

This referred to the confusion over the booking of a meeting hall when Whitlam arrived to take part in Hayden's first campaign.

The interaction between Hayden and Whitlam, would, of course, provide a rich ore lode for psychohistorians, but the simple facts of their circumstances, the stark contrasts between their childhoods and their pasts, are not only fascinating in their differences, but in an essential way reveal something both about the two men and about Australia. And perhaps in that difference is a clue to the paradox of why the radical underprivileged boy from Mabel Street is now Governor-General; there were the elements of envy of Whitlam's social polish and self-confidence in the attitude of Hayden the battler who was determined to win public recognition and respect for his own abilities, and to acquire by remorseless toil the easy familiarity with literature, art and music that had been a natural part of Whitlam's life. 'Bill always wanted you to know he read good,' commented a former Whitlam Government minister recently.

As is well known, Whitlam was the son of one of Australia's most distinguished public servants, Fred Whitlam, Crown Solicitor from 1936, and one of Canberra's leading citizens during Gough's youth. The

Whitlams at meal times would have reference books at hand to support points they made in debate. When Bill Hayden was sneaking into the railway meal room in police uniform to study matriculation algebra, Whitlam, who had married the daughter of a leading Sydney King's Counsel, already had behind him a distinguished university career, creditable service in the RAAF as a navigator on active combat in World War II, and had made a mark as a barrister before entering politics and becoming deputy leader of his party. The fact that Whitlam's mother was deaf led to his clear, distinctive articulation and his effective and characteristic gestures;[3] Hayden's own partial deafness contributed to his whining delivery and his solitary habits.

Bob Hawke, similarly, was a man who had a secure childhood, a conviction always that he was loved, and excellent educational opportunities. By the time Hayden had left school and got a job filing invoices in the State Government stores, Hawke, aged twenty-one, had a degree in law. Some of the awkward edges of Hayden's personality, which in the end contributed to loss of support for his leadership of the Labor Party, resulted from his own attitude to his background. Paul Keating started work as a clerk with the Sydney County Council two days after his fifteenth birthday, a job not noted for providing opportunity or intellectual satisfaction; he had little interest in study, but is not known to agonise about the inadequacy of his formal education. Keating did, however, have a close and supportive family who eventually accumulated moderate wealth.

Hayden's background prejudiced him against Whitlam, whom he believed did not have the credentials of a genuine Labor man, and he maintained those almost comical suspicions for many years: 'I remember when we won the election in 1972,' Hayden recalled later, 'Whitlam's sister said at the time that one of the greatest influences of Gough's life had been Napoleon. I thought, "Oh, oh, what have we here?" But later I picked up Cronin's biography of Napoleon and was surprised to find out that he was a very impressive man. He was an arrogant little tyrant at times, but he was also a brilliant lawyer and a brilliant innovator of military tactics and strategy. He created a whole new concept of warfare and inspired a whole nation. These are not unimportant things.'[4]

Having failed to win a place in the shadow ministry after the 1966 election, Hayden picked his own targets and set his own goals. In 1968 he was studying international economics while completing the sixth and final year of his economics degree as an external student, and was not reluctant to share his new-found knowledge with his parliamentary colleagues. As early as 1966 he had dismissed a Treasury White Paper on the Australian economy with the words: 'Its analysis is at the level of a first year economics student.'[5] He was himself just a couple of years ahead of the first year students. Hayden completed his economics degree at the end of 1968, having secured two distinctions, four credits and four passes.

During 1968 Hayden warned of his fears of a looming international recession. He was a little premature; it did not materialise until nearly six years later, when Labor was in government and he was about to become Treasurer. Hayden also took a particular interest in defence, partly influenced by the fact that he had an RAAF base at Amberley in his electorate, and made a number of thoughtful and well-researched contributions to the debate at this time, touching on questions of strategy, national interests, foreign policy, and, of course, economic considerations: 'It is well to recollect, when we are discussing defence, as indeed when we consider many other matters which are responsibilities of ours, that the problem is not only one of acquiring adequate equipment; there is also the matter of paying for that equipment — and that is the rub.'[6]

In the same speech he suggested that the Government act to improve the efficiency and cost-effectiveness of defence expenditure to eliminate waste, duplication, extravagance, and unnecessary commitments. 'It would mean standardisation and integration of services wherever this is possible, in the interests of better efficiency and performance. All this means that investment — money if you like it that way — will do more than it did before.' Hayden explained to the House that because $321 million was being spent overseas on defence purchases that year, the reverse multiplier effect would come into operation; if the money had been spent in Australia it would generate activity and be used twice over. He was critical of the strategic location of Orion aircraft for anti-submarine patrols which were to be based in South Australia rather than on the north of the continent: 'I am sure that this arrangement will be handy for the protection of penguins.'

In a speech in October 1968, he neatly analysed the conservative Government's political use of defence issues from the early days of the Menzies era. These tried and tested tactics regularly left the Labor Party electorally embarrassed. 'It has been a repeated claim of the Government at periodic elections that Australia had only a short time in which to prepare to defend herself against external aggression. Of course [the Government was] unable to define just who these aggressors were and how they were likely to get here,' he said.[7] 'I suggest that the record of the Government, as summed up by the state of the defence Services in the 1960s, indicates that, if the Government believed what it said, it had a reckless disregard for the benefit of the country, and that, if it did not believe what it said, it had a reckless disregard for the intelligence of the Australian electors.'

Prime Minister John Gorton had at that time flirted, in his usual imprecise way, with basing Australia's defence planning on a Fortress Australia concept. Hayden opposed this with some passion. It was an approach supported by some radical elements within the Labor Party who would have been content for Australia to spend more on defence equipment if it meant keeping out of conflicts in Asian countries under the banner of forward defence. Hayden disagreed: 'This is a completely irrational approach to Australia's needs. Instead of closing doors, locking windows and drawing shutters to South East Asia we should be opening these things up and developing as many techniques as we can to improve our relationship with the people of South East Asia.'

Hayden again went to the heart of the Liberal Party's use of defence and security as a domestic political weapon in another major defence speech on 20 March 1969, when Australia was considering its future role in Malaysia in the light of Britain's decision to withdraw its forces from east of Suez:

> Let us look at this threat which is impending — which is about to hurtle down upon this country. It is always safe, of course, to exploit the threat of the so-called yellow hordes, because in our rather unflattering background of white Australia, with the emotional racist content which went with this, an easily evoked response is extracted from the Australian public by this sort of propaganda. But which countries are the threats to Australia? Which countries have the industrial base which would allow them to launch a massive attack against this country and, what is more important, to sustain the attack?[8]

The most beneficial way Australia could be involved in the area was, he suggested, to become more closely involved in the economic, political, social and cultural development of its neighbourhood in South East Asia.

The Australian Institute of Political Science selected 'Poverty in Australia' as the theme of its 35th summer school, held in Canberra in

January 1969, and invited Hayden to take part. Hayden had already addressed the problem of poverty in *The Implications of Democratic Socialism*, in which he had analysed a book I had written on poverty in Australia which had been published in 1966.[9] Many years later Hayden offered to do the work necessary to bring the figures and details like changes in social service benefits up to date so that the book could be republished. Hayden's 2000-word speech at the summer school was to mark a further development of his involvement in social welfare policy issues and in his political career.

When he turned his major energies and concern to the problem of poverty in an affluent society his first discovery was that most of the work that had been done, and there had not been a great deal, dealt with aspects of the broader problem in isolation. Nowhere could he find an attempt to develop a broad, coordinated program that was economically realistic and capable of attracting public and political support. Many worthy people were working away with individual victims or sub-groups of those suffering deprivation within the existing system, but the broader problems, he felt, were not being properly tackled.

Hayden's thinking was that there should be a two-pronged approach consisting of an anti-poverty campaign, including housing, health and employment assistance programs, combined with assistance to individuals to help them break the cycle of deprivation through a guaranteed income, improved and more appropriate education, assistance with handling their finances, and other opportunities which would involve them in the decision-making process.

It is difficult these days to distinguish the ventriloquist from the doll as politicians increasingly read speeches and pronounce sentiments and sentences that are the work of others. Hayden was, like Bob Hawke, always an exception, but, unlike Hawke, who took sometimes ludicrously misplaced pride in his conviction that he could make an entertaining and lengthy speech with few notes and little preparation, Hayden worked long and hard preparing and constantly redrafting. Although he always had a natural and slightly quirky sense of humour, ironical and often self-deprecating, this seldom showed in his speeches in those days. They were painfully earnest, and bore the hallmarks of much painstaking research, but were often impressive because the research was original and they were founded on deep personal despair about the plight of others and an undiminished sense of the unfairness and injustice of Australian society.

They were marred, though, by bearing the inky fingerprints of a mature-age economics student.

'He was a striver, you would almost describe him as a slow learner.' said a prominent Queensland Federal parliamentarian of Hayden at this stage of his life. 'He wants to speak on everything. All he does is work on speeches,' another disgruntled political journalist complained to Eric Walsh of the *National Times*.[10]

Hayden's standing within the party had not kept pace with his growing reputation among economic and political commentators; he was not gregarious and he had fallen out with the proponents of high tariffs and other orthodoxies. When a frontbench member resigned in April 1969, creating a vacancy on the Executive, Hayden polled less than a sixth of the vote. It was a timely lesson; he realised that if Labor did manage to win the 1969 election he would not be elected to the ministry. He modified his habits, regularly visiting the members' bar, regularly lunching with Labor colleagues.[11] He also worked on developing a higher public profile and mixed more with journalists, knocking out his own press statements on a portable typewriter with a brisk, two-fingered, policeman-taking-a-statement typing style.[12] He was rewarded by being given a prominent role in the campaign for the House of Representatives election held on 25 October 1969: 'I got thrown into it,' Hayden recalls. 'I don't know why. Television was still novel, probably some of the older people were having trouble handling it. I did all right on a couple of major debates on TV.'

Whitlam led Labor to within seven seats of victory and Hayden was one of the first elected to the shadow ministry in a parliamentary Labor Party that had had an infusion of new blood and enthusiasm, and was on a springboard for victory three years later.

'Some time after the Caucus election [for positions on Labor's front bench] I was leaning on the glass case in Kings Hall which has the Constitutional proclamation in it, and Gough came out, and walked past, picking his teeth,' Hayden recalled later. 'Then he came back and said, "Oh, by the way, comrade, I haven't had the opportunity to talk to you about what shadow portfolio you would like." I said: "I suppose it's a bit hard to expect one of the top economic ones," and he said, "Ah, Crean speaks for himself." I said: "Transport would be beaut, Gough, because it's about using economic resources and I've got an economics degree." He said: "Well, Charlie Jones has got that." Charlie knew more about it than me, you see, because he'd worked in a shipyard as a boilermaker. I thought, well, shit, there's not much left, and said, "Well what is there Gough?" He said: "Well, actually comrade, there's only one job left and that's health and welfare."

'I said, "I've got it, I see".'

NINE

Foundation
for victory

*There used to be times when I was swotting
awfully hard.*

Bill Hayden

LTHOUGH not initially welcomed by Hayden, who saw it as a negligent afterthought by his leader, Gough Whitlam's decision to appoint Hayden as the shadow minister for health and welfare was to have profound effects on Australian society and substantially advance Hayden's career. 'As it turned out, it was a boon,' Hayden said. 'I was in the middle of a continuing debate which gave me a lot of exposure, and it was something where the party faithful responded and were fully behind me; and the general community could perceive a real need. It gave me a chance, and I worked fairly hard at those things. I would go home at weekends with a stack of papers from the library. I was reading widely and deeply.'

Hayden's name will be forever linked with the establishment of tax-funded health insurance schemes in Australia, and it is doubtful whether such schemes would have been introduced and endured without the dedication, economic and political skill and grinding perseverance he brought to their establishment. There is, however, considerable irony in the indelible association of his name with Medibank and its later reincarnation, Medicare. Within months of his appointment as shadow minister after the 1969 election, and more than five years before Medibank was to become reality, Hayden approached Whitlam in an attempt to have the proposal dropped from Labor's 1972 election platform, or drastically modified.

Whitlam had launched plans for a national health scheme as a cornerstone of his campaign for the 1969 election in which he had achieved a national swing of 7.1 per cent to Labor, reducing the Gorton Government's majority from thirty-nine to seven. The origins of Labor's health scheme were, as Graham Freudenberg has pointed out, a paradigm of policy development under Whitlam. 'The provision of free treatment at public hospitals was always the core of Whitlam's health programme. In a sense, Whitlam and the Labor Party became sidetracked on the health insurance issue because the middle class have always been much more concerned about insuring themselves for private treatment than in obtaining free treatment.'[1]

In 1967 Whitlam, who had become Opposition leader in February, met two research workers from the Institute of Applied Economic and Social Research at Melbourne University, John Deeble and Dick Scotton, at the Melbourne home of Dr Moss Cass, a Labor candidate who was elected to Federal Parliament in 1969. The two men had prepared an exhaustive analysis of the deficiencies of the existing voluntary health insurance scheme. Although there was no consultation or dialogue between them at the time, Whitlam's response was very similar to that which Hayden had begun to develop separately but simultaneously as a result of his research into poverty. At the Melbourne dinner, Whitlam urged Scotton and Deeble to go further than criticise the old scheme; he pressed them to develop a workable, more equitable alternative. They agreed to do this and by June 1968 had developed a comprehensive plan which Whitlam used as a keystone in his election campaign. 'The foundations for what became Medibank were well laid in the first twelve months of Whitlam's leadership,' says Freudenberg.[2]

When Hayden took over as health spokesman he automatically became chairman of the health committee of Caucus which at that time included five medical doctors, Dr Moss Cass, Dr Richie Gun, Dr Dick Klugman, Dr Doug Everingham and Dr Harry Jenkins, most of whom were strongly independent radical individuals who had been newly elected. One of the first actions of the committee was to debate and dissect

Whitlam's health plan, and they were not long in coming to agree that they should attempt to kill it, believing that it was open to abuse and would lead to overservicing by private doctors. 'It's little more than a mechanism for subsidising private fee-for-service medical practice and private hospitals,' one doctor said.[3] Cass described Medibank as the very antithesis of a genuine health service for the community. He wanted community health centres staffed by salaried doctors, although he did concede that such a scheme would be attacked by the medical profession and the conservative parties as socialist medicine which they would say was, therefore, bad medicine.

Hayden was given the task of relaying the committee's misgivings to Whitlam, who was outraged. Grinding his teeth with anger, he declared, quite accurately: 'Jesus Christ! I've just nearly won an election on my health package, you pissants.'[4] Hayden accepted Whitlam's view, and from then on went about getting it introduced and making it work; he saw that as both an obligation to the party and to the scheme, as being vastly preferable to the shambles it was designed to replace.

Hayden recalls working on plans for improvements in social services with new members who had entered Parliament at the 1969 election as one of the best and most satisfying experiences of his political life. 'It was a great period. There were so many people imbued with democratic socialist values, and a series of good committees who worked hard; Jesus they worked hard. The arguments would go on: what was fair and equitable, who was paying and who was getting what out of it, how you justified it. The debate was exhausting. The difference we had over Medibank was only one of a number. The party policy also committed us to abolishing the means test for the pension. A lot of us really crunched our consciences because we believed that the means test was a fair system and if we paid pensions to millionaires it would reduce our opportunity to improve benefits for more needy people. I still remember us sitting down for hours in this bloody committee room, and we worked out this complex system about how we could meet the commit-ment to phase out the means test by some complex formula related to income. So my colleagues said: "Well you had better go and tell him."

'So I went and said: "Gough, this is the way we would like to do it, rather than just abolish it," and I explained the formula. He said: "Comrade, nobody will ever fucking well understand it. It's too complex." He was right. Then he said the only way to do it was to abandon the means test by age levels, first cutting it out for those over seventy-five and then for those over seventy and so on. I told him the troops wouldn't like it, but that I would report back to my committee, which I did. We were still in heated debate when we broke for dinner. As we entered the dining room the seven o'clock news came on, and the first item was Gough announcing that Labor's policy would be that the means test would be reduced progressively by age levels. That was the end of that debate, too. I've got a lot of deep affection for Whitlam, and not even all the terrors of hell would budge that, but at the time those sort of things rubbed a bit rawly on one's sensitivities.'

With his university studies completed and his electorate made much safer and easier to work by the excision of much of the rural area in the 1968 redistribution, Hayden had more time to devote to his specialist area of health and social welfare. But his political life was still neither simple nor easy. He was the party's leading parliamentary spokesman on the arts, cultural issues and films, he was still crusading on tariffs and he was ahead of thinking in his own party on social issues.

In one of the early debates at the Queensland Labor Party's annual policy-making Labor in Politics Convention at the Chevron Hotel in Surfers Paradise in January 1971, Hayden argued forcefully for a ban on professional boxing. In a later debate he pressed, equally emotionally, for the decriminalisation of sexual relations between consenting adult homosexuals. 'Delegate Hayden seems confused,' rasped the voice of Jack Egerton, the fat, florid president of the party who had control of the microphone at the top table. 'He's bitterly opposed to a bloke getting a punch in the nose; but he doesn't seem to mind him getting a punch in the bum.' After the laughter subsided, Hayden would not back down and he succeeded in forcing a vote on the issue and having a division called. Egerton narrowly carried the day after he had called for those supporting his point of view to go to one side of the hall and the 'poofters' to the other.[5]

Despite the hostility to social reform in his home State of Queensland, Hayden courageously and consistently played a role as a pioneering advocate of progressive measures. Yet in the years from 1969 through to the 1972 Federal election when crusading party figures led by Clyde Cameron and Gough Whitlam were taking vital steps to achieve internal party reform, Hayden took no part. Jack Egerton, dressed in his trademark outfit which included white shoes and broad maroon tie — its knot often obscured by folds of jowly flesh — dominated the ruling faction of the Queensland Labor Party for more than half of Hayden's political career. Egerton and Frank Waters had been the sponsors of Hayden's entry into politics and Waters had stood aside so Hayden could be elected to the party's Federal Executive in the days when he was identified as a conventional and predictable left-winger. Although he was uncomfortable with Hayden's intellectual interests, social ideals, and increasing pragmatism, Egerton was prepared to tolerate them. 'He was always a bit of a girl guide,' was Egerton's dismissive description of Hayden in a conversation with me in 1988.

Egerton would have been less forgiving, however, if Hayden had supported action that threatened his autocratic control of power within the Queensland Labor organisation. Denis Murphy, a leading campaigner for reform, recalled that

> Hayden exercised caution in dealing with Egerton who, Hayden believed, was sufficiently ruthless to have his endorsement for Oxley withdrawn. Consequently, where Whitlam attempted to 'crash through' with reforms to the party's federal structure, Hayden trod warily and went along with the Queensland central executive which was against the reform.[6]

There were other signs of increasing caution in Hayden's political stance at this time, yet his actions did not spring from ambition or self-interest. His increasingly independent views, widely described by his colleagues as 'quirky', had been arrived at as a result of study, of earnest discussion with informed people, and on his reading of the feelings of ordinary people with whom he was in closer touch than many other parliamentarians.

Hayden was disillusioned both with the self-interested bigotry he found among many of his fellow Australians when he attempted to promote schemes that would give deprived people a fairer share and a better chance, and with his Labor colleagues who were equally resistant to change and new ideas. He was still as caustically critical of Australia's involvement in what he described as the 'Vietnam Civil War'. He signed moratorium petitions and addressed rallies, but he would not take part in demonstrations; he believed strongly that, in Queensland in particular, protest marches were politically damaging to the anti-war cause and to the Labor Party. 'I would support any move to end the war in Vietnam,' he told the Brisbane afternoon newspaper, The *Telegraph*, on 31 March 1970, at the time of national marches organised by Jim Cairns, one of his original political heroes.

But I think demonstrations like this do not achieve anything because of the selfishness of the Australian public which remains largely unmoved at the awful slaughter in this unjustifiable war, as long, of course, as they are not involved in the fighting. I support all reasonable and responsibly controlled demonstrations against the completely unjustified intrusion of western powers into the Vietnam Civil War.

Hayden lost the support of some members of the hard-core Left over his views on demonstrations, but that was not his only area of conflict at that time: he fought publicly with fellow Queenslander and northern development advocate Rex Patterson over rural subsidies, and with New South Wales strongman Rex Connor on tariffs. When asked in 1972 why, despite the immense amount of work he had done and the influence he appeared to have in the media, he was not particularly popular among his parliamentary colleagues, Hayden answered:

I suspect it's because many of the things I've taken up haven't been popular. Maybe I've got an abrasive personality with some people in Caucus — a matter of empathy, social relations and so on, I'm not sure. I would like to say many more radical things than I do say, many more, but I don't because I get into enough trouble already. It's not only a matter of getting into trouble with one's Caucus colleagues — one's just got to be realistic.[7]

Hayden's definition of his position as radical was a correct one. He was questioning and challenging the foundations of a number of accepted beliefs, but his definition differed from that of most of his party colleagues. Personalities rather than policies have long been a commanding factor in Australian politics, and at that time a number of the more racist and sexist Labor parliamentarians were leading figures in the Left, the self-anointed progressive section of the party. 'There is a tendency in Australia to discourage questioning, penalise non-conformity and threaten and intimidate dissent,' he told the Federal Conference of the Young Labor Association on 12 April 1971. 'The dun-coloured standards of a conforming mediocrity are preferred to the stimulating challenge and exciting contribution which individual originality and creativity can offer. Too many Australians lie low when the great and controversial moral issues are being decided.'[8]

Hayden also managed to put himself in an ambivalent position in relation to the timing of independence for Papua New Guinea. He had been a member of the 1964 Federal parliamentary delegation that attended the opening of Papua New Guinea's new House of Assembly.

The visit had sparked an intense and continuing interest in that country: by 1972 he had been there five times. In January 1970 he accompanied Whitlam on the historic fifteen-day visit which was to set the country's timetable for early independence. He studied the country's economy intensively. A staff member who once accompanied him to the Trobriand Islands recalls a banquet on a balmy night, with dancers in grass skirts twirling in the firelight and smoke from the cooking fires where the pigs were being roasted drifting through the coconut palms, and Hayden returning to his hut to study reports on the local economy.

Although he did not take the issue up publicly, he had reservations about Australia pushing Papua New Guinea too rapidly towards independence, and was concerned that the withdrawal of Australian administrators could be followed by violence between different sections of the indigenous population. Whitlam was unshakeable, firmly believing Papua New Guinea was producing more capable leaders than Australia was able to supply for it, and that violence was more likely to result from continued Australian dominance.

Hayden anticipated accurately the approach future governments there would take in a report to Caucus after a visit in July 1972 when he said:

> Probably the most important lesson for Australia to learn, however, is that come self government, Papua New Guinea will be doing things in many ways quite different to the way we are used to doing them or expect them to be done. That is, there will be a Papuan New Guinean way. The next thing is that an independent Papua New Guinea will quickly become involved in a wider world than we have allowed and we will be vying for influence with other nations, perhaps even Japan.[9]

He showed his strong feelings for the Papua New Guinean people during a messy debate in Parliament over the fact that an Australian public servant convicted of wounding a Papuan received a suspended sentence while members of the Mataungan Association, a popular political movement among the indigenous people of Rabaul, had been gaoled for up to a year for minor assaults that had occurred during a demonstration. 'Public servants in the Administration took the opportunity to influence the way in which the native people expressed themselves at discussions which we had with them,' he said in Parliament in March 1970. 'We had to tell those public servants firmly to desist from that sort of thing, that we had come to the Territory to speak with native people and find out what they felt.'[10]

The Minister for Territories, C.E. Barnes, who was better known and more successful as the breeder and owner of the great racehorse Tails, interrupted Hayden, saying: 'The honourable member is not concerned about the reputation of the public servant.' Hayden snapped back: 'I am concerned about the reputation of human beings. I get terribly sensitive and emotionally concerned about it. Some people restrict this concern and emotional discomfort to the welfare of racehorses.'

Despite distractions, however, Hayden's prime concern and the focus of his serious work was the health and social welfare field of his shadow portfolio. As he had made clear earlier in his work on poverty, he wanted to go beyond simple solutions designed to deal with isolated categories of need; by 1970 he was proposing that the national health insurance scheme should be complemented by national superannuation and national compensation schemes. He had spent the parliamentary recess of 1970 visiting the United States, Canada, Sweden, Britain and Israel to study the strengths and weaknesses of their health and social welfare systems.

'What are the kind of experiences you enjoy?' John Edwards asked Hayden in 1972. 'Sex,' answered Hayden. 'But apart from that, what are the experiences that most exhilarate you?' Hayden: 'Well I guess I got exhilarated when I did that first thing on superannuation, because I worked hard at it. It was exciting because people had been saying you couldn't cost a national superannuation scheme, which I realised was nonsense.'[11] There is something of the essence of the Hayden of the period leading up to Labor's election victory of 1972 there, in the association of sex and superannuation when discussing pleasure and satisfaction. 'I used to find study exhilarating when I was finding out something new. There used to be times when I was swotting awfully hard and I used to come away feeling wrung-out, but with that really wonderful feeling that you could get in the chest,' he said.

On the surface the ten-page 'National Superannuation Scheme, Outline of Proposals' document presented by Hayden at St Hilda's College, Melbourne, on 3 March 1972 would give very few people goose bumps. Half of it consisted of figures, detailed costings and tables of proposed benefits, but it was in many ways an extraordinary achievement: he had put together a fair, politically viable and properly costed scheme without the backing or benefit of a government department, a computer or a university.[12] In a less technical explanation of the scheme in a Fabian newsletter he outlined its basic advantages over the existing pension scheme:

It will provide a means test free retirement benefit, for all who are retired; it will be self financing; it will cover the 50 per cent to 60 per cent of employees without any superannuation at all; it will provide benefits for those with private superannuation, including the majority who have inadequate cover; it will provide benefits that increase annually according to movements in average weekly earnings so that the retired fairly share in the growing prosperity of the community.[13]

The scheme provided for the contribution of low-income earners to be paid from internal revenue as a direct welfare benefit, while the bulk of the scheme was to be financed by employee and employer contributions. He said:

It is sometimes argued that the whole proposition should be financed from consolidated revenue, that is, increases in income tax. I am prepared to assert dogmatically that the public will not accept this manner of paying for the scheme, but they will accept an easily understood formula of 'ear-marked' contributions paid by them and funding the proposal.[14]

The wage-earner's contribution was to come from a 1.3 per cent levy on taxable income for the year with the employer's contribution being double that. The basic pension rate was to be 25 per cent of male average weekly earnings. His scheme also provided for an earnings-related supplement of up to 10 per cent of updated average earnings.

Hayden's scheme was not to come to fruition while he was in politics, and part of the reason for that was that time ran out for the Whitlam Government before the lengthy processes of consultation which Hayden thought essential for its acceptance had been completed. In his Fabian pamphlet Hayden said:

Clearly, if there is to be an earnings related superstructure built onto the base benefit then there will have to be a public inquiry. I am thoroughly convinced, after considerable experience speaking with audiences, small groups and well-informed individuals on this aspect that in no other way can full information of all the complex issues involved be obtained. Moreover, in no other way will the community be allowed to adequately voice its opinion on how the scheme will affect them and how best it should be adjusted to improve their position.[15]

Although it was to prove frustrating in this case, it was a foretaste of the ultimately successful style of consultation on the health insurance scheme as shadow minister and then as minister that was to occupy much of Hayden's life for more than three years and was to drive close to despair many of his most vociferous opponents, as well as some of his supporters who were impatient of talk and negotiation and wanted decisive action. In the process Hayden himself was to lose some of his faith in his fellow man and his hair was to start turning grey. At the time he said he had learned from More's *Utopia* a lesson which explained why he thought necessary his constant stream of pamphlets, letters to the editor, appearances in radio and television debates, at meetings in country halls and any other forum at which he could get a hearing: people should never be confronted suddenly with a new idea for it was sure to be rejected. 'They'll be frightened by it; you've got to work round to it slowly.'

In that 1972 election year, in his increasingly rare moments of relaxation at home, he would walk through the scrubby bush near his home or take his family down to the side of a creek near Ipswich. 'It's quite pleasant — clear running water, tall river gums. I think they're probably as beautiful as anything I've ever seen, those tall fat-girthed river gums.'[16]

Whitlam's appeal to the Australian people in that election year was a complex of factors, an important one of which was his own ability, his impressive stature, intelligence and wit compared with that of the incumbent Prime Minister, Bill McMahon.

But there were deeper themes, one of which crucially involved Hayden: Australia had once enjoyed an international reputation as a socially concerned, progressive and caring country, pioneering its pursuit of equality and assistance to those in need. After the greedy sixties and decades of conservative rule this was no longer true: a substantial increase in material prosperity had been marked by a more sharply visible difference in Australian society and an increase in the number of people who found themselves vulnerable to misfortune.

While the gloss, energy and excitement of the Whitlam crusade contrasted vibrantly with the bumbling McMahon performance, the voters also sought responsibility and substance, and many found them in the Hayden schemes. In September 1972 a Gallup poll showed free medical services identified by 46.3 per cent of electors as the most important electoral issue. Next, with 44.5 per cent, came pensions for which Whitlam and Hayden had set a target of 25 per cent of average weekly earnings within the life of two parliaments, with the amount to be bolstered by special supplements in appropriate circumstances. Hayden's work was one of the foundation stones of the It's Time election victory of 2 December 1972.

TEN

The Medibank war

I *told them you didn't have enough brains to*
have a mental breakdown.

Jack Egerton

IN AN ACT that, at the time, was of little moment, Bill Hayden deliberately avoided taking part in the traditional shaking of hands with the Governor-General, Sir Paul Hasluck, after the official opening of Parliament when the Whitlam Government took over the Treasury benches in 1973.[1] He was one of the most senior ministers in a key portfolio but still exhibiting radical and individual traits.

In the ballot for places in the ministry, in which Whitlam and his deputy Lance Barnard had already taken their positions, Hayden tied for second with Frank Crean and then won the toss to become fourth-ranking minister after the two leaders and Jim Cairns. He was thirty-nine, the youngest minister, and was given responsibility for welfare in the renamed portfolio of Social Security by Whitlam who acknowledged that he had 'worked with great diligence in making health policies one of the winning issues in the 1972 election'.[2] Hayden got off to a brisk start, introducing legislation to increase pensions, unemployment and sickness benefits on the first working day of the Parliament.

All his personal staff were women except for Padraic P. McGuinness, a brilliant and mildly eccentric journalist and economist of wide international experience given to wearing dark glasses and cloaks. The influence of McGuinness extended beyond Hayden's office; he assisted Labour Minister Clyde Cameron to prepare the Government's first submission to the Arbitration Commission in the 1973 National Wage Case, a submission that rejected Treasury advice that wages should be frozen. McGuinness, again with Cameron, was one of the early advocates of wage indexation.

Hayden's press secretary, Megan Stoyles, had in 1966 been pictured in *Time* magazine demonstrating against US President Lyndon Johnson in a 'make love not war' T-shirt. His principal private secretary, Gay Raby, had been recruited by Hayden when he was impressed by her work as adviser to a joint parliamentary committee investigating pharmaceutical benefits. Hayden had been a member of the committee which had been established by the Liberal Health Minister, Jim Forbes, as a direct consequence of Hayden's criticisms of the pricing policies of the drug companies and the consequent costs to the Commonwealth. Raby says Hayden thought she was an upper-middle-class Melburnian and that he was disappointed when he discovered she had come from a working-class Brisbane background and had, like him, got her academic qualifications the hard way.

'Social service benefits are a right and not part of a disapproving charity,' Hayden declared in one of his first statements as minister when he directed his department not to suspend benefits to unemployed workers before Christmas. He had not even been sworn in before the doctors declared war on him and the Labor Government's proposed national health insurance scheme. This was to be a cruel and acrimonious battle with what Whitlam has described as 'Australia's most militant trade union and its most self-serving bureaucracy, the medical profession and the health insurance industry'.[3] The struggle dominated much of Hayden's life for nearly two years. It was to win him high praise and exact lasting personal costs: less than a week before he was sworn in as Governor-General Hayden was awarded considerable damages against a Brisbane radio station that had allowed to be broadcast in 1988 a false rumour that he had once been mentally ill, a canard that had first been circulated in 1973 by doctors opposing his health scheme. This was not the first struggle between Labor and the medical community: Australia's doctors had frustrated by legal challenges and passive resistance attempts by the postwar Chifley Labor Government to implement a national health service despite the fact that the Government had won by referendum the right to do so.

Hayden exhibited a characteristic blend of radicalism and caution in his dealings with the private health industry. He won public support in an early row in which he stood up to private nursing home owners who claimed the viability of their industry had been jeopardised by a policy of greater supervision of admissions. The policy had, in fact, been introduced by the previous government to stem abuses by unscrupulous nursing home owners. Having won the public debate Hayden then held out the prospect of compromise in return for cooperation, a technique he was to use with success in other battles.[4] He antagonised some doctors by another early declaration that he was more interested in lowering Aboriginal mortality rates than in raising their incomes.

Hayden was quite aware that he was involved in a full-scale political battle with the medical profession for the support of the Australian people and that the doctors, by the very nature of their job, enjoyed particular advantages in gaining the confidence of their patients. At the time he became minister, Hayden said:

> The pressure the Australian Medical Association can exert on us will depend on the degree of public support and sympathy for them. The doctors have done pretty poorly in getting public support so far. Some of the people on the federal council of the Australian Medical Association are very impressive: there are some good ones who aren't always talking about more money for doctors and guaranteed incomes and all the rest.'[5]

He assured doctors there would be no element of conscription or regimentation and that he could not compel them to enter the scheme, adding, however, that as everyone would be covered by national insurance he did not know how they would fare if they refused to see people who were covered by the scheme.

'I have told the AMA that I would prefer to establish a schedule of fees through negotiation. The challenge now is whether the people can trust the doctors.'[6] He was soon to find that the Government, at least, could not trust the official representatives of the doctors. In April 1973 Deeble presented Hayden with the report of the health insurance planning committee, the basic document on which Medibank and arrangements with private hospitals were to be based. At the same time the AMA announced unilaterally that it had decided doctors' fees for various services should be increased by between 25 and 100 per cent. Hayden acknowledged that there was justification for some increases and in July 1973 appointed a tribunal headed by Mr Justice J.T. Ludeke, a deputy president of the Conciliation and Arbitration Commission, and including two medical professors, to inquire into doctors' fees. He wrote to every doctor in Australia urging them to postpone fee increases until the tribunal had reported, suggesting that if they acted in defiance of the tribunal 'the situation that will arise will destroy all public credibility in the present health insurance system [which was based on voluntary contributions] and do untold damage to the prestige and image of the medical profession.'[7]

For a time Hayden managed to hold the line, largely by fomenting a division on tactics between the AMA and the more extreme General Practitioners Society. But even after Hayden had agreed, in the course of further discussions with the AMA, to widen the terms of the inquiry, the doctors went ahead and on 6 August 1973 increased their fees by an estimated 29 per cent. Hayden, appearing on an ABC television current affairs program[8] that night registered his disappointment and also conceded that the Federal Government had no constitutional power to regulate doctors' fees: 'I have always known that doctors could do this if they wanted to be tough and bloody-minded about it,' he said. 'They haven't given a damn about the public interest. I have appealed, I have proposed concessions, I have proposed compromises. I have done everything I could to try to get some sort of balance, sense of responsibility from the spokesmen for the medical profession and they haven't responded.'

Hayden continued to press ahead with other reforms. In March he had established an inquiry into a national superannuation scheme; in July he had introduced a supporting mothers' benefit to provide assistance to unmarried mothers and deserted and separated wives who had dependent children, removing discrimination against mothers and their children who had previously not been entitled to the same level of assistance as widows with children. It was a reform that had particular significance for him: he had seen his mother forced to go out and scrub floors when his father died and she had no other way of supporting her young family. Her youngest child, Joan, was nine years old when George Hayden died.

By August Hayden had released forty-seven previously secret reports on welfare issues that had been prepared for the previous government. In November he established the Social Welfare Commission, headed by

Marie Coleman who had been director of the Victorian Council of Social Services, and through the commission began the establishment of the Australian Assistance Plan based on locally organised and controlled welfare services.

There was, however, a murky lower level to the opposition being organised against the public debate Hayden had initiated on the whole range of health and welfare issues. As the *Canberra Times* recorded later, 'as Social Security minister Hayden was subjected by elements in the medical fraternity to one of the most vicious campaigns of denigration any contemporary politician has had to face'.[9] Dallas was telephoned at home at night and told not to expect her husband home; he had gone berserk on an aeroplane and had been forcibly removed in Sydney and taken to a mental hospital. Stories were widely circulated that he had been drummed out of the police force as a crooked and violent copper; that he was a dropout from medical school who was wreaking his revenge on all doctors; that he had been undergoing psychiatric treatment, but as minister had been able to have his records destroyed.

'I defended you,' Jack Egerton told him once after informing him of the latest lot of malicious lies. 'I told them you didn't have enough brains to have a mental breakdown.' 'The personal pressure began to show. By the end of 1973 he looked older and his hair, in part, turned a shade greyer,' Denis Murphy recorded.[10] The odious campaign was not confined to private whispering: *The Australian GP*, the journal of the General Practitioners Society, depicted Hayden in Nazi uniform, and engaged in personal vilification of him.

There was also a sectarian tinge to the political and personal campaign against Hayden and it had a significant base in his own electorate of Oxley where the Democratic Labor Party had been active since the Labor Party Split of the 1950s. When abortion became an issue in the 1970s the campaign against Hayden was revived with new virulence. In May 1973 Hayden, who, like other Labor members, was entitled to a conscience vote on the issue, supported a private member's bill which would have liberalised and clarified laws relating to abortion in Commonwealth territories, including the Australian Capital Territory.

Although the proposal was defeated, it was then widely and absurdly suggested that Hayden would require private hospitals to allow abortions to be carried out if the hospitals were to qualify for the generously increased subsidies, from $2 a bed a day to $16, that Hayden was in the process of granting them. The Democratic Labor Party had substantial influence in the Catholic private hospital system and this was a cause of irritation to Hayden in his home town where the relentless anti-abortion campaign the DLP had conducted against him from before the 1972 election campaign was again intensified. Under this provocation Hayden reacted in a manner he was later to regret. In January 1974 he wrote a letter to Dr F.J. Carroll who had been the Hayden family doctor and who had, in November 1973, been endorsed as the DLP candidate for Oxley for the next election.

Hayden wrote on official notepaper bearing the Commonwealth Government crest and the superscription:

Commonwealth of Australia, Minister for Social Security:

Dear Dr Carroll,

You probably don't remember but I dare say your records show that shortly after the birth of [name of child] you carried out [an operation].

Unfortunately the procedure was quite defective ... The upshot was that we recently had Dr Todd, assisted by Dr Garozzo, carry out a proper [operation] at St Andrew's Hospital.

So far we have received an account for $51 from St Andrew's Hospital and accounts for $15.50 from Dr Garozzo and $13 and $21.50 from Dr Todd. That is, we have paid a total of $101. This is an extremely large amount to pay for earlier faulty work.

In the circumstances, and especially in view of the fact that had [the operation] been carried out properly in the first instance this cost would not have arisen, I was wondering if you would care to volunteer meeting the cost of having this repair work done.

Yours sincerely,
Bill Hayden.

On 13 March 1974, Tom Aikens, an Independent Labor rebel from Townsville, read Hayden's letter to the Queensland Parliament, describing it as a despicable act of blackmail and extortion prompted by Dr Carroll's political involvement in the DLP.[11] *The Australian GP* published Hayden's letter to his doctor and the speech of the eccentric Aikens who had also said in Parliament that the letter was shocking, defamatory, scurrilous, extortionate, contemptible, detestable and reprehensible.

Aikens' speech was, in fact, more despicable than anything he had accused Hayden of doing. He had used the coward's castle of Parliament, where he was given free rein by the Bjelke-Petersen Government, to make details of the Hayden family's medical records a matter of public record. Hayden, for his part, had left himself vulnerable by what could be seen as a rather petty act. He had not foreseen the possible consequences.

The manic intensity and the duration of the Queensland campaign against Hayden and Medibank is neatly captured in a statement made by the Premier, Sir Joh Bjelke-Petersen, in the State Parliament on 30 September 1976:

> Throughout history, man has had to cope with many disasters. Some of these disasters have become household names — the Biblical Flood, the eruption of Vesuvius that destroyed Pompeii, the Titanic.
>
> Well, as from Friday we can add another monumental disaster that will affect every household in Queensland and the rest of Australia — Medibank.
>
> For that reason, Mr Speaker, I wish to propose that Friday, 1st October, 1976 be designated Bill Hayden Day.
>
> On this day, each year, from now on, as Queenslanders sit down to fill out their tax forms, they will look back and shudder. They will remember that on Black Friday, like Frankenstein's Monster, Hayden's Horror was officially born.
>
> Its pedigree was by socialism out of mismanagement, sponsors Scott [sic] and Deeble and its fodder your and my tax funds ...

Bjelke-Petersen's biographer Hugh Lunn revealed that the statement was written by Bjelke-Petersen's speechwriter Allen Callaghan who was still in prison for misappropriating taxpayers' funds when Hayden became Governor-General.[12]

Despite the emotional personal campaign being waged against him, Hayden continued working at the details of the scheme and travelling the country explaining it. He was so immersed in the figures and logic of his proposals that he began to acquire a reputation as a thundering bore. 'The trouble is I enjoy detail,' he confessed to Owen Thomson in 1980.

> I enjoy boring the pants off people. The greatest joy I got when I was Minister for Social Services was doing all the detail [sic] work, costing Medibank and so on. I liked conceptualising health insurance programs, and it was intellectually satisfying to talk about it to specialist audiences, though on reflection I realise I was boring a lot of people. When I went to speak to doctors I would think, 'now this is going to be beaut tonight, because they will be interested in how we will make these new health services better.' But when I got into the heart of the thing which I found so fascinating, you could just about see them dropping off into soporific trances. Their eyes were glazed and their shutters were clanging. Their self interest would come out rather nakedly, although they would try to dress

it up with euphemistic self-sacrificing terms like 'patients' rights'. They just wanted the right to charge the patient as much as he could pay. Freedom of choice to them meant having the whole system to their advantage. It was a lesson to me and I am still learning it. People do not want everything explained, they just want to hear what interests them.[13]

Hayden felt there were some influences in his past that contributed to his wish to explain everything in detail:

One was being a cop and having to prepare evidence. I came to accept that if I had the right evidence I would establish the case. This might work when you are in court, but it does not work with people generally. Studying economics also had a desiccating effect on my emotions. The disciplines of economics, by their very nature, make you more rational and disciplined. This came out when I introduced Medibank. I was constantly appearing on television programs and large-scale debates in ampitheatres full of doctors. I was battling it out and I had to get every figure right. At that time and in that sort of debate it was a strength, because, although people might not understand the implications of all that was said, they could see I understood my field and could hold my own.[14]

Apart from the personal campaign against him, there was another, more momentous counterpoint to Hayden's political and personal difficulties with the doctors and social welfare issues: Australia was on the threshold of an extended period of economic and political turbulence. In December 1973 the *Sydney Morning Herald* commissioned a poll, the results of which encapsulated the popular feeling of the time: 74 per cent of the people thought the Whitlam Government was trying to do too many things at once. The Opposition, itself sensing that the honeymoon was over for Labor, was increasingly using its numbers in the Senate to obstruct government legislation; by April 1974 the Senate had rejected ten bills twice and nine other bills once. The bills that had been rejected twice included two health insurance bills that had both been forced through the House of Representatives for the second time on 4 April and which provided the legislative basis for Medibank.[15]

An election for half the Senate was scheduled for 18 May, but events moved with dramatic suddenness as what had shaped up as a political masterstroke turned into a costly political farce. Whitlam learned that a disillusioned Vince Gair, who had been dumped by his own party as leader of the DLP, was prepared to accept a diplomatic appointment, and secretly offered him the post of Ambassador to Ireland. His objective in treating with an aged and despised enemy was to create an election for six rather than five Senate places in Queensland at the May election, giving Labor an excellent chance of winning three of those places and in so doing gaining control of the Senate. He was frustrated by twin circumstances. The plan leaked before Gair had formally resigned and Sir Joh Bjelke-Petersen acted immediately to frustrate Whitlam's scheme by having a special Government Gazette printed at midnight proclaiming that the State Governor had issued writs for the election of five Queensland senators only.

Liberal leader Billy Snedden and National Party leader Doug Anthony then determined to use the issue of Gair's appointment, described by Snedden as 'the most shameful act by any Government in Australia's history' as an excuse for using the Opposition's Senate numbers to force a simultaneous election for the House of Representatives and the full Senate, an act then unprecedented in Australian history. On 10 April the Opposition's leader in the Upper House, Senator Reg Withers, moved that 'because of its maladministration, the Government should not be granted funds until it agrees to submit itself to the people'.

Whitlam took up the gauntlet immediately, and went straight to the Governor-General, Sir Paul Hasluck, who accepted his advice to dissolve both Houses of Parliament. The political crisis coincided with, and caused the Whitlam Government to neglect, a deeply worsening economic situation. In a speech the following year Hayden conceded:

At the time of the double dissolution last year, the administration of national affairs was more or less in a state of suspension for something like three months during the election campaign and the post election uncertainty ... The distraction of the election diverted attention from detailed economic and social management, especially from the latter.[16]

Freudenberg, the Prime Minister's speechwriter during the campaign, confessed later that Whitlam had operated under a serious restraint in the 1974 election, which he judged the most difficult that Whitlam had ever fought. The head of Treasury, Sir Frederick Wheeler, had warned Whitlam that cost-of-living figures for the March quarter which suggested a slowing down in the inflation rate represented a 'false dawn' and that there were deepening economic difficulties ahead. 'It was a knowledge he could hardly share with the public,' said Freudenberg.[17]

For all that, Whitlam campaigned with his customary energy and inspirational flair, and Hayden and the health plans played a prominent role, except in Queensland where at the major rally Bill and Dallas had to share a chair in the audience while Egerton occupied the most prominent position next to Whitlam on the stage.[18] 'Few if any social reforms in Australia's history have had a clearer mandate in terms of acceptance and insistence on the part of the majority of the people than Labor's scheme for universal health insurance and the right of all to free hospitalisation,' Whitlam wrote later. 'Medibank, to use the shorthand for all it stood for, had been one of the decisive issues in the great campaign of 1969. It was crucial to our victory in 1972. Its rejection by the Senate Opposition contributed significantly to victory in May 1974.'[19]

ELEVEN

A short, sharp, shock

Sounds serious, comrade.
What does it mean?

Gough Whitlam

I N THE RELATIVE PRIVACY of the sitting room of The Lodge a couple of months after his great victory in the 1974 election, Gough Whitlam was franker than he had been with the voters. 'It was providential that we had to fight the election when we did,' he said. 'We would have been absolutely rooted if we had run the full three years. We would have lost the last election if it was held next month.'[1]

Whitlam and a group of selected ministers who were at The Lodge on the afternoon of 15 July 1974 for a meeting of the economics committee — the 'kitchen Cabinet' as it was known — had just heard a brutal assessment of the present state of, and future prospects for, the economy from the deputy head of the Treasury, John Stone, who said plainly that Australia was heading for a serious recession. Inflation had been increasing through 1973, having been given a kick along by Prime Minister Bill McMahon in his 1972 election-year Budget; he had overruled the austere and electorally unwelcome measures proposed by Treasury and his Treasurer, Billy Snedden.

Labor's first Budget in 1973 with Frank Crean as Treasurer had been relatively neutral, although it was later criticised by Bob Hawke, among others, as being too expansionary because it had honoured an election promise not to increase taxes. A 25 per cent across-the-board tariff cut on 18 July 1973, which Hayden supported, had among its objectives the reduction of inflation by cutting the price of imported goods.[2] Cuts in the migrant intake by both the McMahon and Whitlam governments in the early 1970s had, by the start of 1974, led to acute shortages of workers in key industries and in turn to sharp wage rises for metal workers in the car industry. To add to the problems, unemployment, attributed in various degrees to wage rises and to employers conducting a labour shake-out in the age of uncertainty, was emerging as an issue.

Earlier that year Whitlam had been forced by the Opposition in the course of the May election campaign to devote some attention to economic issues. Whitlam was at the height of his crusade for social reform; the last thing he wanted to do in an election campaign was to become bogged down in a debate on economic issues, for which he had little feeling or interest. Without other sources of advice which he could evaluate independently, he was inclined to place total reliance on the views of Treasury. On 7 June 1974 he made a rousing speech to the premiers at their annual conference in Canberra at which he adopted the Treasury line and implied that the Labor Government was prepared to abandon full employment in order to deal with inflation.

Hayden was disturbed both by the economic situation and the advice Treasury was giving. He and a group of other ministers and their advisers were convinced it was disastrously wrong. From the start of 1974 Hayden had been playing an increasing role in the development of economic policy, his involvement being dictated both by circumstances and by conviction. Crean, in the intervals between a series of overseas junkets, had proved to be a weak Treasurer, neither strong enough to reject Treasury's advice nor effective enough to convince his fellow ministers that it was right and should be implemented. Hayden and others, including Jim Cairns, Tom Uren and Clyde Cameron, were moving to fill this vacuum, to the despair of Whitlam, who would have preferred to avoid conflict between his most powerful and controversial ministers and Treasury, the linchpin of the Public Service. At one economic discussion the Prime Minister turned to Cameron and said: 'What would a fucking ex-shearer know about economics?'

'As much as a classical Greek scholar,' replied Cameron.

Hayden's major concerns were the likely social and electoral consequences of inflation and the lack of resolve or coherence in the Government's policies. With bad grace Hayden had suffered a significant defeat at a previous and critical meeting of Whitlam's kitchen Cabinet in Sydney on 21 January 1974, when he was acting Treasurer during one of Crean's overseas trips. At that meeting Hayden had strenuously opposed a resolution by Cameron in his role of Labour Minister for the Government to support the reintroduction of automatic quarterly cost-of-living adjustments. Under this system, later better known as wage indexation, workers had their wages adjusted for the effects of inflation without having to go to arbitration or take industrial action. Hayden believed this would simply build inflation into the system, and clashed repeatedly with Cameron. Whitlam intervened and proposed a compromise under which wages would be adjusted twice a year, and with Hayden's support had the motion passed by the committee.

Cameron blew up. He threatened that if the motion was put to the full Cabinet the following day and passed he would immediately report all members of Cabinet to the Federal president of the Labor Party — who happened to also be the president of the ACTU, Bob Hawke — calling on him to put in train action to expel Cabinet members for voting against established party policy. 'I will also ask Caucus to elect a new Cabinet, and get rid of the Treasury stooges now masquerading as a Labor Government,' Cameron warned.

Hayden was not intimidated and said that with inflation running as it was, the economy at that time was 'more important than the bloody platform'. Cameron argued that indexation would give the Government a degree of control over wages, saying that in a time of high inflation the strong unions would get increases outside the system anyway. Cameron's threat succeeded: Whitlam reopened the debate and Hayden was defeated, despite the support of others including Kep Enderby, Rex Patterson, Bill Morrison and Ken Wreidt.

In June, 1974, Hayden was consistent in his opposition to salary increases when he was one of eleven ministers, including Whitlam and Cameron, who were defeated in Cabinet when they moved to defer a proposal for $5500 a year rises for parliamentarians. The next day in Caucus, Hayden was one of a smaller group of ministers who broke the convention of Cabinet solidarity to vote again against accepting the rises. He made an impassioned speech saying such a rise would undermine any attempt by the Government to control inflation by reducing pressure for wage increases, and was heckled and jeered for his trouble.[3] 'How many of you think you could get a better job outside?' he asked, and then added: 'That's where you'll be if you vote for a rise.'[4] The majority voted for a rise, but they didn't get it: the Government was ultimately made to look foolish as well as greedy when the Opposition killed the proposal in the Senate.

At a meeting of the kitchen Cabinet at Kirribilli House in Sydney on 8 July 1974, Hayden had been shaken by an estimate given by a senior Treasury official, Bill Cole, that unemployment would reach 110 000 by July 1975. The meeting at The Lodge on 15 July, at which Whitlam expressed relief at the timing of the May election, had been called to fix the parameters for a mini-budget to be brought down later that month. It was chaired by Whitlam and attended by Hayden, Frank Crean, Jim Cairns, Kep Enderby, and Clyde Cameron. In the week between the two meetings Hayden had prepared a six-page confidential paper which he circulated to the other ministers.

Stone's assessment on 15 July was much grimmer than Cole's had been: inflation would become worse; the balance of payments presented a terrifying picture; there would be a slide in commodity prices from then on, he predicted, before raising the prospect of a forced devaluation which would again boost inflation. Stone urged the ministers to increase taxes to reduce demand, a tactic that Treasury had now been denied in successive Liberal and Labor budgets. He said that, even if the sceptical ministers were correct and Treasury's view of the state of the economy was wrong, it was easier to step up demand than reduce it.

If Gough Whitlam had been an economic genius it is still doubtful that his government would have survived the international economic turmoil of the mid-1970s, but if he had had a more informed involvement in major decisions on economic issues or even a surer touch in deciding which economic advisers to trust, his government would have fared much better. He remained, however, almost perversely remote from the area which set the parameters within which he could responsibly carry out his reforms. Bob Hawke, as Blanche d'Alpuget records,[5] was one of those concerned and mystified by Whitlam's attitude, and he and many others at various times and in various ways offered to help Whitlam to come to terms with economic theory. James Cumes, a public servant who criticised the performance of Australian ministers in his book *A Bunch of Amateurs*, said:

Hawke was right in that Whitlam should at least have given himself the chance. So long as he continued to be totally innocent of economics, he could never form any reasoned or confident judgment, even a wrong one, about whether the advice on which he acted made any sense. He was in a blind alley where it was vital for a Prime Minister to have sharp sight.[6]

A respected economic journalist, Ken Davidson of *The Age*, regards the view that Whitlam was economically illiterate as a corrosive myth, and says he had a clear grasp of the essential principles, including opportunity cost, which means if you spend a dollar on something you can't spend it on something else. Whitlam was himself, as much as anybody else, to blame for his reputation. Cumes records: 'On one occasion when I had put a paper on economic policy to him, he confided to me amiably in a departmental corridor: "Sorry, but I just don't understand it." '[7] At a function to mark Bill Hayden's twenty-five years in Parliament, Whitlam recalled Hayden coming to him anxiously to report that an American agency was considering downgrading Australia's credit rating. Whitlam said: 'Sounds serious, comrade. What does it mean?'[8]

Bill Hayden was Whitlam's direct antithesis: from his first days in Parliament he took an interest in major economic questions. He decided to give economics priority over law in his studies and now had his degree, and his experience as Social Security Minister reinforced his conviction that unless the Government got cohesion in its economic policy it could not extend social justice to the citizens. A consequence of his study, his sceptical nature and his increasing confidence in his ability to question those academics he had once accepted as infallible was that he developed views which conflicted with those he had previously strenuously advanced. This is never a popular course in politics. Too few of his colleagues progressed in their views or knowledge or felt it necessary to rethink their theories in the light of changed circumstances. Hayden agonised, but he did have the capacity to change.

As the ministers and officials settled in the sitting room of The Lodge on 15 July, in the comfortable old armchairs, clutching papers in their laps, Whitlam said he had wanted to do something about the $150 million Post Office deficit, but had postponed action because of two New South Wales by-elections.

Stone's speech had shaken Whitlam, but he responded in political rather than economic terms: 'With 20 per cent inflation and no overseas reserves I couldn't conduct a successful election campaign,' he said. He remarked how successfully he had used the CPI figures for the election just past, saying the March figures had been 'the biggest piece of garbage I ever resorted to'. 'Inflation was a worrying issue, but I was better at defusing it than Snedden was at igniting it,' he boasted. The split over basic economic policy that emerged at the meeting was, within a month, to sour relations between Hayden and Whitlam to the degree that Whitlam not only banished Hayden from key economic discussions but hardly exchanged a word with him for months.

It was a breach that damaged both Hayden and the Government. Whitlam made it clear to the ministers at The Lodge that he still agreed with the Treasury prescription for a 'short, sharp, shock' that he had outlined to the premiers and which would involve Labor abandoning its policy of creating full employment. Hayden would accept neither Treasury's diagnosis nor its remedy. In the weeks leading up to the meeting Peter McCawley had, at Hayden's request, gathered informally and summarised for Hayden the views of economists in the universities, Reserve Bank and dissidents in the Treasury, which reinforced Hayden's own view that the squeeze on money supply was already taking effect, and that the economy was more likely to require boosting than being screwed down further. Unemployment concerned Hayden more than inflation, and he was also worried that Labor parliamentarians would soon start looking for solutions like import quotas, increased tariffs and subsidies to particular industries which in his view would not make any substantial dent in unemployment but would further exacerbate economic problems.[9]

At the key meeting at The Lodge he strongly warned Whitlam and the Treasury officials that the parliamentary Labor Party would not accept policies predicated on 2 per cent unemployment. He wanted the Government to lift the pressure of its monetary policies: 'If you don't, you will find one morning that the Caucus will just go "bang".' Turning to Whitlam he said: 'It's no use you telling us not to lose our nerve and not be frightened of Caucus reaction. That's all very well: but it's just like accusing somebody of being too scared to jump into the fire.' Whitlam shifted ground: 'I'm not accepting unemployment either. I am not having people put on the streets or pensioners starving. I don't want to be a Scullin, or find a Caucus going to pieces.'

In the confidential document Hayden circulated to ministers that day,[10] he correctly predicted that inflation would exceed the 14 per cent it was then running at and that unemployment could easily reach 4 per cent. He also added a cautionary warning about the political realities that governed the Government's scope for effective action: 'It is essential to recognise and respect the role of Caucus in future economic policy. Measures taken which lead the economy in a direction unacceptable to Caucus are certain to be rescinded by Caucus. From now on there will be little time for lengthy decision-making processes involving Caucus committees, so the up-shot of measures unacceptable to Caucus is that they will be rescinded and quite likely replaced with unsuitable, even disastrous substitutes. The first parameter we must acknowledge in assessing future measures is that Caucus will not tolerate significant unemployment, and it may very well be disastrous to the Government, but, more importantly to the nation, if there is any attempt to short-circuit Caucus by ignoring its basic attitude.'

Hayden bluntly warned Whitlam that he would be right in the firing line: 'Caucus will find adequate justification for its opposition and for terminating any measures causing unemployment in the Prime Minister's guarantee that inflation will be cut back to 8 per cent next year and his guarantee also that there would be no increase in unemployment. This means that we would be courting disaster to continue with the present economic measures unmodified, plus, for example, other fiscal measures mentioned by the Prime Minister.'

The economy, Hayden said, was in the process of turning around and that meant that the Treasury measures were no longer appropriate. His own proposals called for stimulation of the private sector by cuts in company tax and by allowing more foreign capital into the country. He had also, by now, accepted Cameron's argument that wage indexation would moderate the wages scramble, but wanted productivity increases to be traded off for tax cuts which would stimulate demand.

Whitlam responded to the thrust of Hayden's case with some measure of frustration. At the kitchen Cabinet meeting he acknowledged that he did not seem to have support for an immediate increase in postal charges. In one of his classic performances which combined anger, stagecraft, self-mockery and also a threat, Whitlam ground his teeth and said: 'I don't mind being a bastard as long as you other bastards are prepared to be bastards with me. I'm not going to be *the* bastard anymore.'

The Treasury head Sir Frederick Wheeler, a clever politician and manipulator of men in his own right, could see Treasury's position slipping away, and commented that, while it was not for him to advise on political matters, he had never seen difficulties being resolved by being deferred. His tactic failed. The full Cabinet met on the night of 22 July, threw out the Treasury taxation proposals and endorsed the line Hayden, Cameron and Uren had advocated. 'There followed what can only be described as farce,' Barry Hughes wrote later.

> On the evening of 23 July Frank Crean stood up to deliver a mini-Budget to Parliament. It was full of the same sort of rhetoric that was included in Whitlam's Premiers' Conference address. But the actual measures announced had little in common with the rhetoric. The Cabinet had vetoed the Treasury plan. Gone were the higher income tax rates and extra petrol taxes, and added was an increase in the weekly pension rate amounting to $5 for single people.[11]

Whitlam's patience was at an end. He had lost control of the war that had developed between his ministers and his powerful Public Service economic advisers. It was a struggle for which Whitlam had no appetite and so he turned away both from the debate on economic policy formation and from those he blamed for the complex and critical situation that had arisen, Hayden and Crean. Whitlam blamed Crean for not being forceful enough to sell Treasury's policies to the Cabinet, while Hayden was cast out for being effective in using his sources of wider advice to convince his colleagues that Treasury was wrong. Later, when fulsomely praising Hayden's performance as Treasurer, Whitlam was to acknowledge that his Government may have fared better if he had given Hayden a central economic portfolio much sooner than he did. Now Hayden had ceased to be the Prime Minister's chosen successor, and was excluded from Whitlam's circle.

A little melodrama on the night of 7 August 1974 sealed the breach between Whitlam and Hayden. A joint sitting of the House of Representatives and Senate, called to pass the legislation which had triggered the double dissolution, had dragged on for two days, and Hayden had been out to dinner where he had had more to drink than he usually did. Returning to Parliament he was met by a large group of migrants demonstrating against the decision Whitlam had made recognising the incorporation of the Baltic states of Estonia, Latvia and Lithuania into the Soviet Union. Hayden regarded Whitlam's decision as being unnecessary and gratitously offensive to migrants from those states, and was flushed with anger, 'the effects of the wine and the heat from the candles on the restaurant table' when he strode into the chamber and planted himself beside Whitlam who was sitting in conversation with Senator John Wheeldon.[12] Hayden proceeded to give Whitlam a piece of his mind on the Baltic issue and then went on to attack the Budget strategy then under consideration. Whitlam took the attitude that many of the demonstrators belonged to extreme right-wing groups, and believed that the opposition of some among them to Russia dated back to sympathy with the Nazi cause. Hayden didn't back away from his support for the demonstrators, but, with his temper up, he took the opportunity to expand the argument and get a few other worries off his chest. He told Whitlam the Government was overspending and that this was creating an intolerable squeeze on the private sector in a time of tight money supply. Just to make sure Whitlam had got the message he marched back to his office and dictated a long letter to Whitlam, putting his angry views on the record.[13] That was it as far as Whitlam was concerned. 'He barely spoke to me for more than six months,' Hayden later said.

TWELVE

A tainted chalice

What I had once upheld as a virtue ...
I denounced as sin.

Bill Hayden

'**I** SUPPOSE that with the benefit of experience that I've had now with colleagues I might, for instance, have put Bill Hayden in as Treasurer right from the beginning,' Gough Whitlam acknowledged after his first major Cabinet reshuffle on 6 June 1975.[1] Hayden had got the job he had trained himself for; the one office short of being Prime Minister that allowed him the maximum opportunity to give shape to his vision of a fairer society: at the age of forty-two he was Treasurer of Australia.

But Hayden had been handed a tainted chalice in a government already doomed, and had achieved his ambition as the result of a personal and political tragedy befalling one of his early political models and benefactors, Dr James Ford Cairns. Cairns had in the space of a year taken the full roller-coaster ride of politics from the peak of triumph and adulation to the depths of isolation and bitterness. After the 1974 election he had on 10 June successfully challenged Lance Barnard for the deputy leadership, supported, ironically, by parliamentarians who expected him to provide a responsible check on the enthusiasms of the autocratic Whitlam.[2]

While Whitlam was overseas for six weeks during December 1974 and January 1975 Cairns as Acting Prime Minister handled a number of critical situations, including the destruction of Darwin by Cyclone Tracy, with warmth and effectiveness. But he had been brought undone by his involvement with an extraordinary woman, Junie Morosi, whom he appointed as his office coordinator on 2 December 1974.

Morosi isolated him from his friends, from his party colleagues and his professional advisers, and together she and Cairns created a sort of sexual and racial chemistry that dominated much political discussion and diverted their attention from their critical responsibilities. Cairns had been one of Hayden's earliest and closest political friends; he was, like Hayden, a former policeman who had become a crusader. He had travelled to Ipswich to help Hayden in his first election campaigns. In his earliest years as the youngest politician in Canberra, the raw novice Bill Hayden had dogged Cairns' footsteps, and been politically guided by the man who had now left the second most powerful office in the nation in disgrace.

The end of Cairns' political career, like the aftermath of death in a family, had been formalised by a ritual cleaning of his offices, in the spacious Treasurer's suite immediately under the Prime Minister's office on the north-east corner of Parliament House. 'It looked as if it had been sanitised by a CIA clean-up squad. There wasn't a picture on the wall, there wasn't even a single sheet of blank paper,' a staff member recalled. But in the bottom of a wardrobe in one of the staff offices, his press secretary, Norm Harriden, found an old classical record in a battered cover. It happened to be a recording he knew Hayden had been seeking for his collection and thought the new Treasurer might like it as a souvenir of an important event which had some personal emotional as well as political significance for him. Harriden and Gay Raby took the record in to present to Hayden. 'He was shocked, he was on the verge of real anger. It wasn't our property, it belonged to someone else. We withdrew somewhat stunned. It was partly his personal puritanism; but later it also became clear he had instinctively decided he wasn't going to be linked in any way to the Cairns era,' Harriden said in 1988.[3]

Hayden also immediately increased security measures in the Treasurer's office, having new locks installed and arming himself with a large bunch of keys which he took some time to master. A few evenings after he had taken up the job, Whitlam walked into Hayden's outer office unannounced for a brief confidential discussion just as Hayden had completed locking all doors before leaving for a diplomatic reception. As was his custom with all visitors, Hayden introduced all his staff to the Prime Minister while still shuffling with his new keys. Eventually he had to lead the Prime Minister out onto the office verandah to enter the inner sanctum by an outside door. As he departed the general office, the great man was heard to advise, in a reference to the position that had been created for Junie Morosi: 'Comrade, what you want is an office coordinator.'[4]

Seldom has an Australian Treasurer come to office in more difficult circumstances. The international economic turbulence precipitated by the oil crisis and a war between gold and the US dollar was at its height and would at successive elections soon result in most incumbent governments in the democratic world being turfed out of office. The Australian Treasury was at war with the Government over economic policy and the Arab Loans affair, an unsuccessful and ludicrously bungled attempt to raise massive loans overseas through unconventional channels. Treasury's concern for the damage it believed the dubious intermediaries were doing to Australia's international financial reputation was matched only by their anger at being excluded from the negotiations. The people that had been trusted by some ministers, and Connor in particular, became known collectively as the men in green sunglasses. They had no recognised credentials, no international standing or known achievements. They went beyond what Treasury officers regarded as even the fringe of acceptable international financial dealings. They had been spawned by the age of uncertainty that shifted vast financial power to the Arab oil nations.

Hayden, who had by now served as acting Treasurer on nine occasions, was aware that Treasury had been strengthened in its distrust of the Government by the increasingly sloppy, opinionated and idiosyncratic way in which Cairns and his personal staff had carried out the job. The bureaucrats had also been incensed by the fact that Cairns had succeeded at the Terrigal Federal Conference of the Labor Party in early February 1975 in getting approval to establish a Department of Economic Planning which would have threatened Treasury's hegemony over economic advice to the Government.

Hayden got to occupy the Treasurer's office in two stages. First, Cairns was demoted from Treasury to the Environment portfolio on 6 June 1975, but he retained his large office. Whitlam had attempted to capitalise as best he could politically on the removal of Cairns from Treasury by simultaneous and sweeping changes to the ministry in an attempt to give his already tottering Government a fresh public face. The most tortured of these moves, never properly justified, was to replace the tough and wily Clyde Cameron as Minister for Labour with the smooth Sydney lawyer, Senator James McClelland. This precipitated scenes of high drama. Cameron was forewarned by Bill Morrison, who was at the same time being promoted to the Defence portfolio, that he was to be offered the lowly job Morrison had held as Minister for Science and Consumer Affairs. Cameron refused to go to Whitlam's office, and after a series of tense phone calls between John Bannon, then Cameron's private secretary, and Whitlam's principal private secretary Jim Spiegelman, the Prime Minister descended on Cameron's office. He had not been there before and burst in the wrong door over a pile of papers into the room I occupied as press secretary. Then, seated opposite Cameron on the smallest chair Bannon had been able to find in the building, he declined to give reasons for the transfer. Cameron, for his part, made it clear he did not accept the decision and did not intend to go to Government House to be sworn into the portfolio he had been allotted.

With this dramatic deadlock still unresolved, the division bells rang in the House of Representatives and the principal participants assembled on the front benches. As debate continued in the chamber Cameron moved to ensure, as part of the price of his compliance, a guarantee that one of his treasured projects, the proposed Trade Union Training College, would go ahead. He summoned Hayden to his assistance and received his immediate support. What is now the Clyde Cameron College at Albury is the result of perhaps Hayden's first allocation of funds as Treasurer.

Then, evidence was produced that Cairns had misled the Parliament on 4 June when he had denied that letters he had handed to a businessman, George Harris, had offered Harris or his company a commission of 2½ per cent on any loan money arranged by him. On 2 July, Whitlam advised Governor-General John Kerr to withdraw Cairns' commission as Minister for Environment and Conservation. A special and dramatic sitting of the House of Representatives was held on 9 July to allow Whitlam to explain his decisions. Cairns replied, saying he had answered the question truthfully and to the best of his knowledge, but had now seen evidence that perhaps he had been wrong. In his book on the Loans Affair, *Oil in Troubled Waters*, Cairns said that while he had been in Paris in May he had been informed by Whitlam that the head of Treasury, Sir Frederick Wheeler, had obtained the Harris letter and had sent it to the secretary of the Attorney-General's Department, Clarrie Harders, for a legal opinion. On 3 June Whitlam confronted Cairns with a legal opinion, stating that the letter created an agency between the Australian Government and Harris.

> I said [to Whitlam] I understood there was some doubt about that, but even if the letters did create an agency, it was within my authority to do so, and in the light of decisions taken regarding Khemlani [another person engaged in dubious loan-raising activities under the sponsorship of Mines and Energy Minister Rex Connor] it was a matter of insignificance. The Prime Minister said that Mr Connor had not done anything without the advice of his department, but I had not told my department. I said I had not kept anything from anybody — but my department was Treasury, and no one more than he [Whitlam] had wanted to keep Treasury out.[5]

That was the atmosphere in which Hayden came to Treasury.

These were months of enormous strain for Hayden. His staff estimated he was averaging less than three hours sleep a night, working until past midnight in his ministerial office, often interrupted by questions, debates and urgency motions in the nearby chamber, and a succession of Cabinet and other Budget committee meetings. The old Parliament House, with its red and green lights shining over the Senate and House of Representatives chambers, was something like a ship at sea: packed with human life and passion in all its variety, where enemies, lovers, rivals and friends, politicians, journalists, barmaids, librarians, cooks and media lived in forced propinquity, almost intimacy, all with their own separate concerns and agendas.

Hayden privately recognised and appreciated the calibre of senior Treasury people he was dealing with, and talking to his own staff contrasted them with the Social Services Department bureaucrats he had worked with for more than two years. 'They have a certain elan that the people in Social Security didn't possess,' he once remarked. A staff member said: 'He had been making salient comments on the margins of documents that passed between himself and Social Security: they covered the whole range of human nature. Now he found that when he made comments to Treasury, they were acted on.'[6]

Hayden would work in his ministerial office until well past midnight, and then take papers home to his apartment at Swinger Hill in the Woden Valley, then a new and fairly fashionable low-rise cluster of self-contained units. Returning in the morning he would have read and annotated masses of reports and have lists of requirements. 'I was out in the unit by myself. Dallas was up here [at Ipswich] with the kids, who had started school by then, of course. We'd always had a rather old-fashioned thing that, as much as possible, one of us at least should be with them. I was only getting a few hours' sleep a night. I had this huge pile of documents and I had to go through all of them, not once, but several times, so I was on top of every argument. In those days you were Treasurer and Minister for Finance, and you were by yourself. I quite enjoyed it. It has always made me sceptical of people in the education field who argue opposition to exams and tests. That seemed to me to be the most important major test I had faced, up to that time anyway. I had to meet deadlines. I had to drive myself. It reminded me of doing a major assignment on a very tight deadline in which I was going for the best marks I could get, at university. And I always thought to myself, this is an important part of the training of young people: to meet those deadlines, and to perform to set standards, you've got to really push yourself.'

A feature article in the *Australian* under the heading 'Superswot' two months after he had become Treasurer provides a snapshot of the Hayden of those days: 'Bill Hayden is a hard man to find. The nearer one gets to him the harder he is to see,' it begins.

> His close friends in politics are few, so few that one hand would do to count them ... He has a tendency to lecture colleagues about economics, like many people who've lately discovered a good thing, which makes some of them wonder whether or not he might be a bit of an intellectual snob ... He still gives off the old aura of super-energy barely confined. And he's as willing as ever to have a go ... One of the biggest drawbacks to Hayden becoming the next Labor PM is one of his strengths as a person; his distaste for what he calls 'pop politics' which means his refusal to go in for those old Caucus charismatics. It mightn't be a bad trait in a leader, giving us all the chance to settle down and work it out; but it makes it difficult for the person who has to attract the necessary following from those who like to be attracted.[7]

The author suggested that a potential obstacle in his way to becoming leader was his anxiety about becoming alienated by power from his constituency:

> An admirer speculates that his strong awareness of his background and his working-class loyalties cause him to be suspicious of the middle class. He's

said sometimes to need to be persuaded that environmental issues, for example, aren't bourgeois affairs which operate against the true interests of the working class.

The stress Hayden was working under at the time surfaced occasionally in relations with his personal staff and officers of Treasury; there were incidents which reflect the sort of collective deviation from normal working life patterns that affects Parliament House, or sections of it, at times of sustained crisis. 'You all get a little bit crazy,' is the way one of Hayden's former staff member puts it.[8] Hayden's relationship with his staff and bureaucrats over the years has been one of the most discussed but least documented of the subjects that arise in any private conversation about him. The illustrative incidents that are raised range from trivial and farcical to those that show traits that may have had significance when, in the end, he did not reach his ultimate political goal. A Commonwealth car driver who had worked for years for Hayden was once directed to drive Bob Hawke for a brief period. Hayden refused to allow him to return to his old job. 'He invited intimacy, and dropped the curtain when you least expected it,' one sensitive long-term staff member said.

Two of the internal office disputes in which Peter McCawley, his senior economic adviser, was involved give an indication of the atmosphere of the Hayden office of the time. Hayden reacted with distress to the Indonesian invasion of Timor, and Whitlam's reported attitude of compliance with it. Hayden now sees the situation as having been less dramatic than do some of those who were close to him at the time. Now as a result of a subsequent close relationship with senior Foreign Affairs officers who were involved in the discussions between Whitlam and Indonesian President Soeharto before the Indonesian action in 1975, Hayden privately asserts that Whitlam, in fact, pressed powerfully for Indonesian guarantees that there would be a properly supervised act of self-determination in Timor. Whitlam's position on the events involving Timor in 1975 was seen by Graham Freudenberg as an echo of events in 1962 when the then Labor leader, Arthur Calwell, had through a strange combination of circumstances come close to threatening war against Indonesia if it incorporated West New Guinea, as it inevitably did. Calwell was painted by Menzies as a warmonger and a blusterer and his decline was from then on irreversible, says Freudenberg, who added: 'The Calwell catastrophe would deeply affect the attitude of Whitlam, as Prime Minister, to the problem posed by Indonesia's desire to incorporate

East Timor. Whitlam, as Prime Minister, was determined never again to have a bar of the humbug humiliation and hypocrisy which had occurred over West Irian.'[9]

One of Hayden's senior staff members at that time said recently: 'Bill was outraged by the invasion and by the Government's attitude; he was off his brain about it. McCawley saw no alternative for the economic forces of the world. Bill wouldn't wear it. He had a serious falling out with his economic adviser.' Hayden does not recall the differences with McCawley as being of major proportions: 'I had a few arguments with him. I thought he was less critical than he could have been where the Indonesians were concerned, and I think in retrospect that, while there is more than a grain of truth in that, I was a bit harsh on him too.'

Hayden's further more recent comments on his stance at that time, when he held passionate views on the morality of actions by foreign governments, shed light on the changes that have taken place in him: 'This is a problem for Westerners, particularly people in this country, a young country. We haven't rubbed up hard against other countries and learnt that we've got to make adjustments and accommodations. There is a tendency for us to be so moral that we're moralisers, almost hand-wringing do-gooders, a bit like *The Life of Brian*, where the radicals meet over cheap red in their little villa in Jerusalem hiding from the Centurions who don't give a damn about them and carrying resolutions and amendments and then, at the end of the day, moving an adjournment of the revolution until the following weekend.'

Not all conflicts were over matters of such lasting moment and moral complexity; staff of the Treasurer's office in 1975 still discuss the incident of the cake of soap. Di Fingleton, who subsequently followed her former employer's advice and qualified in law and now runs a community legal service in Brisbane, was Hayden's steno-secretary.

'I would go into his office each morning and he would give me dictation on about a dozen different subjects. They would range from buying a canoe for a family holiday, through Oxley electorate matters to submissions for Cabinet and letters to Caucus. I would go back to my desk and start on what I thought was the most important thing of the day, usually Cabinet. I was starting to become political: a socialist and a blooming feminist. It would turn out that, in Bill's view, the canoe was really the most important. He was a bit of a nag: "How is the canoe going?" he would ask every time he passed. He ran out of soap in his ensuite bathroom. We started the same routine: "Would you get some soap?", "How is the soap going?", "Why don't you get some soap?", eventually, "I want some soap!". Before we got to the stage of me telling him to get his own bloody soap, Peter McCawley decided to defuse the situation and went across the hallway and took an old cake of soap out of the guests' lavatory. Bill came out with the soap in his hand and ordered us into his office. He had a sort of suppressed anger that you could be scared of. He told us in no uncertain terms that we were there to do what he wanted us to do. Peter was furious — he was an old friend — he didn't expect to be treated like that.' Most versions of the story end with Hayden flinging the aged cake of soap onto the floor and jumping on it.[10]

Other staff members believe that in those days Hayden's relations with those around him were governed not only by the immense pressure he was under but by what they describe as working-class hang-ups that have since almost disappeared as a result of travel, experience and continued education. With his staff and visitors, in Di Fingleton's words, at most times he showed a strong egalitarian streak: all were part of a team and all were introduced. Yet with Treasury officials, even those whose ability he privately admired, he was often abrasively rude. 'He abused them like they were kids at school — he would psyche himself up before meetings,' another staff member said. Denis Murphy put forward the theory that some of his anger with Treasury was caused by his deafness.

> . . . Hayden was very demanding of his staff and his department. He was often impatient for instant answers and could produce, sometimes deliberately, one of his 'emotional outbursts' if these were not forthcoming. One senior public servant thought this was because, through his partial deafness in one ear, Hayden did not always hear clearly the answers given to him.[11]

A former staff member, recalling that period recently, said she had observed a significant difference between Hayden's social behaviour — in which he was often ill at ease and sometimes seeming to be masking insecurity with a degree of bluster — and his professional demeanour in which, she said, he would not try either to impress bureaucrats with his knowledge, or pretend to understand something that he hadn't grasped. 'In professional situations he seemed to find it easy to say to young bureaucrats in Treasury: "I'm sorry, I still don't understand this proposal." He would keep on going until either he understood it, or, sometimes, discovered that they didn't understand it either, or that, when it was properly explained, it was hopeless. What was an inadequacy in his private life did not carry over into his professional life.'

It was to Hayden's credit throughout his political career that he selected as staff talented, opinionated individuals. They were never subservient, and some, particularly later when he was leader, alienated other Labor parliamentarians by being forceful to the point of aggression. The great majority were fiercely loyal to him and his cause but also had their own ideas about how the office and the country should be run. At some stage during the preparation of the 1975 Budget his staff discovered that they were the only ministerial office that did not have a rostered night off. A one-night-off-a-week roster was unilaterally instituted, and, on the night of its introduction, a Sydney journalist who was friendly with members of Hayden's staff dropped into the office. He and the staff member who was to have the night off went to the old Wellington Hotel, then a popular watering hole for media and political people. During the dinner break they were joined there by the rest of Hayden's staff with the exception of his principal private secretary, Gay Raby. They became quite relaxed, until they got a call from the Treasurer: 'If you're not back here by nine o'clock you're all sacked.'

The girl who was supposed to have had the night off joined them and they were all still in the office typing at midnight. But one member was critical of Hayden: 'I thought that his attitude was: "If I have to stay back here working, then everybody else should be here too"; he didn't appreciate that the rewards for him and for us were fundamentally different.' But Hayden's reaction was fuelled by other pressures. At that time forces opposed to the Labor Government were leaking damaging Treasury documents to the media and the Opposition, and Treasury was attempting to claim that the leaks were coming from Parliament House rather than their department. This acrimonious interplay between Hayden's staff and some senior officials in Treasury was reflected in a note sent by the first assistant secretary of Treasury, Bill Cole, to the head of Treasury, Sir Frederick Wheeler, with copies to John Stone, on 30 October 1975, after Cole had visited the Treasurer's suite. 'The outer office was deserted,' the memo said. 'The door to Ms Raby's office was open and there was nobody there. The door to the Treasurer's office was open and there was nobody there. Anybody walking in could have picked up papers lying around and walked out with them and nobody would have seen him. I draw this to your attention because Mr Stone told me a somewhat similar story about a visit he made to the Treasurer's office the other day. On that occasion, however, the Treasurer was in his office but the outer office was completely deserted and there was a journalist waiting in that outer office. I do not know whether you are aware that this situation prevails but I thought it appropriate to draw it to your attention.'[12]

Gay Raby, Hayden's principal private secretary, was the only staff member in the office when the Treasurer read this memo and within minutes also became aware that most of his staff were at the pub. Hayden told her he intended to sack one of the staff, and Raby said that if he did there would be nobody there in the morning. Hayden said the Treasury people would be there, and Raby said they wouldn't because they were more frightened of her than they were of him. Hayden hurled a pot plant at the wall. Raby drafted a reply for Hayden that said: 'If your FASs were more interested in our VDRs and our SDRs than they are in my PPS we mightn't be as RS as we are now,' but Hayden declined to send it.[13]

Wheeler, however, was punctilious in requiring his officers to observe the correct form in dealing with their political boss. 'Young Treasury officers would try to grab the bags off him so they could carry them,' recalls Raby. 'At one stage I had to go into Bill and say, "Can you let the Treasury bloke carry your bags onto the plane?". He said, "Why?". I said: "If Sir Frederick Wheeler sees you carry them on, and not him, this man's whole life will be ruined; his whole career's at stake. If you don't his wife and children will starve. It's not too much to ask." Bill agreed.'

Another staff member says that she suspects Hayden's police background had enhanced a quality in his make-up that allowed him, deliberately or otherwise, to make people feel uncomfortable. 'Like when you are stopped while driving, and you haven't even been drinking,' she said. 'Years later one of Hawke's senior staff members said Bob was often nervy in Hayden's presence.'

The real test for a treasurer, particularly in a Labor Government, and quite critical at that time, was the ability to impose discipline, by force of personality and argument, on the expenditure proposals of other ministers. They could, as Hayden, Uren and Cameron had shown the year previously, combine to outvote the Treasurer and Prime Minister, and, even if beaten, then appeal to Caucus. 'I expected it to be tough,' Hayden said, 'because some of the ministers had a faith in spending that would have been inspirational to Colonel Douglas.[14] I reckoned I had to win a big battle early, to establish my credentials, and, if I didn't, of course we were in a jam.

'So the first one we pulled on was with the Education Minister, Kim Beazley [senior], because he was very tough. He was passionately committed to the Education portfolio, and I think one of the great Education ministers. He is an eminently reasonable man. We won that argument, but my regard for his integrity was such that when he said quite firmly there would be retrenchments among schoolteachers as a result of what we first decided, I became concerned. I moved on to other items, and other ministers: but it was in my mind that Beazley wasn't a man to indulge in hyperbole on important facts to win his argument. I called the Treasury up when we had the morning tea break and said they better check it. The people concerned said they had done the exercise carefully and there was no point in doing it again: it was just Education bleating again. I instructed them to meet the Education people again and work it out. They were put out over that. They met the Education people, and at the next break came over to me and said there had been a mistake and in fact the cuts they had recommended, and which I had got, would have been much more severe than they had presumed. Beazley was right, and so we made adjustments there.

'We weren't in the business of blowing things up with sticks of dynamite. We were in the process of putting the brakes on the cumbersome big monster that got under way under Cairns in particular. I told Wheeler that a deficit of around $2500 million was what we'd aim at. He said that would be altogether too severe, too sudden. The consequences would be severely adverse, and he suggested I should aim at the figure we got, about $2000 million.[15] It has to be said the Cabinet was better than I expected, and better than they had been in earlier times. Whitlam, of course, chides me by saying that I was the biggest-spending Social Security Minister in the history of the Commonwealth, and the meanest Treasurer, and what I had once upheld as a virtue in one ministry, I denounced as sin in the next.'

There is more than an element of truth in Whitlam's observation, although Hayden, while attempting to deal with accelerating inflation, did protect the position of the vulnerable: 'One thing I was concerned about, even in the 1975 Budget, was that there should be a full cost-of-living adjustment for social service beneficiaries. There were some who were prepared to go along with less, including Wheeldon who was Social

Security Minister,' he recalled. Outside the Budget process, Hayden had to deal with the towering figure of the Prime Minister, about whom he said in 1988, while discussing the final days of the Whitlam Government: 'My regard and affection for Gough Whitlam is still extremely high; even when he took you on a bloody disastrous course, Jesus it was exciting.' Contrasting Whitlam with other politicians, he added: 'He had a vision.'

One of the most spectacular expressions of Whitlam's vision, which represented a continuing nightmare to Treasury, was given form in a plan to buy a major shipping company, with the whole scheme culminating in a scene Hayden later privately described with a sort of fascinated detachment: 'He had a great idea he was going to buy the Furness Whitney shipping company. He had Frank Crean in, and he was opposed to it, so he had me in. He had the support of the Transport Minister Charlie Jones; he and Gough just loved ships, planes and trains; they were still big boys at heart. I ran through a list of reasons straight off the cuff why I thought it would be unwise, not least of which was that we would have to get legislation through a hostile Senate, and then there were potential industrial problems ... a whole range of things. And, lo and behold, I found Frank Crean had said almost exactly the same things. He had been briefed by Treasury, I hadn't. Gough was still trying to get the numbers on side, so I got dumped a little bit later because I wasn't on side. However, I was sitting there one day and got called up with a big team of people and Peter Abeles was there, and all of the Treasury fellows were there: and when I say all, their style was always to have six people, or, for something really big, up to ten or a dozen people even, to try and duress you if they could. They were terrified of Gough's harebrained schemes, and rightly so. We were all sitting there and, all of a sudden, Gough said something like: "Jesus Christ, you Treasury people lack imagination: you lack creativeness. What I want is ideas. What I want is the dramatic gesture: like Disraeli buying the Suez Canal!"'

Hayden said it was the only time he had seen the faces of the whole Treasury group fall apart: 'You could hear the clunk as all their jaws simultaneously hit the floor: the louder thumps were from people like myself who fell out of our chairs.' Hayden had a number of stand-up confrontations with Whitlam after he became Treasurer and believed he survived only because the Government was in dire straits. 'It wasn't so much that we fell out. It was the first time, I think, that anyone had been able to exercise some clout against Gough. And, frankly, I don't think I would have got away with it earlier, anyway. He would have got rid of me.'

In his earlier days as Treasurer, Hayden called Whitlam up over a number of decisions and discussions he had been involved in without consulting Hayden or other ministers. One involved a guarantee to a Perth entrepreneurial family about the Government buying an entertainment centre. Hayden wrote Whitlam a sharp letter asserting his authority as Treasurer, telling Whitlam he should discuss such matters and saying he would have opposed such a commitment if he had been consulted. Hayden was more disturbed when he received a phone call from London from the Queensland primary industry leader, Sir William Gunn, which Hayden took as suggesting that Whitlam or his senior staff were aware that people purporting to be acting with Whitlam's tacit consent were still engaged in a search for the elusive Arab oil dollars. Hayden forcefully told Whitlam and his staff that all the shonky deals were over, there would be no more negotiations with men in green sunglasses, and all undertakings already given to Parliament on such matters would be observed. But it was already too late.

THIRTEEN

The dismissal

Oh, Mr Hayden, we must get your coat orf.

Princess Margaret

HAYDEN was sipping a Jim Beam bourbon in the mushroom-walled study at Government House while the Governor-General, Sir John Kerr, gazing at him across his ornately carved desk, seemed to be taking more interest in ordering another huge Scotch whisky than in listening to the Treasurer's account of the economic situation. It was the afternoon of Thursday, 6 November 1975, and it was then that Bill Hayden's instinct warned him that Kerr was planning action against the Whitlam Government. Australia's greatest political crisis was drawing rapidly to its climax, and, despite the fact that Hayden's Budget had been well received, the Opposition led by Malcolm Fraser had determined to use it as the instrument to force Whitlam's Government to the polls.

Early in October the Opposition parties had decided to use their numbers in the Senate and on 15 October Fraser asked Whitlam in Parliament to 'resign decently in the interests of the political health of Australia'. Whitlam answered:

> I will not relieve the honourable gentleman of the odium which will flow from any reprehensible conduct which he aids and abets his colleagues in

the Senate in perpetrating ... He will have to tell his colleagues to do the unspeakable, the unprecedented, the reprehensible, of rejecting a Budget. If a Budget is rejected there is very likely to be an election of one sort or another.[1]

Fraser and his advisers feared that Whitlam would attempt to resolve the deadlock by holding an election for half the Senate. This would present Labor with the possibility of winning a majority in the Upper House, and not only solve the problem of Supply but allow it to enact all its other controversial proposals and, most significantly, carry out an electoral redistribution to remove the bias then existing in favour of the conservative parties. It was a colossal battle of wills between two proud and wilful men.

As the deadlock continued, with neither Whitlam nor Fraser showing signs of bending, there emerged a real prospect of the Government running out of money, and Hayden began preparing contingency plans to pay public servants and meet other government obligations. Whitlam had, however, discounted the potential role of the man he had appointed as Governor-General, Sir John Kerr, who began to take an active interest in the situation with the avowed intention at the beginning of finding a formula that would allow Fraser to back down without losing face.[2]

'I remember during this period [of the constitutional crisis] that Gough threw a dinner party at The Lodge for Princess Margaret who had chosen quite by accident (since the visit had been arranged long before the crisis blew up) to be a guest of the Governor-General at Yarralumla,' James McClelland recalled in his 1988 biography. 'I found myself seated next to the Princess with Bill Hayden on her other side.' The socially relaxed McClelland asked Princess Margaret whether she had been following the crisis, and she replied that she had, avidly — which produced temporary confusion as she pronounced it 'evidly'. McClelland goes on:

> Before I could develop the theme, the maid arrived with the soup. Whether she became flustered on drawing so close to royalty or for whatever cause, she stumbled as she was holding Bill's soup above his head and let him have it all over his dinner jacket. This, I thought later, is what princesses are trained to cope with. Margaret did not bat an eyelid, but said; 'Oh, Mr Hayden, we must get your coat orf,' and proceeded to peel the sodden garment off with her royal hands. Bill was covered with confusion because the removal of the coat revealed a very Ipswichian pair of police-and-firemen braces. He sat there while his coat was taken away to be sponged down, but the princess insisted: 'Oh, these have to come orf too.' She removed the braces, hopped into her soup and then lit up another cigarette.[3]

Hayden's discomfort was not only caused by his braces; unbeknown to McClelland, Hayden had asked a member of his staff as he rushed off to the dinner whether his shirt was clean enough to wear. She had told him it was good enough as long as he kept his coat on.[4]

As he watched Sir John Kerr, sitting in his study at Yarralumla downing his whisky under the Aboriginal bark paintings and copper shield from New Guinea, Hayden was unaware that the Governor-General had held discussions with a more significant audience in the same room earlier that day. On the morning of 6 November, without the knowledge of any members of the Government, Malcolm Fraser had been at Yarralumla and had lengthy and perhaps decisive talks with Kerr in the same room. On the same day Whitlam also went to Government House where Kerr presided over a brief meeting of the Executive Council and then joked with the Prime Minister about a row then going on between the Chief Justice, Sir Garfield Barwick, and Whitlam's former Attorney-General, Lionel Murphy, who had recently been appointed to the High Court bench. Murphy had appointed a female tipstaff and was insisting that Barwick provide a uniform for her. Whitlam's impression was that he and Kerr had agreed that Barwick and Murphy deserved each other; yet within days Barwick was to play a key role in stiffening Kerr's resolve to act.

Hayden had been made aware of the animosity between Murphy and Barwick some weeks earlier when Barwick had telephoned him to complain about Murphy's appointment. Hayden arrived late at Cabinet as a result of the phone call and when asked by Whitlam what had delayed him, replied: 'I've had Garfield Barwick haranguing me for almost an hour over what a mess we've made of the High Court.' Whitlam snapped back: 'Yes, but did you tell him how much we'd improved Cabinet?'[5]

After Whitlam had returned to Parliament House on the afternoon of 6 November, Hayden recalls that the Attorney-General, Kep Enderby, called on him in his Parliament House office and said: 'Gough wants you to go out and talk to Kerr and outline for him the details of how the mechanism for financing the continuing operations of Government would work. You can be candid with him, Gough believes he can be trusted.' Hayden still remembers the meeting with great clarity:

'Kerr started by saying, "Would you like a drink?" and when I accepted asked if I wanted coffee or something hard. I said something hard, and, when he asked what I wanted, nominated a Jim Beam

141

bourbon. In came a tumbler full of bourbon for me and a tumbler full of Scotch for him. They were real men's tumblers. I was a third of the way through mine when he asked: "Would you like another one?" His was empty. I outlined to him what was happening. He said there was a worry about whether it was legal. I said: "I have to tell you this: it is a pretty scrappy arrangement, but I am assured by Attorney-General's that it is absolutely legal. I'm to tell you that my people looked at it and it will work, even though it is scrappy. Gough has not told me what he has in mind, but I don't believe he thinks he can run a Government for twelve months on this arrangement; what I believe he is on about is breaking through the political front that Fraser has established against him on this, because there are senators who I believe don't agree with Fraser's tactics; they are very worried about forcing a very serious confrontation." '

Hayden remembers again assuring Kerr the scheme was legal and that it would work, and work for some time. 'Then Kerr said, and I remember the conversation episodically: "If an election were called now, there is no doubt that, with his back against the wall, Gough is a magnificent fighter — he fights like a lion — he would be back within a term at the most, I would expect." I said: "Jesus Christ, it's not as easy as that; when you go out it's bloody hard to get back, and it usually takes more than one term. We've just had twenty-three years trying to get back." Anyway, that was the conversation. I got very uneasy about that. I had to catch a plane home. Being Treasurer had its distinctly different demands from Social Security, which took me all around Australia — sometimes I would be away from home for two or three weeks on the run during that Medibank debate, which was pretty awful for Dallas, but I had no choice. With Treasury you could get home, but the workload would follow you. I didn't want to miss the plane, so as I left Government House I said to the driver: "Go flat out, I want to see the Prime Minister."

'At Parliament House I hurried to the Prime Minister's office, and in there were Freddie Daly, Gough and the Commonwealth Electoral Officer, and I thought "Oh, oh, what are they up to?". In fact they were sorting out when an election could be held if one were forced on us, and what were the problems — there are always problems like school holidays and so on. I said: "Gough, I've got to talk to you", and he came out of the room. I said: "This was the conversation, this is what Kerr said. I'm telling you now, my copper's instinct tells me that this guy is going to sack you. He's thinking of an early election to sort this thing out." Gough had his spectacles in his hand, and his striped shirt on as I remember, and he drew himself up and boomed: "Comrade, he wouldn't have the guts," and he walked back into the room. And I said, "Okay", and I headed off ... and next week we were out of a job ... not that there was anything Gough could have done to stop it.'

It was later revealed, by Gough Whitlam in his book on the dismissal, *The Truth of the Matter*, that, immediately after Hayden had left Government House, officers who had been summoned on Kerr's orders were instructed to proceed with sound-proofing the Governor-General's study.[6] The work was continued throughout the weekend and completed on the Sunday. As Hayden had suspected, by the time he had told Whitlam of his suspicions, Kerr had already made up his mind. Kerr was sitting at his desk in his study when he dismissed Whitlam on Tuesday, 11 November. Whitlam has always acknowledged that Hayden did approach him and warn him of his suspicions of Kerr, but has suggested in private that he suspected that Hayden, with hindsight, had sharpened up his account of the substance of the warning he had given his Prime Minister. Yet Whitlam quotes at length and as an essential part of his case to show both Kerr's duplicity and lack of proper basis for intervention an article by Hayden in the *Australian* on 3 December 1978, in which Hayden detailed his discussions with Kerr in a way that agrees in every detail with all accounts he has given of the meeting which preceded his unheeded warning.

In his 1978 article, Hayden touched on some of the concrete information he presented to Kerr, saying:

> It was explained to Sir John that Supply would last to about December 11 but that the Treasurer's advance would sustain the Government's liability to fund the public and defence forces' payrolls for a few more weeks after that ... I was taken by surprise to find Sir John apparently little, if at all, interested in much of what I said.

Hayden pointed out in that article that some 60 per cent of each year's expenditure by the national Government is covered by automatic appropriations which do not come before the Parliament. Kerr has apparently tried subsequently to suggest that Hayden gave a more alarmist, or at least much more pessimistic, view of the Government's dilemma. Sir Garfield Barwick, in a letter to Clyde Cameron dated 1 December 1983, wrote: 'I am not sure that Supply would have lasted to

November 30. I think from a conversation I subsequently had with Kerr that Hayden had given him an earlier date for its exhaustion.'[7] Hayden responds by saying, 'What I explained to him was that only 40 per cent of Government spending was in the Budget. The other 60 per cent was right, automatically funded, and it was important to understand that. Supply would run down, but the proposed financing arrangements would keep it going. It would be a scrappy arrangement, but it would work. It boiled down to the banks providing credit for the Government. If Kerr said that, he was trying to justify his actions.'

On Monday, 10 November, Hayden got telex messages from the Commercial Banking Company of Sydney and the Bank of New South Wales making it clear they would not participate in the proposed scheme to advance funds to keep the Government afloat. He was, perhaps, the first to know the Government was finished. Hayden was on the steps of Parliament House the following afternoon when David Smith, official secretary to the Governor-General then and now, read the proclamation dissolving the Parliament. Years later, in March 1983, in an interview after he was appointed Foreign Minister, Hayden recalled the impression Whitlam's performance then had on him:

> There are some things in the Australian political scene which are memorable for the courage which is shown. Whitlam ... was a magnificent and amazing creature standing on the steps of the House in 1975 and declaring 'Well might you say God Save the Queen.' The conservatives shook in their boots. But what he was doing was rallying the troops for a battle he well knew was hopeless.[8]

Hayden, in my view, was wrong in judging that Whitlam at that time thought defeat was inevitable: it was not until the afternoon of the twilight rally on the Parliament House lawns on the Wednesday before the election that I saw signs that he had conceded that defeat was possible, and then he did so reluctantly. After a sad and desultory conversation with Bruce Grant, the former Ambassador to India, in the anteroom to his office on the last full day he was to spend there, he suddenly turned to me and said: 'Comrade, if the polls are right, it looks as though we are gone,' and then turned and walked off, leaving an air of ineffable sadness.

Hayden was convinced from the start that Labor would be smashed at the election, although on the night of 11 November he was one of those who was most aggressive in urging Whitlam to fight with all his might. 'Although the polls were showing us as being quite high, I found that hard to believe: I believed we were in diabolical trouble, and this is why Kerr and Fraser were silly in forcing the issue,' Hayden says. 'Among many things which would have happened was that, while the Labor Government and Caucus had gone along with what for them had been a quite severe and dramatic turnaround in economic management, they would probably not stay in there in the early New Year when they saw unemployment starting to go up. We would have had a rerun of the problems with getting supplementary Supply [through the Senate]. We were in a terminal stage.'

Next morning, with a hangover, Hayden flew back to Brisbane, already trying to develop a strategy for the future.

He got an early taste of how life had changed. When he had travelled as Treasurer, the Trans Australian Airlines manager would meet his car as it arrived at the airport, a ground hostess would be standing by to meet him and his staff and escort them to the VIP room, while others took care of luggage and seating arrangements. 'Bill hated special treatment, but had come to accept it,' a staff member said. When he and his press secretary Harriden arrived at Canberra airport on 12 November, there was nobody to greet them, nobody to look after the luggage, and no invitation to the VIP room. As he sat in the plastic seats waiting for the flight to be called, he turned to Harriden and said: 'It just goes to prove what I've been saying for the last three years: they don't care who you are as a person, as long as you hold the position.'[9]

'It happened overnight; he went from the treatment which he didn't really like — he wasn't comfortable with it — to being nothing,' said Harriden. Having to travel to and from his Ipswich electorate, and later selling his health plans across Australia, Hayden spent hours on end in planes and at airports. He was never known to sleep during a flight, and virtually all his time was spent working on documents. The work would begin in his car on the way to the airport, a practice that continued even on his way from Ipswich to begin international journeys as Foreign Minister. He developed strong views about how the airlines were run, and how their employees were treated. When he arrived late at a function he would frequently make a reference in his speech to the poor performance of the socialist airline. A combination of two practices he encountered almost weekly on the early morning flight from Sydney to Canberra, often on Mondays, particularly upset him: more than half the first-class section, which he walked through on his way to his economy-class seat, would be occupied by public servants, many of them returning from weekends they had managed to subsidise by carrying out some brief official business in Sydney on the previous Friday; and they all insisted on being served breakfast on the flight.

'He thought it obnoxious and thoroughly immoral,' Harriden said. 'He used to describe to colleagues how the poor stewardesses, as he called them, on the half-hour flight had to run down the plane throwing down plates, then draw a breath, and then run down the plane again picking the plates up again and storing them for landing.' Hayden eventually succeeded against strong Public Service and some ministerial resistance, in making public servants and politicians fly economy. Working on planes on sensitive matters had its lighter moments. On one flight from Sydney to Brisbane when he was Treasurer, he was sitting in a window seat working on a confidential Budget document with Harriden sitting beside him and a middle-aged woman in the aisle seat. Midway through the flight the woman nudged Harriden and, nodding towards a section of the document Hayden was working on said: 'I wouldn't do that if I was the Government.'

As soon as he arrived in Brisbane on 12 November 1975, Hayden went straight from the airport to the Brisbane Trades Hall. He met leaders including Harry Haunschild in a ground-floor office, and his message was blunt: 'We are going to lose this election. The important thing is to win the next one.' Hayden then argued that for the next three years the unions had to confront Fraser. There is some disagreement now on the strength of the measures he urged at that time, but those present believed that they were being urged to let loose, if not run amok, for the term of the Fraser Government. 'You have got to scare the business community — and convince them that only a Labor Government can work with the unions,' was the theme of his proposal, and one which, in modified form, helped Bob Hawke to office less than eight years later.

Hayden was dismally unhappy with the way the 1975 election campaign was fought, and his despair was compounded by the problems he faced in his own electorate. He recalls vividly his first confirmation of the foreboding he held about the way in which the Australian people would interpret the dismissal of the Government by the Governor-General. 'I was going to a meeting at Nunawading, and first of all I booked in at the Travelodge at St Kilda, in Melbourne, and Lenore

Nicklin [a journalist] was booking in at the same time, and she said: "You've had it." I said: "Look at the polls, they look good", and she said: "Wait till the polls come out that were taken after you were sacked." And I thought to myself, "Here I am trying to put on a brave face, and Lenore, who is a nice person, has devastated me in front of other people". The next night we were out at Nunawading in the school assembly hall. It was packed: a good feeling, the crowd are cheering, and all of a sudden my instincts came into play. I thought: "Hey, wait a second: there is something wrong here. This is not spontaneous enthusiasm; this is tense, it's almost hysteria." I realised it was all tight, jaded, and people were frightened. I realised then that not only were we in trouble, but that the troops in the field knew we were in trouble, in serious trouble. And of course that replicated itself wherever I went. The meetings were getting worse and more tense as the campaign went on.'

Hayden was campaigning in Perth when he got a call from Queensland State ALP organiser Bob Gibbs, a rugged, no-nonsense ex-boilermaker who now holds a State seat that overlaps the Oxley electorate. Gibbs: 'Bill, for Christ's sake, you better come home, mate. There is only one guy who's got a chance of surviving in Queensland, and that's you. I tell you, it's awful up here, and you've only got a chance if you come home and fight.' Hayden stayed briefly, committed to his program, and Gibbs rang again, and told Hayden he had arranged television appearances for him and again told him it was his only hope of saving his seat. Hayden: 'We have had differences since, but I'll always be grateful to him.

'There was a guy in Sydney who I had agreed to spend a day campaigning for, and there was some bloody awful function like a fund-raising dance, and I cancelled out; I had got the message all right. He rang me back, and said: "Bill, Bill, if you don't come to my electorate I will lose, I will lose. Do you want that on your conscience?" I said: "I'll tell you something: if I go to your electorate, I will lose; I don't know whether you want that on your conscience: I don't want it on my bloody conscience." End of conversation. For the first time in my life, I think — I'm probably kidding myself — I was really tough; I generally didn't like to be rude or abrupt to colleagues, because it's not an easy life, especially in marginal seats.'

Only with great difficulty were Labor's Federal campaign organisers able to conscript Hayden to fly to Canberra where he would be accessible to the national television networks, to hold a press conference on economic issues. Because of the way Kerr had acted, staffs of ministers in the Whitlam Government had lost all travel rights. Hayden's press secretary, Harriden, was grounded in Ipswich producing a regular newsletter that reminded locals of every cent they had got in benefits from the Whitlam Government, the tax benefits they were due to get in January from his Budget, the social service improvements, the wonders of Medibank. Hayden's Ipswich campaign staff were told to keep out of the debate on the morality or constitutional validity of Kerr's action.

On the morning of the election, 13 December 1975, Bill Hayden said to Dallas: 'Look, I think we are likely to lose Oxley. We saw what happened with some of our State members when they got defeated in '74; they were abusive and offensive to the electorate. You don't do that, because, firstly, Australians have no respect for you if you behave like that; secondly, they have been very good to us in this electorate. We can never complain. We went into a seat that we didn't think we could win, and when we won it, didn't think we could hold it for very long because of its history. It's been very good to us, and we've got to remember the positive side.'

The Haydens went to a polling booth at the Brassall State School in their home suburb. The Hayden children had all gone to school there; they were a well-known local couple. 'There were long queues and people were shuffling and looking away and trying to avoid us, and literally nobody outside the party faithful wanted to speak to us,' Bill Hayden still remembers.

The tension of the count that night was relieved by an incident that Hayden gets a better laugh out of now than he did at the time. 'There was a vital booth at Dinmore State School, and one of our guys rang in and gave us our vote, and I said "What did the other candidates get?" and he said "Oh, fuck them. I'm only going to count for you, Bill. I'm in the Labor Party."' Looking back on that election now, Hayden says: 'It was a great experience, and the Liberals would have had similar experiences of the way the troops rally to the flag and support it when it is in real trouble. People took time off work, pensioners came out.'

Bob Gibbs had been right: Hayden was the only Queensland Labor Member of the House of Representatives to hold his seat. He had introduced Medibank, increased pensions to their highest level for twenty-five years, introduced a whole range of new social service benefits, and brought down a responsible Budget. He received 50.2 per cent of the primary vote compared with the 68.9 per cent he polled in 1972.

FOURTEEN

Like a
languishing lover

*How bloody crazy — Hawke's not even
in the Parliament.*

Bill Hayden

THE POPULARLY accepted version of the event that most
damaged Hayden's political career, and which forms an un-
challenged canon of Australian political history, is significantly
different from the truth of the matter as Hayden saw it. The fact is that
Hayden never believed that Gough Whitlam sincerely offered him the
leadership of the Australian Labor Party after Labor's disastrous 1975
election defeat. But he is convinced that Whitlam sounded him out about
taking over as Prime Minister before the dismissal in 1975. Hayden
believes quite firmly that Whitlam was considering standing down as
Prime Minister well before he was sacked by Sir John Kerr.

Whitlam was in a state of profound shock after the stresses of the
previous months which culminated in his dismissal by his own appointee
Kerr, a harrowing election campaign and a shattering rejection by the
Australian people at the ballot box. He was also due to enter hospital in
less than two days for haemorrhoid surgery he had been forced to postpone
because of the crisis.[1] It is also the judgment of many participants, and
of Hayden himself in retrospect, that the dismissal and election results,

which gave the sanction of the vast majority of the Australian people to the actions of Kerr and Fraser, had a more devastating and lasting effect on Hayden than on any of his colleagues. The conversation took place between two men who were under severe emotional stress at a time Freudenberg has described as 'the morning of anguish'.

Whitlam genuinely believes that when he telephoned Hayden on the Sunday morning, 14 December — when both men had had just a few hours' sleep on the night of Labor's election disaster — he made a firm offer: if Hayden would contest the leadership Whitlam would stand aside and support his candidature. The leadership was, of course, not his to offer, although his backing would have been a powerful advantage.

The version of events that has gained wide acceptance is that which is told in the words of Bob Hawke as related to Blanche d'Alpuget. Hawke had been summoned to The Lodge and sat with Whitlam beside the swimming pool. Hawke later recalled:

> The essence of what Gough said to me was that his leadership had been rejected and that he had to accept that he was finished. And that in his view Bill Hayden was the man to take over as Leader, that he'd spoken to Hayden already, and Hayden had rejected the leadership. So that now I was the person to lead the party ...[2]

Hayden has in public always accepted the Whitlam version, but in private on more than a dozen occasions told friends that it was not correct. 'The important thing to understand is that Gough, like anybody else in the Labor Party, is in no position to offer anybody the leadership; it is a privilege of Caucus and their judgment,' Hayden said. 'You may recall that after one election Gough nominated Manfred Cross as a suitable Minister for Aboriginal Affairs. As soon as Gough did that the forces closed up — you know what the Labor Party is like: they knocked over the favourite son; it's their way of teaching the leader a lesson without hurting the party or him. So the first thing is that Gough was in no position to offer the leadership. What he did was he rang up. He didn't say "I'm offering it to you". I still remember it quite clearly. I was in this room I'm in now. I had a team of people outside and I was running them through how to count preferences, using their fingers as scorecards and making notes on bits of paper, because I knew we were in trouble. Gough's words were almost exactly these: "You're still not interested in being leader, are you?"'

Hayden then commented that Whitlam's reference to him as still not being interested was significant. 'When we were going into the bunker, in late 1975, before the dismissal, with the bloody flame-throwers flashing in against any openings that were presented, Gough called me into his office, and he said: "Comrade, I am thinking of moving to become chairman of the Inter-State Commission."'

'I thought to myself, Jesus Christ, Gough, you've always had a hang-up about the Inter-State Commission: I'm buggered if I can see the Inter-State Commission as a formula for centralising economic activity in this country and rationalising economic performance and getting around the States. It's not as simple as that. Even though there are some powers [for gaining more centralised control of the economy] in the Constitution, they are balanced by attitudes in the community. Also, I would not have thought it was big beer for a prime minister. But I didn't say anything to him.'

Hayden said that at the 1975 meeting Whitlam had gone on to say: 'I think you would be a suitable leader to succeed me.' Hayden commented in 1988: 'Now, I'm not absolutely stupid ... although I was pretty green in the eyes and pink around the gills in those days. As near as I can remember, I said something like: "Come on. I'm not interested: I think you should stay where you are." Of course, what he was thinking very seriously of doing was bailing out.' Gough Whitlam has made a principle, even in his own writings, of not revealing the details of private conversations he has had with others. He made an exception of John Kerr, who published his version of their exchanges first. However, he has told me that he did consider at one time that he might at some stage seek to head the Inter-State Commission. He would have only considered doing this after he had substantially implemented the program on which he had been elected. He may have mentioned this to one or two people, but has no clear recollection of doing so. Although legislation to establish the commission was passed by the House of Representatives during Whitlam's second term it was emasculated by Opposition senators acting on Fraser's instructions. It was later given some form by the Hawke Government, but never became the powerful body Whitlam had planned.

Hayden said that, when he told Whitlam on the Sunday after the 1975 election that he was still not sure whether he would hold his seat of Oxley, and that the only thing he was interested in at that moment was counting votes, Whitlam had given an exasperated sigh, and said: 'Oh, very well, comrade. I suppose I'll have to talk to Bob Hawke.' Hayden recalls: 'I instantly thought, ''How bloody crazy — Hawke's not even in the Parliament''. It was just Gough going through a self-indulgent, *mea culpa* performance, showing contrition and guilt but not really feeling anything, and holding on for dear life. There was no further discussion. He said he was going to ring someone else, and hung up.'

Twelve years before he spoke to me, Hayden had given an identical account of his conversation with Whitlam to another Labor parliamentarian who recorded it on the same day in his diary. In the 1976 retelling of the conversation with Whitlam, Hayden had said that at the end of the call, just before hanging up, Whitlam had said he was going to then telephone Doug Everingham. Dr Everingham, like every other Queensland Labor parliamentarian except Hayden, lost his seat at the 1975 election. Whitlam did in fact spend some hours on that Sunday ringing Labor politicians who had lost their seats. Several say he mentioned to them that he had spoken to Hayden but did not make any reference to having offered him the leadership.

Some weeks afterwards, when Whitlam's leadership appeared in jeopardy again because of a fresh political scandal, there was speculation that Hayden was considering competing for his job. Queensland Labor figures claim that Whitlam rang them then and called on them to put pressure on Hayden to stay out of the leadership stakes. Whitlam, with typical formidable resilience, had bounced back: if the job had ever been on offer to anyone it was not for long.

Early in 1976, by his public statements, Hayden was soon to give credence, even though sometimes ambiguously, to the Whitlam version of the events of 14 December. In Canberra he gave a long interview to Peter Bowers for an article printed in the *Sydney Morning Herald* on 14 January. Bowers asked Hayden bluntly why he had not taken the leadership when 'it seemed his for the asking' and had subsequently decided not to contest a position on the front bench. ''I have always marvelled at people who say in politics that they're going to contest a particular position of significance because they have been persuaded by people who have approached them. I sit down like a languishing lover, but no sweethearts ever phone in,'' he answered.'

There was a faint suggestion there of the truth of the version he had put forward privately, that the leadership had never, in fact, been offered to him. But much of the rest of the interview, and even the account of the period put forward later by his biographer and friend Denis Murphy, accords more closely with the Whitlam belief. And it was this accepted view that was to cast a shadow in the minds of others over the rest of his career.

Here was a man who admired resilience and tenacity and who appeared, through his struggle with ministers over the Budget as with the doctors over Medibank, to have epitomised those qualities, and who now appeared to have lost them, to have failed the test when there was strong support for him to take over the Labor Party and rebuild it in what was then its darkest hour.

Denis Murphy has explained Hayden's actions as being almost entirely based on a decision to reunite his family as a unit after a long period of enforced absence and almost unconscious neglect.[3] There is evidence that Hayden recognised that he had drifted away from his family, that he had become a stranger as a result of his continual absences and his total immersion in work, study and politics. This recognition was a strong motivating factor in his decisions, first not to fight for the leadership, and then not to contest a position as a shadow minister. The very private Dallas even made a public reference later, reported in the *Queensland Times*, to an occasion on which Hayden had been given a symbolic representation of how his family was working. His son, Kirk, then nine, had been asked at school to draw a picture of his family. Kirk drew his mother and his sisters on one page with dad, quite separate, on another.

But a more serious, and politically relevant, core of rationalisation, self-analysis and personal doubt surfaced in the probing interview conducted by Peter Bowers in 1976. Hayden was in a relaxed, reflective, even expansive, mood that some of his party critics characterised as his self-indulgent mode: the immediate traumas of the election result and its aftermath had subsided. Bowers asked Hayden why he had not made a bid for the leadership. 'Some people are just not interested in wanting to run things from the top seat. Some people like to be technicians close to the top, playing a worthwhile role — at least I hope I have played a worthwhile role — in contributing. I like to have a task, and give myself to that task fairly single-mindedly.'[4]

Hayden later went on to make an unflattering and almost prophetic self-assessment of his own leadership qualities: 'I am not sure that I would be a satisfactory leader in the sense of working with a team of people. I have a record of being in conflict with the Caucus fairly frequently.'[5] He attributed his unpopularity with fellow parliamentarians in part to the fact that he had frequently taken a Cassandra role, often warning them that courses of action they were taking would present problems later on.

Hayden had decided to study law. Like a number of other journalists who had been working for Whitlam Government ministers as advisers, speech writers and press secretaries, I had been sacked, and shared something of Hayden's despair about the implications of the election result after the dismissal. There didn't seem to be much of a future for people advocating what they saw as fairly moderate and sensible reforms if the Australian people preferred Kerr and Fraser and what they represented. During a couple of conversations with Hayden over several afternoons in the modest backbenchers' office on the wrong side of Parliament to which he had been moved, I found his enthusiasm for law — and the importance he placed on it as an essential tool for understanding government and implementing change — so infectious that I enrolled for a law course also, with the necessary two members of the New South Wales Bar of good standing, from memory Senator Jim McClelland and Tony Whitlam, being enlisted to make the required declaration, or marginal perjury, that I was a person of good repute. That was about as far as I got, and Hayden didn't get much further, studying for only one year through circumstances beyond his control, although his fascination for the law continued.

'When I came into politics I had then recently matriculated and had enrolled, in 1962, for a law course,' he recalled in January 1976.

> I had to suspend it in the first year adjusting to a completely new vocation, with implications completely beyond anticipation. I learnt in that first year, particularly at Budget time, that very few people — fewer than a half-dozen in the parliament — understood economics and they had the game by the throat at Budget time. I decided then that I would study economics rather than law. There was no shortage of lawyers. The contribution of lawyers seemed less broadly constructive than that of economists.[6]

Experience in Cabinet had convinced Hayden that in the most powerful decision-making forum in the nation the lawyers came into their own in a way that excluded him. Another, and more biting, interpretation was later put on Hayden's decision to study law in 1976. 'I found it obnoxious that Hayden, in so safe a seat as Oxley, should use his parliamentary salary to prepare himself for an outside job and flaunt his contempt of his electors by bringing, as was reported, his law books on the Opposition benches,' George Munster wrote in a polemic against Hayden in the *Nation Review* on 29 September 1977.

Hayden saw a law degree as a form of insurance that would give him an option outside politics. After fourteen years as a parliamentarian he had come within the shadow of defeat and had seen the difficulties other colleagues who had held supposedly safe seats faced in trying to find satisfactory jobs outside Parliament. He had a young family and was not interested in, and not suited to, a business career. Several people who have known him well over the years see both his decision to study law in 1976 and his acceptance of the office of Governor-General as springing from the same well of insecurity that arises in his childhood. In 1976, his fears for the future of himself and his family had been magnified by the devastating 1975 election result, but he felt he was giving himself options, rather than abandoning politics. His game plan then was to qualify for law within three years and then review his position; but he added, 'I don't find myself attracted to the leadership in three or four years' time either, incidentally'.

In his interview with Bowers he showed only a mild awareness of the political dangers of his decision: 'It's a risk in the sense that I may have an opportunity pass me by. But you take risks in life and you weigh up the consequences. People who always take the safe course, I guess, are rewarded and get to the top but there's some satisfaction in taking risks and pulling them off.'

Although he now had an economics degree, and at the age of forty-three had revolutionised Australia's health system and shaped a widely acclaimed budget, in discussing his attitude to law he again agonised over what he saw as personal inadequacies that were the result of his lack of education early in life. 'I am concerned that there are so many gaps in my intellectual grasp of so many issues. I just wish, looking back on life, that I had had the opportunity of gaining a very broad, multi-disciplinary sort of study, just to prepare for life. It's a thing that makes a better person.'[7]

Political events and growing frustration at being removed from the heart of the action combined within months to force him to abandon his plans to remain on the back bench. The consequent pressures of the additional political workload caused him to give up his law studies at the end of the first year. Dallas played a role in this after coming to realise that she would have to encourage him if he was to rejoin the team in a positive way. She had begun accompanying Bill to Canberra more often, spending time with the wives of other politicians and getting a closer understanding of the realities of politics and her husband's situation. 'I knew he had so much to offer, and I told him we'd be perfectly happy if he wanted to go back,' she said later.[8]

One of the more bizarre episodes in Australian political history propelled Hayden back into the fray, and at the same time thrust Bob Hawke into a central role in national Labor Party affairs. In November 1975, as Labor began its election campaign without the resources of government, Bill Hartley, a Victorian left-wing Senate candidate, Arab sympathiser and bitter enemy of Hawke's, had suggested to the Labor Party's national secretary, David Combe, that there could be a prospect of Labor obtaining substantial funds to finance its campaign from the Ba'ath Socialist Party which was in government in Iraq. Once more, through a combination of almost wilful naivety and political misjudgment, Whitlam became a party to another secret Arab funny-money affair, and once again there wasn't any money. The exercise began with Hartley, who acted as a correspondent for the Iraq Government, as he had for Libya, introducing an intermediary named Henri Fischer. Whitlam, while leaving the details to Combe and Hartley, had three meetings with Fischer, the last, which was probably taped by Fischer, taking place in Fischer's unit in Blue's Point Towers at McMahon's Point overlooking Sydney Harbour, where Rupert Murdoch also had an apartment.

The stage was set, according to Fischer, for him to go to Baghdad to raise the money and remit it in laundered form to the Labor Party in Australia. Without telling other party officials of this plan, Combe authorised a sharp increase in campaign spending. The result was that by January, when Hayden was contemplating his navel and starting to study law, the ALP had debts of more than $300 000 and advertising agencies and others were pressing for payment. No money had arrived and Fischer was nowhere to be found. On 28 January Jack Egerton found out about the affair and immediately alerted Hawke, who wanted to make the details public, believing, rightly, that they would be leaked, and call a special meeting of the party's Federal Executive to deal with the situation.

Hawke was overruled at that stage, and went ahead with a planned overseas trip. He had just arrived as an honoured guest in Israel when he was telephoned by Rupert Murdoch, who had been given full details of the saga by Fischer.[9] The Labor Party, already demoralised, was devastated. It was at its lowest ebb. A special meeting of the Federal Executive was called to begin on 5 March and attempt to sort out the mess. On the eve of this critical meeting Hawke himself made a political misjudgment: after a press conference at his house at which he gave a brief and formal announcement that the matter would be thoroughly investigated, he continued drinking with some journalists and made it clear that he and other executives expected those involved to be expelled from the party.

The ethical convention that such discussions are not reported was breached and the headline in Murdoch's Sydney *Daily Telegraph* next day read: 'Hawke to Axe Whitlam'. There was a surge of sympathy within the party for the leader.

Hawke's indiscretion and the public exposure of his intentions influenced the history of the Labor leadership, and did so in a way that formed part of a pattern in the interaction over the years between the three major Labor figures, Hawke, Whitlam and Hayden. Hawke's restless ambition, particularly in the period when he was still drinking, led him to public excesses that would cause alarm to his supporters, and his plans to advance to the leadership would be delayed. Then he would recover, and the advance would continue. Whitlam, who himself was more calculating when he created situations of conflict, also proved much more adept than Hayden at protecting his leadership from challenge.

Part III

A Leader Wasted

FIFTEEN

The challenge

*I'd understand if you just could not bring
yourself to chop off Gough's head.*

Bill Hayden

GOUGH WHITLAM had suffered enough from the enemies of Labor; he should not now be dumped and humiliated by the party he had led to power after it had spent two perishing decades in the wilderness. That sentiment, shared by Hayden and the majority of the rank and file of the Labor Party early in 1976, allowed a diminished Gough Whitlam to retain the Labor leadership despite the twin humiliations of the 1975 election defeat and the Iraqi loan fiasco. But, even after his confused dealings with Hawke and Hayden on the hangover Sunday following Fraser's election triumph, Whitlam had to go through double jeopardy before cementing his grip on the leadership at the start of the 1976 parliamentary year.

Whitlam was re-elected as leader in a close contest with Lionel Bowen on 27 January, before parliamentarians were aware of the Iraqi affair; but, at the moment of confirming him, Caucus also decided that the leadership positions should be declared vacant and recontested after eighteen months, midway through the scheduled term of the Parliament. By doing so, commented Freudenberg, Caucus damaged and diminished the

161

leadership and ensured instability at the leadership level for the whole parliamentary term.[1] The scene was set for two painful, wasted years for Whitlam, Hayden and the Australian Labor Party.

Whitlam showed a measure of contrition at the special meeting of the National Executive convened to discuss the Iraqi matter, which began in Canberra on 5 March and lasted for three days. Hayden's opportunity to return to the front bench and a relevant role in politics was sparked by the same events; Kim Beazley senior, who had in January been elected shadow defence minister, resigned his post on 14 March over the involvement of his colleagues with the Iraqis, and in protest at the National Executive's lack of decisive action. The Executive had made the details of the loan discussions public, and cleared those involved of wrongdoing, though condemning them for errors of judgment. Hawke had softened his initial agitation for stronger action against Whitlam and had been rolled by the Executive when he attempted to direct all the blame at his Victorian left-wing enemy Bill Hartley, who had been one of the instigators of the farce.

Sentimental support for Whitlam in the Labor Party was bolstered by the fact that the two leading bogeymen of the 1975 election campaign, Rupert Murdoch and Malcolm Fraser, were leading the calls for his blood. Whitlam made several television appearances on the eve of the Caucus meeting and was restrained and mildly penitent:

> This matter would never have proceeded if I had scotched it at the outset, as I could have done ... The only question is whether this mistake of mine — the only mistake of this character that can ever be alleged against me in nine years of leadership — is such as to make them change their mind that I should contest the next election campaign. That's up to Caucus to decide.[2]

Hayden was under pressure from Whitlam's enemies in the parliamentary party to challenge for the leadership. The *Australian Financial Review*, on 26 February, had reported that he was set to become the new Labor leader. He found himself in an awkward position: he had barely reconciled himself to his proposed furlough of study and reflection out of the mainstream of politics; he was bored and felt guilty that he was not making the contribution he should. Now an opportunity had been thrust at him not just to return to the front bench but to challenge for the leadership from a strong position. He wisely resisted. 'In the revivalist emotional state of the Labor Party then, Hayden showed good political sense in not challenging Whitlam. The last years of Calwell's leadership had left acute memories with him. When he became leader he wanted the party united behind him, not at war with him,' Denis Murphy commented.[3] Hayden did, however, agree to contest the front bench vacancy, believing that he could no longer stand aside in Labor's dark hour if he wanted to preserve options for a significant future in politics.

By the time of the Caucus meeting on 17 March 1976, three days after Beazley's resignation, Labor was still groggy and reeling from the accumulated shocks of the previous six months, and neither Whitlam nor Hayden were popular figures with a considerable number of their parliamentary colleagues. Whitlam obviously believed he had done enough explaining and apologising to the National Executive: he brushed aside a call by Dick Klugman for him to consider recontesting a leadership ballot, and easily survived a motion by George Georges that he should 'resign at a time convenient to the party'.

There was palpable resentment over what was now accepted as Hayden's indulgent withdrawal from the battle, and, when Caucus was officially notified of Beazley's resignation and a ballot called to fill the front bench vacancy, two minor parliamentary figures, Keith Johnson and Ken Fry, nominated against Hayden. Hayden received only twenty-nine of the sixty primary votes, defeating Fry by thirty-six to twenty-four on preferences. At Hayden's request, Whitlam gave him responsibility for defence, but it wasn't long before he was taking a tough and prominent line in Caucus debates that involved economic considerations. Hayden had developed strong views about the education establishment and something approaching prejudice against university students from privileged backgrounds: he thought those who benefited from the considerable advances the Whitlam Government had made in funding education had done little to defend that Government when it was fighting for its life, and when it was sacked. He had been particularly upset by a demonstration against his Budget by university students at Monash when he had visited the university on 22 September 1975, to deliver the first Arthur Calwell memorial lecture.

When, in Caucus debate in April, Senator Susan Ryan proposed that schools be allowed to determine how they would spend 5 per cent of their recurrent cash grants, Hayden objected strongly, saying he was concerned about Federal money being given in an undefined way; accountability was not observed and minority groups had taken control of many bodies that were supposed to be representative. 'Do not let the role of the Government's importance in these matters be downgraded,' he said.[4] Many of Hayden's actions over the years have been explained as being motivated by an interest in money, a tight-fisted reluctance to spend that some think stems from his early experiences and insecurity: there are, however, many examples of occasions when he has acted generously or against his own financial interest. When the issue of parliamentary salary increases came before the Caucus meeting on 16 February 1977, he intervened as he had in Cabinet and Caucus in 1974, agreeing this time with Mick Young that it would be politically reckless for the Labor Party to support a suggestion that politicians' salaries be linked to those of judges and senior levels of the Public Service.

Hayden's comparative silence on defence issues during most of 1976 was a deliberate strategy: he believed Labor could not win arguments on defence and security if they became matters of heated national controversy involving conservative tub-thumpers; he believed it was to Labor's advantage to avoid political conflict on the security of the nation. He was assisted in this aim by the fact that he enjoyed a friendly, bantering relationship with the Defence Minister and fellow Queenslander, Jim Killen. They regularly sent messages to each other across the floor of Parliament while the debate raged around them. A typical exchange took place while a Labor member was feverishly claiming the Defence Department had records of sightings of Unidentified Flying Objects which it would not release; Killen sent a folded card by messenger across the chamber to Hayden saying: 'If I can find the U.F.O. I would be sorely tempted to get on it.' Hayden's return message said: 'Your company would be neither stranger nor more unbelievable than you have to bear with here.'[5]

More than personal regard for Killen underlay Hayden's reluctance to tackle the minister aggressively. Denis Murphy says: 'Hayden did not want ... Jim Killen, whom he saw as a "good club man" rather than a tough warlike defence minister, replaced by a Liberal hawk who would commit Australia to expansive defence purchases which would tie up budget flexibility for years ahead.'[6] Commentators at the time made different interpretations, some suggesting that this had been one of the few areas in which Hayden had failed to make an impression, having been handled with ease by the wily Killen.

Hayden later said: 'There were two areas that worried me, and they later worried Bob Hawke, who is a product of the same generation of experiences: the Labor Party used to give electoral prospects away over issues of defence and foreign policy, usually in areas where it was unnecessary. In defence there frankly was no difference: we weren't going to cut defence spending in any major way, if at all, or in any way differently from them. They weren't extending themselves. Menzies' genius was to sound as though he had this impregnable fortress here, when consistently he maintained an extremely modest rate of defence spending. On foreign policy we used to allow ourselves to be skewered in the public square on the shafts of rhetoric: we'd leap onto them. I look back, and those were important years for me, I was learning lessons; I had been part of that leaping onto the sharp end of the pikestaff of that awful rhetoric of Menzies and his colleagues, and a lot of others were doing it. There were a lot of lessons.'

As shadow defence minister in 1976 Hayden continued to issue statements on Medibank and the economy, without getting in the way of Chris Hurford, who had been appointed shadow treasurer when Hayden earlier declined to take a position on the front bench and with whom he shared compatible views.

The less demanding workload Hayden was carrying as defence spokesman had allowed him more time for family life, but it was not long before the family's harmony was shattered. On 22 September at about ten o'clock in the morning while Dallas was at home alone working in the secluded garden of their home in Ipswich a gangling youth approached her. He said he was making inquiries about a car that had been stolen, and then asked for a drink of water and followed Mrs Hayden when she went into the house to get it for him. Then he walked away from the house, but returned a few minutes later and asked if he could use the phone to contact police. Mrs Hayden took him into the house and he dialled a number, although Ipswich police said later they had not been contacted. Mrs Hayden was showing him out the door when he suddenly grasped her round the throat from behind and dragged her to the ground. A desperate struggle followed. The youth grasped a bush rock in his hand and was trying to batter her on the head.

Although she sustained injuries to her neck and back that were to be a continuing problem, Mrs Hayden managed to break free of her attacker, who then fled. She managed to phone police and was taken to Ipswich General Hospital and admitted. Bill Hayden put forward a speech he was scheduled to make to the Returned Services League national congress and flew home. Inspector Dick Muir had called in the police dog tracker unit, and the youth, who had run through neighbouring backyards and the grounds of the Brassall Village nursing home, was caught in the early afternoon. He later appeared in Ipswich Children's Court and was sentenced to a short period of detention in an institution. Several months later while tidying up a large golden palm tree near the front door in their garden, the Haydens found an ivory-handled carving knife concealed among its fronds. They believe it belonged to the attacker. Some time later the youth attacked and raped an Ipswich woman who had employed him to paint her house. Friends believe the attack had a lasting effect on the naturally reserved and hospitable Dallas Hayden.

Through the latter half of the year Hayden had been more aggressive on economic issues, and after analysing the Budget brought down by Phillip Lynch he forecast early in September that there would be a devaluation by the end of the year of around 15 per cent. In explaining his reasoning on ABC television he coined one of his memorable canine images: 'blind Freddie and his dog' were aware of the inevitability of devaluation. In November 1976, Australia devalued by 17.5 per cent. There were mixed views about the consequences and propriety of Hayden, as a recent Treasurer, forecasting a devaluation; he was open to the accusation that he was damaging Australia's financial position by what could amount to a self-fulfilling prophecy. Most Labor parliamentarians regarded Hayden's accurate devaluation prediction as Labor's most effective political exercise of the year, and contrasted the impact Hayden had made with the dispirited performance Whitlam was providing. Others thought it irresponsible. George Munster said: 'I happened to agree with that forecast, and in public, but I didn't then, and don't now, think that a man ten months out of our Treasury should have made it. Whitlam is constantly criticised for his foot in mouth antics. Since he's been in Opposition, none of them have been as bad as Hayden's September gaffe.'[7]

Hayden's increasing concern about the economic policies of the Fraser Government, its reversal of some of the social equity measures he had initiated, and its efforts to drive down real wages brought into focus the increasing dichotomy in the leadership of the Opposition. Gough Whitlam was still, understandably, viewing the Australian political scene through the lens of the dismissal. He had been betrayed and wronged by the Governor-General he had appointed, acting, he believed, in alliance with Fraser; both were scoundrels not fit for office. He sought vindication and revenge. Hayden wanted to put the past aside — or at least into perspective — while beginning the work of organisation and policy development that was necessary for Labor to regain power. Whitlam's attitude was understandable; Hayden's was the one that more closely matched the mood of the Australian people.

An article in the *Bulletin* assessed the attitudes of the two men:

> [Hayden] has said that 'incompetence' was the cause of Labor's defeat, that it was 'nonsense' to try to run a Cabinet with the full twenty-seven ministers and that the unwieldy Cabinet produced 'endless chatter'. He has openly criticised ministers 'appointing members of their families or becoming too closely involved with friends or personal appointments' — an obvious reference to Cairns. Whitlam's approach has been the opposite. He has made no admissions of error or that he regretted anything of substance that was done in the three years of his government. That is an attitude which frightens middle-ground voters because they see him as having learned nothing from his mistakes.[8]

This article neatly pinpointed the dilemma that faced Labor people who would be involved in determining the course of events when the leadership of the party was declared vacant midway through 1977:

> Jack Egerton expressed a common view in the Labor Party recently in describing Hayden as a 'very nice, conscientious and hardworking follower who made and will make a good minister,' and adding, 'but Bill's not strong enough to be a leader.' The other view in the Labor Party is that Whitlam has to go, that he is an impossible electoral liability, and that too many middle-ground voters vowed in 1975 never to vote Labor again while Whitlam led the Opposition.

Hayden seriously considered his position over the Christmas break, but did not at that stage firmly decide to challenge Whitlam. He did, however, reduce the number of law subjects he intended to study in 1977 from three to one. He was given a high distinction for the law subject he had taken in 1976.[9] Hayden was also becoming more aware and concerned about the role Bob Hawke was playing. Early in 1976 he had dropped a memorable bucket on Hawke who was irritating many Labor parliamentarians by appearing to be cooperating more closely with the Fraser Government than he had with the Whitlam team. Hawke, while drinking late at The Lodge with Malcolm Fraser, was also publicly offering gratuitous advice from the sidelines to the parliamentary party.

There was a clear scornful reference in Hayden's remarks to Hawke's public behaviour while drinking:

> Mr Hawke was not always terribly helpful to the Labor Government with some of his impulsive, intemperate comments and his occasional emotional outburst.
>
> Given the present industrial situation, Mr Hawke might find it best to give an industrial commitment to the aspirations of the workers of Australia and to save politics for when he becomes a politician.[10]

Early in 1977, Hayden confided his reservations about Hawke to Denis Murphy:

> Hayden had more serious reservations about Hawke [than he had about Whitlam]. While he recognised Hawke's public popularity and his capacity for work, he thought that too many of Hawke's serious public speeches were badly prepared and had a middle, but no beginning and no end; he felt that Hawke's ambition was geared too much to Hawke's own future and that this plus Hawke's abrasiveness would create great difficulties in a Labor caucus or in cabinet.[11]

At this stage Whitlam believed, as a result of a private conversation he had had with Hayden, that Hayden would never run against him. He thought it was, however, quite possible that Hayden would contest the deputy leadership against Tom Uren.[12] This was not in Hayden's mind. On 8 March 1977, Hayden had a meeting with Hawke that had been arranged by the party's national secretary, David Combe. He was interested in enlisting Hawke's cooperation to reform the Queensland Labor Party, believing Labor had no chance of achieving power nationally without reform in his home State when he held Labor's only seat. Hawke, who had been drinking, wanted only to discuss his own chances of succeeding Whitlam as leader. Hayden made up his mind to move. On the following day he told Uren he would contest the leadership against Whitlam and then, about 13 March, he went privately to Whitlam and told him of his decision, returning to Paul Keating's office then for a quick glass of Scotch. 'Hayden has crossed the Rubicon,' Clyde Cameron noted in his diary. After a meeting of the party's Federal Executive on 14 March, Hayden went to EJ's restaurant in Canberra, then owned by Whitlam's former press secretary Eric Walsh, and under pressure from journalists and parliamentarian friends over an excellent dinner and several bottles of fine wine, confirmed that he would run for the leadership.

The contest between Whitlam and Hayden provided a set-piece study in internal party politics played with all the intensity, and often more subtlety and vindictiveness, than the open public contest between rival parties. The ever-changing coalitions that formed in support of Whitlam and of Hayden crossed all factional lines and forged unlikely alliances between traditional enemies while simultaneously rending old and close friendships. An institution unknown to outsiders, but referred to at that time within Labor's parliamentary ranks as the White Wine Club, whose core members were on the Right of the party, played the principal organisational role in getting, and keeping, numbers for Whitlam among parliamentarians in the lead-up to the ballot. Its secretary was Frank Crean who had been sacked by Whitlam as Treasurer, but held a deeper grudge against Hayden who had been acclaimed for his performance in that office. Whitlam's chief allies outside Parliament included the unlikely combination of the right-wing New South Wales machine and most Victorian ALP officials led by the extreme left-winger Bill Hartley who had been involved with Whitlam in the Iraqi business.

Hayden had the solid support of the New South Wales left-wing steering committee, master tacticians like Lionel Bowen and Clyde Cameron, and unlikely adherents like the West Australian right-winger and born-again Christian Kim Beazley. Whitlam had the added advantage of a dedicated, politically committed staff who cultivated the media, leaked documents unfavourable to Hayden and spread rumours about him. It was back to the days of Medibank and the doctors again for Hayden. Members of the White Wine Club, which included the influential New South Wales right-wingers Frank Stewart, Les McMahon, Les Johnson, Vince Martin and Senator Doug McClelland, dined well at a select table in the parliamentary dining room. Queensland Senator Ron McAuliffe would sometimes arrange for fresh barramundi to be flown down for the members, and there would be sampling of other select delicacies and vintages. Individual guests would be invited to join them, often ostensibly for discussion on a specialist subject, and then attempts would be made to seduce the guest to the Whitlam cause.

At an early meeting during the campaign Chris Hurford was persuaded to approach Hayden and suggest that he run against Tom Uren for the deputy leadership if he lost the ballot against Whitlam. The backing of the White Wine Club would be guaranteed. Clyde Cameron saw through the strategy instantly: if Hayden had accepted it would give the significant group who wanted to get rid of Uren an excuse to vote for Whitlam in the leadership ballot, as Hayden would have more chance than any other candidate of beating Uren. Whitlam was a master of the art of dispensation of patronage, whether or not the means to provide it were immediately at hand. Hayden supporters were convinced that promises were made to some vulnerable souls, including Bert James who had long cherished an ambition to be Administrator of Norfolk Island. He was told to pack his bags — he would be off as soon as the next Whitlam Government took power.

During the nerve-stretching campaign, Hayden also became convinced that Whitlam's staff were briefing accommodating journalists to ask him questions to gain information about his intentions and attitudes. As Clyde Cameron remarked to me, it is a well-known tactic, and slightly more ethical than tapping telephones. Despite the pressures, at the start of May there was a strong belief within Caucus that Hayden was comfortably ahead of Whitlam. Fred Daly told colleagues that once he was sure Hayden had the numbers he would approach Whitlam and tell him he ought to resign.

Then on 5 May, Hayden made one of his typical blunders in human relations through underestimating the appetites of his fellows. Parliament was due to rise early to celebrate the fiftieth anniversary of the old Parliament House; but, while the ice melted, the tomato sandwiches wilted and his colleagues yearned for a drink, Hayden decided to take constant points of order against the Government in a futile exercise that delayed the celebrations by more than an hour.

Whitlam had used his time more effectively, cajoling and entertaining supporters, and had made three visits to the hospital bedside of Dick Klugman's daughter who had been injured in a car accident. Klugman was one of Hayden's few close friends.

Things got much rougher. While Whitlam deployed all his formidable political and personal skills, was in turn devious, manipulative, charming and ruthless, some of his supporters, without Whitlam's knowledge, subjected Hayden to such pressure that his supporters waited daily for him to show signs of cracking. 'No established leader has so far been overthrown and Whitlam and his supporters are fighting a hard — some say dirty — campaign to ensure Gough is not the first,' Samuel and Rees recorded.[13] 'Someone rang up my home here,' Hayden told me later, 'and said to Dallas something like: "How would you like the newspapers to get stories of your husband's affairs — plural — with women in Canberra?" The message was to pull off the challenge to Gough. Whitlam would not have had anything to do with it. My regard and affection for him is extremely high.'

Some of Hayden's supporters, described fittingly by Paul Kelly as members of an oddly assorted alliance of hate and hope — hate for Whitlam and hope for the future — spread a story designed to show that the Hayden camp was capable of fighting in the gutter if necessary. In an interesting display of tactics they claimed Hayden was sick of Whitlam supporters tipping shit on him and if it continued he had the documents to 'wipe Whitlam out of the water'. The suggestion was that the documents related to Whitlam's knowledge of overseas loans negotiations when he was Prime Minister. No documents were ever produced.

By the second week of May, less than three weeks before the vote was to be taken, there was a growing belief among Hayden supporters that Whitlam had taken the lead in the contest, but that there was a group, including former ministers Rex Connor and Frank Stewart, who wanted to get rid of Whitlam but who harboured even deeper grudges against Hayden. The animosity against Hayden came largely from the hard line he had taken in Cabinet as Treasurer, cutting back expenditure on ministers' favourite projects, and often doing it with apparent relish. Jim McClelland has told a story of a clash between the bulky Rex Connor and Hayden in the last months of 1975.

> By this stage Connor had become tetchy and paranoid. I remember one occasion when he was worsted in a debate and he began irascibly to collect his papers, preparatory to walking out. Bill Hayden, from the other side of the table, shouted at him: 'I'm sick of seeing you get away with bullying this Cabinet, Connor. You're not going to bully me any more.' 'The Strangler' as he was dubbed in the media, gathered up his papers and flounced out like a fat tenor who has been hissed off the stage.[14]

Connor's feud with Hayden dated from the days of the Arab Loan affair during which Hayden had, often at Whitlam's instigation, taken a tougher line in standing up to Connor than the Prime Minister had been prepared to take. Once he had been encouraged to be so tough on Connor that Connor would bluff as he had before by offering his resignation to Whitlam. This time, however, Whitlam was prepared to call the bluff and accept the resignation. Connor became aware of the tactics and swore revenge on Hayden. During Cabinet debates Hayden had also been hurtful and vicious in his attacks on some of the slower-witted, conservative and less talented ministers. He had deep ideological differences with Frank Stewart, a strict Catholic, on social issues including abortion, homosexuality and divorce.

It became clear some of the former ministers who had been demoted and humiliated by Whitlam would vote for Lionel Bowen, but would not wear Hayden. Bowen was approached again, but said it would be a breach of faith on his part to ask Hayden to step aside now that he had gone so far out on a limb. Bowen also felt that Whitlam supporters had earlier so smeared him with false allegations that he couldn't win. Liberal Government members were advised by their leaders not to refer publicly to the guerilla war raging in the Opposition ranks; Liberal strategists believed Whitlam was the Fraser Government's best electoral asset and were frightened Hayden would win. They had seen how Whitlam, by constantly humiliating and ridiculing Billy Snedden, had helped Fraser to the leadership. They didn't want to repeat the mistake by attempting to embarrass Whitlam.

While the contest was at a high pitch Whitlam was approached by Jim Cairns to give evidence in a libel case involving Junie Morosi, and readily agreed. The Whitlam forces fed out a story that if Whitlam was defeated for the leadership he would run for the deputy leadership, and if he lost that would run for the shadow Cabinet, hoping to get the shadow portfolio of Foreign Affairs. This was seen as an attempt to enlist some Uren supporters who feared Whitlam as a rival for the deputy leadership. Cameron saw the Whitlam camp's tactics as a double-edged weapon: he felt there were more people who were more dedicated to getting rid of Uren than saving Whitlam, and felt they might see a vote for Hayden as leader as a way of achieving this.

As the ballot approached, Whitlam, who had been transformed into an affable, approachable man-of-the-people, made an unscheduled late-night visit to the non-members' bar at Parliament House only to find it deserted except for a couple of attendants and journalist Brian Toohey, who later had some fun sending up the attempts of the minders to rustle up a few drinkers to share the leader's hospitality.

Hayden refused suggestions by some of his more nakedly political supporters that he should follow Whitlam's example and start a few hospital visits, starting with former minister Gordon Bryant who was in Canberra Hospital, and also that he should entertain a few of the waverers. To the deep frustration of his backers, some of whom had reservations about him but who saw him as their best chance to get Whitlam, Hayden continued to mix only with his customary acquaintances. He did, however, agree to a number of lengthy interviews. Toni McRae of the Sydney *Sun* captured something of the intricacy of his character in a lengthy feature in which she asked: 'Can someone as much a softie as Bill Hayden survive the coming battle and then convince the electorate he's the man to lead the country?' ... 'Hayden has integrity — and an irritating degree of self doubt. Like when you're talking to him and he tells you you must be "bored" with his answers. He's often worried you're not interested.'[15]

But she added that at times Hayden showed a surprising degree of self-confidence, quoting him as saying: 'I know that I can do what I want to do in the time which might be available to me — if I'm given that time. I know that because I've been in government and I've taken pretty severe strain without buckling under.' McRae went on: 'From comments like that you discover Hayden is as concerned about people wondering if he can take strain or not as he is about his media portrayal.' She said that Hayden wanted a society with compassion and regard for itself; he knew from his days as a policeman, when derelicts got to him on the beat and pleaded to be locked up for a night of warmth and shelter and food that there were less fortunate people around, and that those people were not always responsible for their plight.

The resilient, uncrushable Gough Whitlam was first in the queue when the Caucus vote for the leadership began soon after 9.30 on the morning of 31 May 1977. Not far behind him, and towering over everybody else in the queue was Tony Whitlam, taller, more heavily built, darker and more handsome than his father. Tony Whitlam had replaced Fred Daly at the last minute before the 1975 election as Labor's successful candidate for the Sydney seat of Grayndler.

At the back of the Caucus room, shrunken, slumped in a chair and too weak to collect his own ballot paper was the critically ill Gordon Bryant who had been brought to Parliament House from hospital. His silver hair crowned a pinched and pallid face. Dark, beetle-browed Rex Connor, 'the Strangler', who had been too sick to attend any of the parliamentary sittings in the previous week, had also left his sickbed; he was not going to miss his chance to even the score with Hayden.

Supporters of Hayden had declined an offer from the equally ill Martin Nicholls from South Australia to attend and vote for Hayden. On such small decisions do fortunes turn.

Whitlam looked stunned, but only for a moment, when the result was read to the meeting: he had beaten Hayden by only two votes, thirty-two to thirty. If Hayden had convinced one more voter there would have been a tie and Whitlam would have followed the example of John Gorton and resigned. Bill Hayden would have been Labor leader. Hayden remained outwardly calm and when Cameron suggested that, because of the volatility of politics, he would be unwise to make any public commitment not to challenge Whitlam again before the election, Hayden said he had already made that decision.

The result of the ballot for the deputy leadership provided another surprise for Whitlam when Uren defeated Keating by thirty-four votes to twenty-eight after Chris Hurford's preferences had been distributed. Paul Keating, then a little over a month away from his thirty-third birthday, immediately told colleagues he was not at all concerned: he did not have any ambitions for the leadership until he was at least forty years of age, and would run then only if, presumably in his own judgment, he was better than the person then in command.

When Whitlam rose to ask the first question when the House of Representatives met after lunch, Government members cheered. There were two celebrations that night: the Liberals drank champagne until the early hours while Whitlam, his staff and some key supporters went to Zorba's restaurant for a victory dinner. Cameron had predicted to Hayden that Whitlam would attempt to mollify him to forestall another challenge, and simultaneously heap work on him to keep him too busy either to think about a challenge or maintain contacts with his parliamentary supporters. The predictions did not take long to be realised, and as soon as Whitlam had returned from dinner he summoned Hurford to his office and informed him that some of his responsibilities were being immediately transferred to Hayden.

'I've dined well and am less inhibited than ever,' he said to Hurford before beginning a less than flattering assessment of Hurford's abilities which, to Hurford's relief, was interrupted by the ringing of the division bells. The new apportionment of duties between Hayden and Hurford, in which Hayden was given responsibility for some economic matters while retaining his job as shadow Defence minister, was both hasty and sloppy and led to a major embarrassment during the election campaign later that year.

Several of the participants in the ballot have since written their accounts of Hayden's challenge to Whitlam. Two of the most revealing are those by Jim McClelland who was a minister in the Whitlam Government and Barry Cohen who was to become a minister in the Hawke Government. Cohen's account, published in 1988, gives an insight into the emotions of the time.[16]

> Initially, I was one of those who encouraged Bill to run, but as the contest drew nearer I was torn between my affection and admiration for Gough and my growing conviction that Bill was our only hope of bringing us back from the massacre of 75. Few of us expected that we had much chance of defeating Malcolm Fraser, no matter who led the party at the next election, but many had anticipated that Bill could win enough seats to put us in a good position to tackle him at the following election.

Cohen said he had decided to vote for Hayden, and had told Senator Jim McClelland this as they strolled across the road from Parliament House to lunch at The Lobby restaurant. McClelland agreed, saying:

> You're right, Gough's had it. He's one of yesterday's men. The future lies with the Haydens and Bowens and Bill's clearly the outstanding performer in the Caucus. You've got to forget about sentiment and support the man that can get you back into Government, and Gough can't do that. Bill can.'
>
> I knew then that I had made the right decision.
>
> 'I really am glad that you've decided to support Bill,' said Jim, once again emphasising his admiration for the former Treasurer. 'But,' and there was a long pause, 'I want to tell you the reason I am going to vote for Gough ... I just couldn't do it to the big bastard. After what the mongrel Kerr and Fraser did to him, I couldn't do it.'

When he returned home to Gosford, Cohen found his wife felt the same way:

> 'How could you do it to him? After all he's been through?' she demanded.
>
> 'Look. I feel the same way about him as you do, but we're talking about the future of the Australian Labor Party.
>
> 'Bugger the Labor Party. You're talking about the greatest Prime Minister this country's ever had and you're going to give him another kick in the teeth.'

Cohen says he told Richard Butler, Whitlam's private secretary, on Monday night that he would be voting for Whitlam and adds: 'I often wonder just how different our history may have been if I had stuck to my original 'firm' decision ... Hayden would have been the Leader. There almost certainly would not have been an election until 1978. Hayden would have won seats and led us into a 1981 election, and so it goes on ... what if only ...?'

McClelland records Hayden's response when he told him that he was going to vote for Whitlam:

> Though I realised that Labor's enemies had done a first-class job on the satanization of Gough, which would almost certainly deny him the Prime Ministership again, and though I had become closer to Hayden than to almost any of the leading Labor figures, I just could not bring myself to join the execution party. Bill sensed what I was going through. On the day before the vote he came to my room in Parliament House and said: 'Jim, I have a feeling you are not going to vote for me. I'd be wounded if I thought it was because you did not consider me up to the job, but I'd understand if you just could not bring yourself to chop off Gough's head.' I assured him it was for the latter reason and we remained close friends.[17]

Hayden spent much of his time in the following months working on the development of an economic policy designed to reduce unemployment without too excessively increasing the Budget deficit and stimulating inflation. In July 1977 he played a central role at the party's Federal Conference in Perth and was instrumental in getting Labor to modify its commitment to nationalisation. There was no constitutional authority for a Labor Government to nationalise banks and no hope of getting the power by referendum. Labor's nationalisation plank was already moribund, except in the propaganda of the conservative parties, and Hayden had found it had been used with telling effect to frighten a considerable section of the electorate when Labor was in power. Continuing to include it in the platform was, he told the conference, 'like belting your big toe with a hammer to give pleasure to your opponents.'

Journalist Laurie Oakes described Hayden's performance at the conference as 'sparkling', and added: 'In terms of influencing proceedings Mr Hayden was by far the most important figure at this conference. He also showed commendable courage and independence, particularly in the debate on the way a future Labor Government should handle the economy.'[18] On 11 August Hayden appeared at a press conference with Whitlam to launch the economic package he had developed, now in document form entitled *A Proposal to get Australia Working Again*.

That night George Negus asked Whitlam during a television appearance with Hayden whether he still saw Hayden as his heir apparent.

Hayden interjected: 'Oh, no favourites in my presence. Modesty is always a problem. I can't handle it.'

Whitlam: 'I give you the same answer here as I have for some time. Yes, I do.'

The possibility of a succession being necessary was more immediate than Whitlam realised. By mid-September 1977, panic and despair about the lack of purpose of the Opposition under Whitlam's leadership had reached such a pitch among members of the parliamentary Labor Party that members began again discussing the prospects of change. Tom Uren was at the hub of the unrest and by 22 September he had had discussions with Don Grimes, Clyde Cameron, Chris Hurford, Peter Walsh and Ralph Willis, all of whom supported a change of leadership. Discussions then began in an attempt to settle tactics and it was agreed that when Parliament resumed after a break early in October an approach would be made to Whitlam giving him the opportunity to step down voluntarily and gracefully.

At that stage planning was proceeding on the basis that an election would not be held until the end of the following year, 1978. When those involved found support across the factions for a coup they approached Lionel Bowen who immediately agreed, and at that stage Uren approached Hayden and asked him whether he would be prepared to contest a leadership ballot. Hayden agreed but did not become involved in organising any move against Whitlam. Uren also approached Ken Wreidt, leader of the Opposition in the Senate who said he would agree to sign a petition calling on Whitlam to stand down provided a majority in Caucus would support the move. The plan then was to sound out informally those members of Caucus who were likely to be sympathetic and, when it was established that there was a majority, circulate a petition quickly for signature.

The move gained impetus in the same week from two small events: Barry Cohen told one of the organisers he had voted for Whitlam in the May challenge, but was now prepared to support a change; and in Parliament Whitlam handled badly an exchange in which the Government produced documents showing that Margaret Whitlam had travelled alone in a VIP plane in February 1974. Events, however, overtook the plot and an unexpected twist of fate saved Whitlam. From the perspective of

Hayden's eventual loss of the party leadership on the day Fraser called his final election in 1983, the end of the second challenge to Whitlam assumes the proportions of supreme irony: it was abandoned because Fraser in October 1977 called an election a year before it was due.

For Hayden there was to be one final damaging incident involving Whitlam before the defeat of 1977 and his election to Labor's leadership. Fraser had promised extensive tax cuts, mainly to benefit the middle class, which were not to come into effect until after the election, but which had been heavily promoted with fistfuls of dollars being thrust out of advertisements towards the electors. Ken Davidson, the respected economic columnist of *The Age* in Melbourne, had written about and discussed with Whitlam's advisers an alternative strategy involving the abolition of payroll tax. The chief attraction to Whitlam was that it would stimulate employment and had enjoyed the ringing endorsement of major business and industry groups. He did not feel confident in proceeding without political backing, however, and summoned Hayden, Hurford and Ralph Willis to his office. All rejected the idea as an alternative to tax cuts because tax cuts would directly benefit a far greater number of voters.

After he returned to Queensland Hayden reconsidered and later rang Whitlam to say he would support the idea. He said later: 'Against my original better judgment, I changed my mind. We had nothing else going at all, and this was going to be the leitmotif of the whole campaign. But, I repeat, there was nothing else going on at all. It was the policy of a whole range of organisations, employers and so on.

'I remember Ken Davidson ringing me up and going to town, saying surely I realised that these pressure groups were on side on it. I said: "They'll bail out once it's politicised by becoming the central issue in an election campaign." Davidson said: "No they can't. They're on record as supporting it." Of course, they did bail out.'

Hayden said he had come round to supporting Whitlam's proposal to promote payroll tax concessions as his major election promise rather than match Fraser's fistful of dollars in personal tax cuts. In 1988 he said frankly: 'I must say it was a bad judgment. Chris Hurford rang me up and abused me and said it was awful, and he was right. I knew we were in trouble with it at the campaign opening in Sydney. Gough, with flair, announced the abolition [of payroll tax] and people looked starkly surprised: they didn't know what the bloody hell it was.

'And I thought: Oh, oh. Our key point has foundered, we're in trouble.'

SIXTEEN

The leader

*We must not be seen as a collection
of narks.*

Bill Hayden

WHEN the towering figure of Gough Whitlam left the centre stage of Australian politics with grace and dignity an hour before midnight on 10 December 1977 — the night of his worst election defeat — he left behind a demoralised, directionless Labor Party. When Bill Hayden was elected as his successor on 22 December he became, at the age of forty-four, the youngest leader in the party's history, and, as is a recurrent theme in his life, achieved a dream that carried with it a taste of ashes.

Whitlam had held on to Labor's leadership in the belief that a majority of the Australian people had an affection and admiration for him. He was right, but they didn't want him to be their Prime Minister again. The Labor Party had won only thirty-eight seats in the House of Representatives compared with the Fraser Government's eighty-six; even Hayden believed the party was two elections away from hope of victory.

As Mick Young said later, 'We had missed a step on the ladder'.[1] Hayden brought to the most testing and difficult job in Australian politics, that of Opposition leader, an enormous range of human experience, and, arising from it, a compassion for the weak and needy. He had, as well, a substantial record of concrete achievement; he had already put in place enduring reforms and extensions of Australia's health and social welfare services. In the Budget of 1975 he had, with the support of Gough Whitlam, introduced new concepts of fairness and equity into Australia's tax structure.

Hayden's radicalism had been tempered by first-hand experience of government and he had passed the stage when, as he later said disparagingly of himself, he thought the world could be changed with magic mirrors; yet he had a powerful belief in the responsibility of the Labor Party to protect the underdog, to promote tolerance, freedom of choice and equality of opportunity.

'Bill Hayden indicated the honour he felt in his election and indicated the commitment he felt to the party and the community,' is the rather dry introduction in the official Federal parliamentary Labor Party minutes of 22 December 1977, recording his victory in the ballot for the vacant party leadership by thirty-five votes to twenty-two over Lionel Bowen. Hayden's victory speech was brief and without ornament. After congratulating Lionel Bowen on the way he had conducted his campaign in the brief contest they had engaged in for the job, Hayden assured Bowen of his respect. The minutes record also that he acknowledged Whitlam's qualities and role in shaping the modern Labor Party and said he had been inspired by his untiring application and industry in achieving targets Labor had set.

Hayden put the task that confronted him and the party in an historical context:

> We have a demanding challenge ahead of us, but no more demanding than Curtin faced. We were faced with the daunting challenge of Vietnam in defeat in 1966, yet attained Government in 1972 ... We have a dreadful government ahead of us for three years and a responsibility to overturn it for the sake of the ordinary people.

Hayden returned home to Ipswich and began drawing up plans for reshaping the party and its platform, and in the first week in January went to the Gold Coast to discuss staff appointments and strategies with Mick Young and Eric Walsh who were holidaying there and had resisted Hayden's invitation to spend time in Ipswich. In the holiday weeks he also took full advantage of the opportunities of the honeymoon period traditionally offered by the media to new leaders. In a series of lengthy interviews he was able to outline in some detail his approach to the job, his aims and priorities. 'What I propose to do is raise some sort of theme about where this country ought to be going and what we should be trying to do to fulfill people's expectations of a better future,' he told the *Australian*.[2] Although he displayed no glittering mirrors or magic lanterns there was a firm commitment to social equity, a pledge that the party would not move to the Right while he held the reins and a prophetic expression of concern for the effects on young people of the economic policies of the Fraser Government.

> We are committed to welfare programmes — they are the basic reasons for the existence of the party. It's a party of social conscience. I believe the sort of policies which the government has, and which it shows no sign of deviating from, are such that we will still be wallowing in the economic doldrums into the 1980s. The costs of lost production are enormous, the costs of lost opportunity could easily be to the despair of this country, especially in creating not only an unemployed generation, but an unemployable generation. We have got to start worrying about the possible consequences of substantial social alienation of this young generation — well qualified, coming from good homes, but facing hopeless job prospects and therefore a depressing outlook. That's one of the most worrisome features I find in the present climate.[3]

He was at pains to reject suggestions that he was a technocrat, but there was a cautious, responsible, and to a degree boring, tone to many of his responses, and although some of that was the essential Hayden emerging, there was some political deliberation involved: the electorate, including a massive number of traditional Labor voters, had just indicated at the ballot box that they had had enough of the fireworks of the Whitlam era, that they were no longer interested in grand gestures or in righting historic constitutional wrongs. They were worried about inflation and jobs, the bread and butter of Hayden-style politics.

Michelle Grattan of *The Age* in Melbourne, who was then — as she remained when Hayden became Governor-General — one of the country's most diligent and knowledgeable political commentators, went to Ipswich with a more probing and analytical eye than most of those who interviewed Hayden at that time:

> He stresses the need for priorities, the gradualness of change, the importance of keeping in step with public opinion. What comes through strongly is the man's caution, his awareness of the difficulty of producing change —

and winning power to get the opportunity for it ... Mr Hayden is approaching his new job carefully and determinedly. He belies those who see him as a 'nice man' not ruthless enough to handle the rough political world. He is both tough and organised — though whether enough to match Mr Fraser remains to be seen over the coming years.[4]

In a perceptive aside, Grattan noted: 'As a personality Mr Hayden is interesting because, at forty-four, the learning process is still going on. This applies to other areas besides his politics — as shown by his reading. One feels interested in what Mr Hayden's views will be in 10 years' time.'

Hayden called a special meeting of Caucus in Canberra on 2 February to begin the huge task of bringing the Labor Party back to credibility as an alternative government. There were few new members; the bulk of those who assembled were battle-weary survivors of the disasters of 1975 and 1977, the two worst electoral defeats in Labor's history. Hayden told the parliamentarians that he wanted a year spent on the development of policies, to allow two years for them to be patiently presented to the Australian people, and cited Medibank as a successful example of the preparation and marketing of a difficult policy.[5] He explained what was, and remained, his political creed: Labor had to get its economic policies right if it was to be trusted with government and so given the opportunity to improve the lot of ordinary Australians.

The Caucus minutes record that he said:

> Economic growth is necessary for us to be able to do all the things we wish in the field of Aboriginal affairs, social welfare, the arts and many other areas. The community considers us as a party with compassionate concern for people, but not good economic managers. They suspect we want to collectively level things down rather than allow individual enterprise. We must change our attitude that we want nothing to do with the citadels of capitalism; we must know how they operate so we can correct them.

It wasn't the speech of a dewy-eyed idealist; there was more than a trace of political cynicism, a recognition of the role of greed and ambition in human affairs, when he added: 'The well-springs of material aspirations must be tapped, and people encouraged in their attitudes to believe they can develop excellence.'

Hayden's speech lifted the mood of the parliamentarians. Clyde Cameron, perhaps in a mischievous reference to Gough Whitlam's reputation on economic matters, described Hayden's address as the best statement to Caucus on the economy since the days of Chifley. Hayden had, in fact, admitted that his lengthy analysis of the economy had been a gloomy one. He ended it with some advice that he was, himself, in the public view at least, not able to put into practice: 'We must not be seen as a collection of narks. Our role is to show that these problems have been building up for a time and depend for a solution on proper management of our natural resources.'

Hayden took with him to the leadership, as well as his positive qualities and achievements, some severe handicaps that included a voice which, partly as a result of his deafness, had a thin, whining quality. It was a major reason for a false perception of him by some opponents as being weak, and it allowed Fraser to attempt to label him as 'whingeing Willy' or 'belly-aching Bill' a few months later when Hayden started drawing attention to the very real economic problems the Government was facing. Another handicap Hayden took to the leadership resulted from an inherent tendency to be suspicious of the motives of others and to be solitary by nature. Both characteristics were reinforced by his partial deafness and the fact that he lived away from the major centres of industrial and political activity and intrigue, Sydney and Melbourne. He was physically and emotionally on the periphery of the circle of power-brokers, yet closer than them to the concerns of the ordinary Australian suburban electors and rank-and-file members of the Labor Party.

At that first meeting he called as Labor leader in February, 1978, there was already the hint of a cloud on the horizon that resulted from a combination of these factors, and it was to shadow his days: Sydney backbencher Les McMahon asked what channels of communication were being established with the trade union movement. Hayden said he would arrange meetings with Trades and Labor Council leaders in each State and trusted this would lead to appropriate consultative mechanisms.

'I don't think he had the temperament for leadership,' said Graham Richardson, at the time a senior official and numbers man, one of the movers and shakers in the powerful New South Wales right-wing Labor Party machine. 'He always had the brains, but you've got to have more than brains ... I don't think that temperamentally Bill was the right bloke to be leader. In the old days if you told Bill that one and one made two, he'd look at you very suspiciously to see how you were trying to con him. Just after he was elected leader, I rang him up and arranged a meeting. John Ducker [then president of the New South Wales Labor Party and a powerful figure in the trade union movement] and I took him to dinner at Le Cafe. I remember Ducker and I were quite staggered, because what we did was sort of take him out and be very friendly, and virtually say to him: ''Well, you've got the Right with you.'' Our record of supporting leaders up to then had been pretty good. Hayden told us he had been warned not to trust us. As soon as we had parted, Ducker said: ''You better watch that bloke, Graham. He doesn't like us at all, and it may come to the stage when we've got to do something about him.'' [6]

Ducker was quoted later as having described one of his typical exchanges with the Labor leader in these terms:

> Hayden would say to me, 'Uren and Gietzelt tell me not to trust you because you are too treacherous. You seem all right to me but I just wonder what you're doing behind my back.' I just tell Hayden that we support the leader of the Labor Party. But he seems to have a bit of trouble accepting this. He'd better bloody well make up his mind. [7]

Despite problems he may have been having in communicating with sections of the party organisation, the judgment in the cockpit of politics in Canberra was that Hayden performed from the start better than most independent observers had expected, although he had deliberately avoided attempting to raise high expectations. He had told Wally Brown of the *Courier Mail*, the dean of Queensland political journalists, on 17 January 1978, that he believed that for the first half of the year the people were going to be interested in the re-elected government and what it was going to do about the economic situation:

> I don't believe, as a matter of timing — and that's what these sort of things are all about — that the first half at least of this calendar year is the right time for us to be producing detailed policies. I don't believe we will have, and I as leader will have, the greatest impact in what we want to do if we rush in immediately and try to go flat out right from the start.

Yet within four months, Peter Bowers, writing his 'Canberra Commentary' in the *Sydney Morning Herald* under the heading 'Hayden Rides High' said:

> Mr Hayden's harping doesn't seem to have hurt his public popularity. According to the latest Morgan Poll, Mr Hayden has a popularity rating of 49 points, four points higher than Mr Fraser's ... So far, so good for Mr Hayden. He has been moderately successful in Parliament, and remarkably successful in settling the Labor Party down ... Labor MPs confide that, to their surprise, discussion now takes place in Caucus and in the shadow

executive, whereas Mr Whitlam was principally concerned that his opinion prevailed. In terms of performance, Mr Whitlam's was a hard act to follow ... Mr Hayden decided from the outset that the only way to follow the Whitlam act was not to act at all; he would be himself.[8]

Michelle Grattan in *The Age* gave Hayden a B plus for his first six months. Like Bowers she pointed out that he had enjoyed a couple of lucky breaks. The first was provided, ironically, by the Governor-General, Sir John Kerr, who had become something of an embarrassment to Malcolm Fraser, the man he had installed in office.

After Kerr's national exhibition of himself as a garrulous public drunk at the 1977 Melbourne Cup presentation, Fraser was anxious to remove from the scene this reminder of his past. In January 1978, Fraser appointed Kerr as Ambassador to UNESCO in Paris. There was such a public storm that Kerr, who had initially accepted the appointment, resigned and went into voluntary exile. Fraser had also intervened clumsily in a dispute between companies tendering to supply computers to the government. 'Labor exploited the Facom-IBM computer row, and Mr Fraser's intervention in it, with consummate skill. It squeezed out every bit of mileage, and more,' Grattan said. She went on to offer some advice to Hayden. She was not the first to do this, nor was she the last, and she had no more success than most of the others.

His speaking style remains poor — fast and high pitched. He also interjects and makes points of order and personal explanations too often. Like Mr Whitlam, but rather less successfully, he insists on setting the record right after every Government jibe. There is a danger that he will come to sound querulous and fail to establish that vital presence in Parliament. In the past, Mr Hayden has resisted suggestions that he should get some professional coaching on his speaking and presentation. But, as a leader, he needs to work on this if he is not to become ineffective or even ultimately a joke in Parliament.[9]

Hayden was getting, and largely ignoring, similar advice from other quarters. A member of his staff at that time later recalled: 'After Gough they didn't want a one-man party, and Bill didn't either. He got a good team together and worked on policies. The policies were largely developed in his office, and by him, but he sought advice and genuinely listened. He did want to involve people. But he was reluctant to take any advice about presentation, what he regarded as 'cosmetic' advice. He regarded any suggestion about fixing up his clothes with amusement. We would tell him to ask the make-up girls at the television studio to use yellow-base make-up, because the pink-based stuff they normally used would make him look red in the face. He would just laugh at us. Yet I think he was vain about his hearing aid. He only used it once and put it back in the drawer. He had matured before the age of television; it was not introduced into Ipswich until he was in his mid-twenties. He was, in a strange sort of way, in a time warp. He was young to be Leader, but an increasing number of the people coming through in the Labor Party were university graduates who had grown up with the sort of concepts he had fought so hard to become familiar with.' In contrast, Hayden looked old-fashioned.

Bob Hawke, who as Whitlam and Hayden had both intuitively known for years was a potential party leader and Prime Minister, had been born in remote Bordertown in South Australia three years before Hayden; yet he had adapted to the political age of electronic image-building as naturally as a duckling to a pond. It was only when Hawke entered Parliament that Hayden's staff noticed that their boss paid slightly more attention to their cosmetic advice.

Grattan also suggested that while parliamentary performance was only a small part of the political scene, it was important for the troops to be able to see their leader performing well. No parliamentarian of the era could match Whitlam's flair in the House, but Hayden had a deep feeling for the institution. After Labor members had disrupted a sitting and shouted abuse at Malcolm Fraser, he wrote a note to Jim Killen, saying: 'You've been here long enough to know what the behaviour this morning means (it's spontaneous) — Fraser doesn't have any more respect on this side of the House, and that's serious for him, and for the House I suspect.'[10]

Relations between Fraser and the Opposition remained acrimonious throughout Hayden's term as leader. Within weeks of Hayden becoming Opposition leader, Fraser summoned him and his deputy, Lionel Bowen, to his office to inform them of some matters connected with security. Hayden nodded his head occasionally as Fraser spoke, but there was no response at all from Bowen. Eventually Fraser asked Bowen what was wrong with him. Bowen answered: 'I'm listening. It's just that I don't trust you, you bastard.' As they left Hayden congratulated Bowen for being so direct with the Prime Minister.[11]

On 14 August 1978, for the first time since he had entered Parliament, Hayden addressed a Caucus of which Gough Whitlam, who had retired from politics, was not a member. He gave a sombre, if realistic, assessment of the state of play:

> We haven't so far greatly impressed people outside where sections of the community still query whether or not we can be trusted. It is felt that we may not have the sorts of programs that will hang together in an economic framework. Some committees have worked, some have not, perhaps because, as in 1969, we think we cannot win.[12]

The best prospect he could offer was that the party could win in 1980 if members did work and started feeding constructive ideas into debates. A Caucus member confided to a journalist: 'We've got to keep our morale high, because if we don't and Bill sees this, he gets even more depressed.' In fact Hayden had periods of justified optimism during his initial years as leader and he was consistently ahead of Fraser in the polls.

'When he was going well, he'd decide to be generous to the staff,' a secretary recalled. 'He would stop his driver, Ray, at this shop in Woden on the way to Parliament House and buy these revolting donuts. He'd buy dozens. They'd be cold and covered in candy pink or sickly green icing. He'd think it was a really generous gesture. When he was really feeling good some poor unsuspecting Lib who was wandering by would be dragged in: I remember Phil Lynch being brought in and presented with a garish, cold sticky donut.'[13]

Hayden for long retained his preference for simple food. His lunch every Friday when he returned to his Ipswich electorate office to work, would be a hamburger and a can of coke. As leader, while being driven from Brisbane Airport to his city office he would often stop the car at a fish and chip shop at Hendra and buy buttered bread and chips and make his own hot chip sandwiches and eat them in the Commonwealth car. 'When he did start drinking wine with meals he would often make some sort of self-conscious remark about it, as if it was betraying his working-class background to be drinking anything but beer,' commented a Brisbane Labor activist.

One of the developments in Hayden's early years of leadership was the formation of a Centre group of bright, pragmatic young frontbench figures, few of whom were rigidly factional. This period saw the emergence as a force in politics of John Button, who was to remain close to Hayden until the last six months of his leadership. Hayden's staff always had instructions to put Button's telephone calls through, no matter what the difficulties. Key figures in the group that emerged from a depleted post-Whitlam parliamentary party to play a role in policy formation were Mick Young, Paul Keating, Ralph Willis, Chris Hurford, Don Grimes, Peter Walsh, John Dawkins, and Dick Klugman. In a long article in the *Bulletin* on 13 March 1979, Bob Carr, then a journalist who had become leader of the Labor Party in New South Wales by the time Hayden became Governor-General, said:

> By consulting people and encouraging debate Hayden has built a better working relationship on the frontbench [than Whitlam].
>
> In fact there are reasons for seeing Hayden as a stronger Labor leader — and, potentially, Prime Minister — than his predecessor. Even National Executive meetings come and go barely noticed, without melodrama or crisis. Arguably, Hayden has been better at the job of bringing stability and consensus to the Federal ALP — better at the task of party leadership — than anyone since Chifley.

Significantly, though, Carr made the observation that the fact that Hayden's defenders were constantly talking about his hidden strengths was evidence in itself of a serious image problem. Apart from the gaudy sportscoats, clashing ties and reedy voice, there was Hayden's insistence on using quite technical jargon in everyday conversation, in speeches and interviews, and, in Carr's presence in a talk-back radio session on station 2BS in Bathurst, telling the country folk about 'massive diseconomies' and 'utilisation profiles'.

> When the spots are as deeply ingrained as they are on my hide it's very hard to change some of these things. I would get letters from time to time saying 'For God's sake, why don't you smile on TV?'. So I smile and then people say 'For God's sake, these matters are serious.' Can I say just one thing: the important thing is to be yourself and not get into the hands of people who want to mould you as a sort of cellophane packet and present you as soap powder or that sort of commodity. That's artificial: I couldn't bear with that.[14]

He was not repentant, either, about his use of technical terms when dealing the complex matters:

> I know from the time of the Medibank debate and the period when I was Treasurer this criticism was directed against me — that I tend to resort to some technical jargon. On the other hand, the market research showed that people had confidence in me on the basis that I knew what I was talking about, that I always briefed myself well, that I didn't fulminate about these things or resort to blustering rhetoric. That's very important: it's the integrity with which you present something.

Hayden was uncompromising too, in the privacy of Caucus, on a number of issues that were not necessarily popular with some of his colleagues but about which he felt strongly. In the early years of his leadership refugees fleeing Vietnam in overcrowded boats and landing on Australia's northern shores had created a political issue made emotive by smouldering Australian racism of which the Labor Party, which had only dropped White Australia from its policy in the mid-1960s, was not free. When there was a suggestion that there was support for a policy of intercepting the boats and turning them back, Hayden made a telling intervention: 'They can't be turned back; nobody will let them land. We must think of the consequences if a boat sank on the way back. Rampant racism is rife, but we must not accede to that pressure. There are great moral issues involved and our basic principles must be our guidelines.'

Neither would he compromise on another image-building suggestion that staff members made to him over the years: they wanted him to identify strongly with sport. Hayden had been an enthusiastic competitive footballer, rower and woodchopper and had remained physically fit and strong, mainly by working in his garden. He had once taken up jogging, got halfway around the block and decided it was a boring waste of time. 'We used to have enormous rows about sport,' Gay Raby said. 'It is such a central part of the Australian ethos, but Bill would never, ever, have anything to do with it politically, except occasionally and often reluctantly watch a grand final. Once when there was an opportunity to have a picture of him taken on Melbourne Grand Final day with two Labor people who had been great footballers, Geoff Prior and Ken Bennett, he slipped off somewhere to buy presents for Dallas. He used to tell me I didn't know what I was talking about, that it wasn't fashionable. He said sport might have been fashionable once but that was no longer true. I always blamed people from the 'intellectual Left' of the party; I knew he was being influenced by people who thought you should be reading Camus instead of going to watch a football game, whereas I didn't see them as being mutually exclusive.'[15] The politics of sport is a fairly complicated issue, of course: as Michael Sexton commented: 'It's fairly obvious if you're interested or if you're not; the reason John Howard can't go and upstage Bob Hawke by doing cricket commentaries is that everyone would think it was silly.'[16] Hayden's lack of interest in sport was a limiting factor in his relations even with fellow Labor parliamentarians. His friend Dick Klugman said:

'I often find it easier to talk to Hawke than to Bill, because we can talk about racing.'[17]

While Hayden was working relentlessly on the development of policies and travelling around rural Australia, where Labor held only three of the 40 House of Representatives seats, he faced entrenched problems with the ambitions of some of his colleagues outside the Parliament and in the Labor machines. Bob Hawke and Neville Wran shared Hayden's private assessment that Labor could not win the 1980 election; both saw that his failure would present them with the opportunity to lead the party. This was the unspoken precept that governed relations between the three men and their ambitious retinues. There was not necessarily anything venal in this classic political situation; each group saw themselves as representing the best hope of victory for Labor, and winning elections was the only way to give any party the opportunity to put its policies into force.

Media speculation about Hawke entering Parliament reached one of its frequent pitches of intensity in the period leading up to the Federal Conference of the Labor Party in Adelaide in July 1979. It was the first meeting of the party's supreme policy-making body since Hayden had become leader. He had played an influential role at most of the conferences, normally held every two years, since he was first elected to it as a promising young left-winger with the support of Jack Egerton in the early 1960s. He placed great importance on conferences and their role in establishing policies that were both progressive and acceptable to the electors, and that could be accommodated by those who made up the party. Peter Walsh, who saw Hayden in action first at the 1973 Federal Conference, said: 'He was a misfit in the Queensland delegation; first he was sober, second he was younger, and third he spoke on policy issues.'[18]

The Adelaide conference, in the Festival Centre with its private meeting rooms and a cocktail bar across the road at the Gateway Inn in North Terrace, was to become the set for the most extraordinary, unpleasant and public row between the two men. It resulted in an apparent victory for Hayden and a public exhibition by a drunk and emotionally overstretched Bob Hawke that threatened to end, then and there, any future for him in politics: yet in the end it was Hayden who sustained the more lasting wound, one that was used to drain him of support until the end.

Hawke's principal involvement in the conference was to be as chairman of the party's economic policy committee, which had drafted and was supporting a resolution that would commit a Labor Government to holding a referendum designed to give the Federal Government power to control incomes as well as prices. This proposition had been rejected by the union movement when proposed by the Whitlam Government, and it was still strongly opposed by the Left unions. Hawke was unable to attend a meeting of the ALP Federal Executive in Adelaide on 12 and 13 July in the lead-up to the conference because he was involved in attempts in Melbourne to resolve a major Telecom dispute which was still going on when the Federal Conference began on Monday, 16 July.

That night the party's national president, Neil Batt, rang Hawke to urge him to fly to Adelaide for the debate. Hayden walked into the room while Batt was on the phone. The Hawke and Hayden recollections of what took place from that point on are sharply different. Hawke has said that it was vital that Hayden have a good win on the issue which would be important to the future of a Labor Government. Blanche d'Alpuget takes up the story:

> Then on Monday night Batt rang me again and handed the phone to Bill who said, 'We've got the numbers, but we want to make sure we win well'. He said he really wanted me to come to Adelaide, although as I'd explained the Telecom dispute was at such a stage that I felt I should stay with it ... I told Bill on Monday night that I'd get over to Adelaide on Tuesday morning ... it was agreed that Ralph Willis would open the session and when I arrived, around 11 o'clock, I'd take over. I had a speech prepared, attacking the Left's position on the issue, which would have devastated them and shown up what a pack of bastards they were.[19]

Hayden tells it: 'I walked into the room while Batt was trying to talk Hawke into coming over. I took the phone and said: 'There's no need to come across. We are in the process of sorting something out that is bearable all round, and it's not going to be a disaster.' He was always one for not turning up if there was going to be a disaster. When I told him it was being sorted out, he said, "Let me have a look at a timetable: Gee, I think I can get across", and he got a bloody plane.'

Hawke never got to deliver his speech.

> We broke for lunch and I went down to say g'day to Bill. He made an extraordinary remark. He said, 'This was never my idea', referring to the recommendation on wages ... I was staggered by what he had said, but I just thought, Oh Jesus. When I returned from lunch I was given the message that Hayden had done a deal with the Left. They had an amendment to the wages policy and Hayden was going to support it.[20]

Graham Richardson says: 'I think the moment that I actually really decided that something would have to be done [to depose Hayden as leader] was at the Adelaide Conference in 1979. Bill approached me to get together a group of like-minded souls. We didn't have a Centre Left, we had what might be called moderate forces or Non-Left. They included the Old Guard Queenslanders like Ed Casey and Harry Haunschild. All I remember is getting the meeting together and getting the agreement; then Bill having lunch with Jim Roulston and totally turning it over, and agreeing to the Left's proposition. There were three votes against the proposition, Ducker, Keating and myself; we just wanted to make the point and we did. That incident really worried me. You don't go out of your way to get a lot of people together, get them to vote on something, and then go to lunch with somebody else and rat on them.'[21]

The leaders of the Left, Roulston, who was president of the Victorian Trades Hall Council and vice president of the ALP, and Tom Uren, who was also at the lunch, had told Hayden they had the numbers to beat the motion for a referendum on incomes. Hayden had to choose between defeat and compromise. He chose to compromise on grounds that then set the foundation for an accord between future Labor governments and the peak union bodies. It was to play an important role in future Australian politics and industrial relations. Hayden said later: 'Before Hawke arrived I had already got things into place with a deal that would accommodate the Left. They had been supporting me and I would be crazy to have turned them upside down and bashed their brains in. I hadn't asked him to come across, and I was not going to go along with some extremely emotional performance that left the Metal Workers bloody and battered on the conference floor. I had done a lot of work with the Metal Workers, and the Labor Government inherited the benefit of a lot of that work. They have been one of the most faithful supporters of a prices and incomes policy.'

But Hayden made a bad mistake in not consulting or adequately informing powerful figures including Hawke, Young, Richardson, Wran and Ducker. He had lit a long-burning fuse; he had beaten the New South Wales Right, the people he later suggested had a code similar to that of the Mafia and leaders who enjoyed tearing the wings off butterflies.

Hayden carried the same conference with another compromise that gave him the numbers, with right-wing support, to thrash a left-wing motion designed to commit the Labor Party to greater nationalisation and public ownership. In attempting to mould Labor's policies as close to the economically responsible but socially progressive blend that he favoured, Hayden was constantly involved in a hazardous balancing act that carried with it the constant threat of disaster. Journalist and author Paul Kelly, discussing Labor Party national conferences during Hayden's period of leadership some years later, analysed how he had made major changes to the party's policies and structure by achieving different alliances for different purposes, and also pinpointed the dangers and consequences of such tactics:

> This technique infuriated the faction leaders, but the approach was sound. Over time it gave both the left and right their own wins within the party. It helped maintain the ALP as a broad coalition of forces. On nearly all these key issues [mainly relating to maintaining his leadership, setting economic policy and intervening to reform the Queensland branch of the party] Hayden's decisions as leader were utterly sound for the party's long-term interests. The technique had one flaw and Hayden was susceptible to it. It had the potential to cast doubt on the leader's personal trustworthiness.[22]

The Right, particularly in New South Wales, took a less charitable view: 'Hayden didn't know how to weld a team together and make them perform,' Graham Richardson said. 'That is mainly due to that aloofness of his. If you don't have the massive charisma to carry you through, like Whitlam, then you have to rely on interpersonal skills, and he had few of those. He relied for his hold on the leadership on courting the Left when he needed them and dropping them when he didn't. He established a small group around him, people like Button, Blewett, Grimes and Dawkins, some of whom considered themselves intellectually superior to everybody else. Nowhere in that equation was a consideration of the trade unions.'

The Adelaide conference was a watershed in the relations between Hawke and Hayden; the intense rivalry between them became a matter of public record in a way that was much to Hawke's disadvantage. It is a measure of Hawke's unique political characteristics that he survived the saga at all, and more remarkable that in the end he was to benefit from it. Such was his frustration at being dumped by Hayden and defeated by an alliance that had at its core his enemies of the Victorian Left that he went out of his way to make a public scene in front of a group of politicians and journalists that was almost immediately publicised across the country and later analysed in depth in the *National Times* under the front-page heading: 'Hawke: The end of the road?'.[23]

It was an almost classic demonstration of the volatility of Bob Hawke in his drinking days at times when he was under strain and in the spotlight. He had lunch at State Parliament House, some wine, a port or two, a cigar, and then, towards the end of the afternoon back at the conference venue not far away joined a group of people I happened to be with that included Mick Young and Eric Walsh. We were in a round of six or eight, drinking stubbies at a price we considered quite excessive in the foyer of the Festival Centre. Somebody arranged for most of us to have dinner with our wives at Ayers House, then considered Adelaide's most prestigious restaurant. I was instructed that Hawke was not to be made aware of the arrangement.

When the group had faded into the night, Hawke went to an improvised television studio and gave a restrained television interview during which he said only that the deal 'was something that occurred over lunch time. I haven't had time to consider it'. Asked about his political future he said that if delegates thought he could serve the party better in another capacity he would expect them to come to him and express their view, adding, 'and so far they haven't'. Ducker had restrained Hawke from attacking Hayden on the conference floor, and Hawke later said, 'John Ducker saved me'. After the calm interview Ducker embraced Hawke. Then, as the *National Times* story said:

> The ABC, sensing they might be on to a story, brought in some bottles of beer to keep the duo around ... but after an hour or so John Ducker, realising Hawke's capacity to exaggerate was leading to overkill, began to play down the incident, telling colleagues, 'It will all be over after a good night's sleep'. But to no avail. Sleep was low on Bob Hawke's priorities.

Hawke had not eaten since his lunch at Parliament House, and Ducker was not in good health and had to retire early from his role as minder.

Hawke went across North Terrace to the Gateway Inn and found in the expensive Rotunda Bar, among the furry red-and-gold wallpaper, a group of delegates and journalists. Hawke's 'temper warmed when he spotted Hugh McBride, original author of the amendment moved by Bill Hayden, and Simon Crean, also a member of the Victorian delegation'. Both were members of the Centre Unity faction. 'You're all bloody gutless,' he told them. Then he told five or six journalists, some of whom had tape recorders: 'As far as Bill Hayden and I are concerned, Hayden is dead', and then, louder: '... as far as Bill Hayden and I are concerned, it's finished ... he is a lying cunt with a limited future.'

Bill Hayden votes at Ipswich on 19
October 1980, the day of the only
election in which he led Labor to
the polls.

Bill and Dallas on holiday on the
Barrier Reef in 1982. (Photo
courtesy of Bill Hayden.)

John Spooner, 1988

Bill at the funeral of Geoff Jackson in June 1982. Geoff, who had been
an economic advisor on Bill's staff, was killed in a tractor accident near
Lismore while helping his parents on their farm. Within two weeks of
this day, Hayden had attended the funerals of three other young men
with whose families he had close personal links. At the end of that
period he made a disastrous television appearance attempting to explain
why he had backed down on the issue of visits to Australian ports by
American nuclear ships. (Tom O'Connor photo.)

On 23 January 1983, as the Hawke forces prepared for the coup that
would end his leadership of the Labor Party on 3 February, Bill Hayden
celebrated his fiftieth birthday in typical style: he paused for a cold beer
while renovating the bathroom at his Ipswich home. NSW Premier
Neville Wran formally advised him that this was not the sort of image
that Australians wanted of their political leaders. (*Sunday Sun* photo.)

Bill pours a drink for Fred Daly
and Gough Whitlam at the
celebration in Ipswich marking his
25th anniversary in Federal
Parliament. (*Daily Sun* photo.)

Hayden, arriving late for the
official picture of members of the
newly elected second Hawke
Government, bends the knee to
Hawke. (Graeme Thompson photo,
News Ltd.)

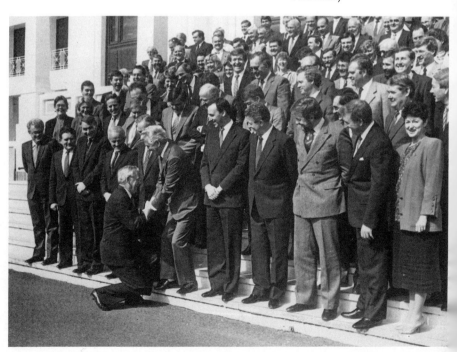

THE LIFE OF BILL

Bruce Petty, the *Age*, 18 February 1989.

Alan Moir, *SMH* 1987

The *National Times* article reflected the common judgment when it commented:

His behaviour probably rules out any chance he will have of becoming Leader and suggests that he will never run for Parliament anyway ... Hayden emerged with the imprimatur of leadership. He put his own indelible stamp on Labor's future direction, formally ended the era of Whitlamism, and ushered in a new era of his own based on the twin themes of sound management and limited reform.

SEVENTEEN

Intervention

There is a seething, festering unhappiness.

Bill Hayden

'**I**'M NOT ONE of those people who foresee some supernova exploding in the world's social and economic system, and everything collapsing into a black hole of disaster,' was the mildly optimistic approach Bill Hayden took to the approach of the decade of the 1980s in an interview published on New Year's Eve, 1979. 'I have quite a healthy respect for what we can do as long as we're sensible about it.'[1] Hayden's consuming aim in the lead-up to the 1980 Federal election was to resurrect the Federal Labor Party by furnishing it with a set of contemporary and coherent policies. His substantial success, marred by some political compromise, was to be one of his towering achievements; his failure was in communicating them.

As there are in all election years, there were to be many alarms and distractions away from the central ground on which he wanted to fight the campaign, which was the change in the standard of living of ordinary families during the five years of Fraser Government. Hayden's political landscape was also seldom free of the menacing shadows of potential challengers for his position, but he did have something of a respite in the later months of 1979. Despite the fact that sections of the Right in the Labor Party had put him on their hit list after his deal with the Left at the Adelaide conference in July that year, he was given a breathing space and saved from any immediate threat of retaliation by Hawke's very public display of bad manners.

Graham Richardson, recalling Hayden's actions in Adelaide, said: 'We walked out of that and said: "We'll get that bastard; we'll do something." And that same night Hawkey goes and does something absolutely atrocious. It made it very hard for us to turn around, point to Hawkey, and say: "There's our man".'[2]

Hayden at this time was getting some conflicting advice about how to deal with the Right and with potential challengers for his position. With Hawke at one of the lowest and most vulnerable points of his turbulent career, there was an opportunity for Hayden to build some bridges to people who had been committed Hawke supporters. They could have had little incentive or prospect of certain political advantage in attaching their futures to Bob Hawke's star at that point in its trajectory. Richardson believed Hayden should instinctively have adopted the tactics most picturesquely described by former US President Lyndon Baines Johnson who said he preferred to have the powerful people inside the tent pissing out than to leave them on the outside pissing in. Others, including some of his staff members, were telling him to take advantage of his victory in Adelaide to put the boots into Hawke and his supporters. Hayden did nothing decisive either way.

But Hawke was not the only person watching Hayden's position with unconcealed ambition. Even before the 1977 Federal election, when Whitlam's leadership was tottering to its end, several New South Wales Federal parliamentarians had twice sounded out Neville Wran urging him to make the move to Canberra. Wran, who had become Premier after winning the New South Wales State election only a year previously, setting Labor back on the road to electoral respectability after the disaster of 1975, told them the approach was premature. But he left no doubt that his ultimate goal was Canberra.

When Wran won his second election in October 1978 the approaches were renewed, and speculation smouldered, encouraged by Wran. 'If and when I decide to enter Federal politics it will be the same way I entered State politics: by sitting down, studying the rules, finding out who has to be moved, who I've got to beat, then coming out smothered in blood and horror.'³ There was no secret about who he had to beat: it was Bill Hayden. Wran's comments were destabilising, and resented by Hayden. The New South Wales Premier was a tough talker:

Unlike in Biblical times, Biblical events, I do no expect the ranks of the Labor Party to divide like the Red Sea to permit my entry into Federal politics. My experience of politics is that you have to fight for everything you get, and largely, unfortunately, you have to clamber over a number of dead bodies to get anywhere.'⁴

Wran was in a powerful position. As Premier he was able to exercise patronage that was not at the command of an Opposition leader, and he had demonstrated in his climb to power with the backing of the New South Wales right-wing machine that he was not reluctant to be ruthless. When asked at an off-the-record dinner with the Canberra press gallery once why he had ruled out going to Canberra for a full parliamentary term, Wran said: 'The great thing about politics in this country is that if you break your promises they don't break your arm.'

Wran's game plan then was to take a Federal seat just before the election due to be held at the end of 1980. In his position he was able to bank on the fact that his machine could safely arrange a seat at the last moment, avoiding a situation in which, having gained normal preselection he would have had to wait more than a year as a lame-duck Premier waiting for Fraser to choose the election date. The whole strategy was predicated on Hayden losing the 1980 election, and Wran made little secret of the fact that he believed this would be the result. Periodically Wran would go public to keep his strategy alive.

In February 1980 he told John Laws, his friend and Australia's most widely listened to radio personality, that Hayden was 'not getting his thoughts, ideas and concepts through to the public'. Hayden replied, with a rather malicious swipe at the older and physically vain Premier, referring to him as an elder statesman whose advice was interesting but adding that he didn't think it would suit his own style 'to cover the grey patches with hair tint'.⁵ It was not to be the last time that Hayden was to make biting public comments about prominent New South Wales Labor figures.

Wran's schemes were frustrated, then and later, by events over which he had no control, but his activities continued to undermine Hayden's confidence and authority. On 16 June 1980, Wran underwent the first of a series of throat operations, and although the worst fears that he was suffering cancer proved false, the quality and strength of his voice was diminished. Nevertheless, while recuperating at a Queensland resort, Wran heard of the unexpected decision by Neil Batt to resign as national president of the Labor Party as well as from his position as Deputy Premier of Tasmania. As a tactic to demonstrate that he was still very much a figure to be reckoned with, Wran immediately decided to go for the party presidency, and stitched it up with one phone call to his deputy press secretary Peter Barron. Barron, later to become Hawke's minder in his first term as Prime Minister, had intimate links with the New South Wales machine and immediately enlisted Graham Richardson who then contacted Mick Young, and within the day he had the numbers.

Wran was using a powerful internal party network that was not at Hayden's disposal. 'The news that Wran would be the next president came as a surprise to Bill Hayden who had been pushing his deputy, Lionel Bowen, for the position,' Steketee and Cockburn wrote.[6] Hayden was in fact on a ship at sea and could not be contacted by the coup organisers, who also neglected to advise Lionel Bowen.

> But presented with a fait accompli, Hayden put the best possible face on it by having his staff feed out the story that Wran's ascension was his idea and that he had asked Richardson to arrange it. This was reported by most newspapers. In fact Hayden was one of the last members of the ALP National Executive to know. When he found out, Hayden had no doubt that, like Hawke, Wran was positioning himself in case he stumbled at the next election.[7]

Later in the year, as the election approached, putting the desire for victory ahead of pride, Hayden willingly cooperated with Wran and Hawke as part of a leadership troika designed to compensate for his lack of charismatic appeal. The use of Wran and Hawke in the campaign may have bolstered Labor's appeal, but it diminished Hayden's leadership. Hawke acted with scrupulous correctness in the discussions that led to his participation in the 1980 campaign. After Hawke had eventually gained preselection for the Melbourne seat of Wills he and Hayden had a face-to-face meeting at Labor's headquarters, John Curtin House in Canberra, and Hawke laid his cards out plainly, saying:

> I will work my guts out in this campaign to get you elected as Prime Minister. I will go to the last ounce of my energy to do this. It would be dishonest of me if I didn't say the embers of Adelaide remain in my mind, but I want you to know I can put this away and work for the party and your success.[8]

Hayden, for his part, attempted to assist Hawke to enter Parliament once he had gained preselection for the safe Melbourne Labor seat of Wills, but the attempt was frustrated when the veteran sitting member, Gordon Bryant, flatly refused to resign. Bryant, who had crawled out of his sickbed to keep Hayden out of the leadership in the 1977 Caucus ballot, added another landmark to an otherwise mediocre career by keeping Hawke out of Parliament.

Another diversion from domestic political issues that arose during the early months of 1980 placed Hayden in a personal and political dilemma. The issue which was to divide the community and dominate much of the debate during the first half of the election year resulted from the invasion of Afghanistan by Russian forces and the response to the invasion by Malcolm Fraser who pressed for Australia to join an international boycott of the Moscow Olympics to be held later that year. There were deeply felt divisions on the issue within the parties on both sides of politics.

Hayden had throughout his political career a record of opposition to Russian armed incursions into neighbouring countries. In August 1968 he had come under attack from sections of the Queensland Labor Party's Old Guard when he moved a resolution at the Queensland Central Executive condemning Russia for invading Czechoslovakia and for attempting to crush the liberalisation of ideas with guns. He was as emotionally opposed to the invasion of Afghanistan as he had been to the Indonesian takeover of East Timor, but he was unwilling to support Fraser's position on the Games. He was deeply suspicious of the Prime Minister's motives, believing that Fraser simply wanted to generate a 'khaki election'.

Fraser would not listen to equivocation in his own party: 'through the first half of the year he single-mindedly pursued a policy that was both unpopular and uncertain of success,' commented his biographer Philip Ayres.[9] Hayden said in 1989: 'I thought it was a stunt from the start. I strongly suspected it was another Cold War stunt from Fraser, undertaken to put us in a difficult position, put us where we allowed ourselves to be positioned throughout the post-Split period of the fifties and sixties, seeming to come down on the side of issues that allowed us to be presented as being soft on the Communists. Frankly, the Russians went into Afghanistan because it was the sort of soft underbelly of their border areas; but it didn't justify them going into another country. I was hostile about it, I was worried about it. It was a very difficult thing to handle.'

Hayden at first said he would support a boycott if it took in a large number of countries. On 18 February Hayden told Caucus that he had been asked by the media whether, in the light of the Government's withdrawal of support, the Labor Party would set up a fund to assist athletes to attend the Games. 'I have said no, because there would be many problems, but of course we could show support for such ideas.'[10] His tough and experienced adviser Clem Lloyd pressed Hayden constantly to take a clear stand in support of Australia sending a team to Moscow. In 1989 Hayden recalled what he had said to Lloyd in their Ipswich office: 'We've got to get a formula that doesn't have us endorsing this awful bloody political stunt, but doesn't get us into hot water with hostility towards those opposing the invasion of Afghanistan.' Hayden had close links with three politically sympathetic officers of the Office of National Assessments which had been established by Fraser as part of a shake-up of Australia's security services, and he was leaked an assessment which was critical of key aspects of Fraser's stand.

Lloyd worked out a formula for handling the issue politically and opposing the Olympic boycott without endorsing the invasion of Afghanistan, and presented it to Hayden while they were working in the Ipswich office. The line, basically, was: 'We condemn the Russians, but want sanctions that actually work.' On 20 February Hayden reported to Caucus that when the issue was raised in Parliament by Fraser he intended to move an amendment to Fraser's resolution which would condemn the Prime Minister's double standards over sanctions, illustrated by his harassment of Australian athletes while permitting continued trade.

The division within Labor's own ranks was given expression by John Dawkins, who did not want it to be inferred he was supporting the invasion of Afghanistan. He asked: 'When our amendment is defeated, what do we do?'

Hayden: 'Vote against the motion.'

Dawkins: 'Is it possible to abstain from voting?'

Hayden: 'The point is that we will not call for a division, so that voting will not be called for.'

Still, on 27 February, there were lingering doubts in Caucus and Gareth Evans asked what response Labor could make if the boycott looked like being effective.

Hayden: 'If there was an effective boycott, we could support it. In any case a really effective boycott would mean no Games.'

He advised parliamentarians against taking initiatives as Labor Party people, but added, 'that doesn't mean we can't participate as people'.

Ken Fry pointed out that Canberra branch members had taken a strong view against the invasion of Afghanistan, and an equally strong view against boycotting the Games. It was an attitude that Hayden shared, but he simply commented: 'There is a vast range of reactions throughout the party. If a boycott could be effective, it might be supported.'

Labor's role was simplified when it was revealed that wool from Fraser's own property Nareen was being exported to Russia at the same time as he was asking athletes to give up their chance of a lifetime. Fraser in private considered imposing an economic boycott: after Hayden had revealed that the Prime Minister was personally selling wool to Russia, 'Fraser got his office to prepare a minute outlining possible implications of a ban on Australian wool, wheat, rutile and other exports'.[11] He backed away when he studied the consequences: in the Australian tradition, sport proved more important than politics and of more concern than the fate of a remote unknown country. The tide of public opinion swung Labor's way, but Hayden's staff say he was never comfortable on the issue.

But his discomfort was less than that of Fraser who became increasingly strident on the issue as his popularity slumped. In June 1980 the Australian Olympic Federation reaffirmed its decision to send an official team to Russia, at the same time saying that individual athletes should consider the Prime Minister's remarks carefully. 'How the executive can reconcile these points of view is beyond comprehension,' Fraser reacted angrily. 'It represents a failure of national leadership and a denial of national responsibility.'[12] In Hayden's office Clem Lloyd poured a celebratory drink and Hayden breathed a quiet sight of relief.

There was a more significant distraction for Hayden throughout 1980 as his running war with the Old Guard controllers of the Queensland branch of the party reached its climax. Hayden had been late to join the moves, made over several years, to reform the branch and make it more democratic and electorally relevant, and had been frustrated and tormented at every turn. But when he went in, he went in hard. It was a tribal factional battle in which ideology remained simply an excuse for the notorious Queensland Inner Executive to maintain iron-fisted control of the branch's affairs and select only candidates who would bend to their commands. The controllers, led by Jack Egerton until he accepted a knighthood from Malcolm Fraser in June 1976, branded their opponents 'Right-wing Groupers', expelled dissenters from the party and discouraged rank-and-file branch members from any real participation in the party. One of the main complaints in Queensland Labor circles about Egerton's knighthood, according to journalist Max Jessop, was that he had knelt before Sir John Kerr to receive his Imperial honour.

'The old Egerton Leftists had become merely opportunists who understood the numbers, personalities and internal party power — but not the issues, principles or ideals,' commented Wayne Swan, an academic who had been a Hayden staff member and in 1988 was campaign director of the Queensland ALP.[13] When the Old Guard narrowly defeated some moderate measures for structural reform of the party which had been proposed by the party's State leader, Tom Burns, and supported by Hayden at a State Conference at the Crest Hotel in Brisbane in January 1977, its members and supporters lined up in the bar chanting:

> The Left got up, the Right went down;
> We stomped the Groupers into the ground.

An indication of the Queensland controlling group's attitude to Hayden's brand of moderate reform and the development of a broadly based party was neatly illustrated when one of its most powerful members, Neal Kane, told a Toowong ALP branch meeting in 1977: 'Professional people such as doctors, lawyers, etc., have no right to be in the ALP.'[14]

Although Hayden was a member of 'the Inner' — as the Inner Executive was known — both it and the Trades and Labor Council had publicly opposed his bid for the party's Federal leadership. Kane, as acting vice-president of the Queensland Trades and Labor Council, helped bring the conflict to a head after Hayden had become leader when he publicly called for his resignation from the party because he 'lacked worker support'. The basis for his claim, he said, was that Hayden had, by endorsing Whitlam's payroll tax promise, opposed tax cuts for the workers. Hayden counter attacked by saying on television that Kane, who was a well-known heavy drinker, should withdraw from the Inner because of 'an unfortunate health problem'.

'Mr Kane does have a problem maintaining his attention on a lot of matters and recalling a lot of these incidents ... He has often denied he has said these things, because he has this serious health problem; and I think in his own interests he ought to retire so that he can recuperate.

He just can't devote the energies and application necessary to fulfil his job these days ... it is very sad.'[15] The standard of debate was shown on the front page of Brisbane's major newspaper, the *Courier Mail*: 'In reply, Mr Kane accused Mr Hayden of involving himself with "Right-wing, Grouper" politics in trying to control the trade unions.'[16] The Queensland Central Executive of the party refused to discipline Kane, who had continued his public attacks on the party's Federal leader, so Hayden took his fight to the Federal Executive. He complained there of the run-down state of the party in Queensland which he said was the result of the way in which influence, power and authority were exercised. 'There is a seething, festering unhappiness,' he said. 'There is an amorphous mass which settles on the party in a thoroughly suffocating way.'[17]

On 31 July 1978, the Federal Executive responded to Hayden's call by authorising a wide-ranging investigation into the affairs of the Queensland branch, but stopped short of intervention. This resulted in a series of minor changes to rules but did not break the power of the Old Guard who took the first opportunity, which came at a State conference in Rockhampton in February 1979, to 'engage in an orgy of recrimination. Reformers were attacked in a vitriolic and personal manner, and several members of the Federal Executive previously unsympathetic to reform decided they could never trust those Queensland bastards ever again.'[18]

Hayden, overreacting to the intransigence of his opponents with a miscalculation of his own, nominated the prominent Socialist Left figure Senator George Georges as his proxy on the party's administrative committee. Georges was at the time playing a leading role in the demonstrations against Joh Bjelke-Petersen's ban on street marches in defiance of a party instruction not to confront the police, and had been arrested, as had 2000 other Queenslanders. 'In the eyes of the Trades Hall grouping, Hayden's nomination of Georges was an extremely provocative act, and it moved swiftly to change the rules denying him his right to appoint an alternative. In one sweep it had publicly belittled Hayden and further discredited Georges.'[19]

The Federal Executive used Hayden's action in attempting to appoint Georges as an excuse not to intervene. The Queensland junta saw this as an invitation to increased displays of arrogance and wilder abuses of power. There was actual violence, with reformers being bashed, and one was attacked with a broken beer glass in a hotel. A young woman reformer who nominated for a minor position against an Old Guard candidate was told she would have her face rearranged if she persisted. Late-night telephone threats and other forms of harassment were constant, but the southern State officials were unmoved. There were several threads to the rationale of Federal Executive members from other States in refusing to endorse intervention; it would set a precedent for interference in their own branches, and, for all its excesses, the Old Guard was opposed to the Socialist Left and therefore in alliance with the New South Wales Right and its allies in other States.

Hayden continued to work for intervention and was ready to move early in 1979 when he postponed action under pressure from Lionel Bowen and Paul Keating. Their argument was similar to that outlined in the *Bulletin* on 13 March 1979, by the veteran conservative political writer Alan Reid who warned that the Georges Affair would trigger a left-wing bid for control of the party nationally:

> The Socialist Left in Victoria scented its opportunity. Its leaders were not so concerned about a loss of face for Hayden as with the opportunity to strengthen their positions on the Federal Executive, the Labor Party's supreme governing body between biennial Conferences and a body to which even an ALP Prime Minister has to bow the knee. If they could secure Federal intervention in Queensland and enforce proportional voting on Queensland, as they had on New South Wales, they would take a further step along the road to national control.

By February 1980, the Old Guard had suspended Georges from the party as well as a prominent reform activist, Peter Beattie, and defied a Federal Executive decision reinstating them, and had also deregistered three party branches in Toowoomba that contained strong reformist elements. The party in Queensland was in a state of open, constant warfare and Hayden was determined to act. He had moved full circle in the byzantine feuding of Queensland Labor politics: first, as a teenager in South Brisbane, he had been denied even membership of the party by Gair's 'Grouper' supporters; then, in Ipswich after the Split, as a trusted left-winger he had advanced rapidly under the sponsorship of Egerton's purists; and now, as the party's national leader he was being vilified by the party's Queensland controllers as a hated 'Grouper'. In fact Hayden's political position had moved less than that of his opponents, a situation that was demonstrated by the fact that while they called themselves members of the Left their national support on bodies like the Federal Executive now came solely from the right wing of the party.

Writing in the *Australian*, journalist Max Jessop, who was close to the Old Guard, reflected how its members were able to brush aside this substantial internal contradiction in their professed ideological stance, without raising any issues of policy, in justifying their attitude to Hayden: he had become a snob and a class traitor.

> The man who used to say: 'Come on sport, let's have a beer' and described himself as a typical product of a deprived socio-economic background had advanced to wine casks in a typical middle class home in Brassall. The Trades Hall boys became increasingly suspicious ... in 1973, after he had become the Minister for Social Security in the Whitlam Government, a union official grumbled: 'He is surrounding himself with bloody academics.' Hayden, the intellectual arrived. Hayden, the man at ease with the Jackie Howe singlet and the 7 oz Fourex glass was a creature of the past.[20]

The outrageous idiocy, blinkered vision and limited horizons of the ruthless ruling Old Guard hacks was clearly shown: the vision of the height of decadence was a cardboard box of wine at Brassall on the outskirts of Ipswich, and hiring Paddy McGuinness rather than a relative or an unemployed electrician was no way to run a minister's office.

While fear of a left-wing takeover seemed to guarantee the Queensland regime's immunity from outside discipline, it continued to belittle and bully its opponents. Then in the early months of 1980 it became involved in a number of financial scandals including clandestine efforts to sell half the party's radio station.[21] Hayden committed himself totally to intervention. 'In taking the most important and toughest stand in his two years as party leader, Hayden judges that most of the talk about a Queensland breakaway party is exaggerated and that any split will be kept to a minimum. If he has misjudged, the consequences will be disastrous,' Paul Kelly wrote in the *National Times*.[22] Kelly recorded that Hayden was speaking to all members of the Federal Executive personally and resisting all moves for compromise which was being demanded by the strong right-wing New South Wales branch which was arguing that full-scale intervention would only strengthen the forces of the Left nationally and in Queensland.

In the period before the decisive meeting of the Federal Executive Hayden made unrelated moves that have shadowed his personal and political life ever since. He demoted two friends, Mick Young and Dick Klugman. Hayden admits he handled the matter badly and is uncomfortable talking about it. He gave no reason at the time and now explains it only in terms of having decided how he wanted Labor's parliamentary team to operate. In recent years the kinship of survivors has brought the three men back into contact. Hayden and Young were at a strategy meeting at John Curtin House in Canberra that had dragged on without apparent direction or purpose for several hours when Hayden told Young he was sacking him as manager of Opposition tactics in the House of Representatives. Young said: 'Well, I hope we are going to make some important decisions at this meeting.' Hayden asked him what he meant. Young answered: 'It's going to look great, we'll really look like an alternative government if we go out after meeting all day and tell the media that all that has been decided is to dump me.'[23]

Young was already closer to Hawke than he was to Hayden and had been critical of Hayden's actions at the Adelaide conference, but had continued to respect his position as leader and work closely with him. Hayden had always envied Young's ready humour and relaxed social confidence, but was as critical of Young's casual working style as Young was of the importance Hayden placed on academic study and theory. By demoting him, Hayden ensured that Hawke had a more formidable ally. 'I must say I don't think I handled it very well at all,' Hayden said in 1988. 'I was under pressure and I felt highly embarrassed because they were friends of mine. I would now regard them as two warm friends whose company I would prefer above many others. In politics you have to be able to forgive and forget pretty bloody quickly. A lot of politicians don't but if you don't you'll just have a poisoned soul. I admired Mick's natural ability, sense of humour, the Irish Catholic style I grew up surrounded by — you were quick on your feet otherwise you got knocked over. Personally he's a nice bloke, but at that time we'd fallen out and were on different sides of the fence.'

On 1 March 1980, Hayden carried the Federal Executive and secured intervention in Queensland. 'A tired, pale and tense Bill Hayden walked out the front door of the Labor Party's Canberra headquarters to be surrounded by television cameras, microphones and reporters,' the *Australian* recorded.

> A few minutes earlier Hayden had secured a costly victory: against the strong arguments of many of his closest supporters and friends he had secured ALP Federal intervention in the affairs of the troubled Queensland branch. 'Being leader of the Labor Party can be a lonely job,' he said. 'Sometimes you have to make decisions you would rather not have to make.'[24]

The Federal Executive had gone the full way with Hayden and sacked the Queensland branch, established an interim administrative committee of twenty-nine members to run its affairs until a special conference could be held to fill all party positions by elections which would be held under a proportional representation system. The leading role was taken by Denis Murphy, reader in history at the University of Queensland, and one of the principal campaigners for reform of the party in Queensland, who was at the time completing his biography of Hayden. Accountants were to conduct an audit of the books of the party and its associated business enterprise.

All this proved more difficult to achieve than Hayden had hoped, but the worst fears were not realised. The Old Guard, with the support of only four unions, including the Electrical Trades Union led by Neil Kane, refused to hand over the assets and in July 1980, took legal action against the federally appointed committee. The action, Murphy said in his report to the party's annual conference in June 1981, 'hung like a pall over the whole Labor movement in Queensland, producing disaffection among unions, branches and supporters'. But at the election that year Labor's primary vote in Queensland rose by 5.1 per cent to 42.8 per cent. 'Labor, despite its still unresolved problems, had returned to the Federal electoral pendulum.'[25]

It is perhaps permissible to move slightly ahead of our chronology at this point to note briefly some further events. On 2 July 1981, the first State conference held under the new structure was meeting for the third day at the Greek Community Centre in Edmondstone Street, South Brisbane, a short walk from where Bill Hayden had grown up, when George Georges took the microphone. He said Denis Murphy and Peter Beattie had just telephoned from a court a couple of kilometres away to report that Mr Justice Lucas had dismissed the Old Guard's challenge. 'This Conference is now legal, our leaders will return soon. We will now have a short adjournment,' Georges said to excited cheering.

The conference had been notable for its display of unity and its serious attention to policy development. Bill Hayden had been forced to leave to meet other engagements by the time the Lucas decision was announced, but he sent a telegram which was cheered by delegates. It said: 'Suddenly our backside has stopped itching. A great victory has been won for our members and for the future of the party.'[26]

The result of intervention was recorded by Paul Kelly: 'Three years later Bob Hawke led the ALP to a sweeping five seat gain in Queensland and so reaped the benefit of the seeds Hayden had fought to sow.'[27] Denis Murphy was elected to the Queensland State House of Assembly in 1983 but died of cancer after having been able to attend the Parliament on only three days.

EIGHTEEN

Hawke swoops

*It was a nasty job ... but with the benefit
of hindsight, I'd have to say I'd do it all
again.*

Graham Richardson

USTRALIA has never had a political phenomenon that remotely
resembles the life and career of Bob Hawke, and there have been
very few people who have matched his particular ability to
communicate with the Australian people. When he was a long-haired
problem drinker, a womaniser and leader of one of the country's least
popular institutions, the trade union movement, public opinion polls
consistently showed that he was the most popular figure in the nation.
They changed little after he entered Parliament in 1980 and became, for
more than a year, a sober, bored and boring, out-of-place and ineffective
Opposition backbencher whose main distinction was that he had cried
when wrongly accused of deserting the cause of Israel.

Hawke had given up drinking in May 1980 and been elected to the
House of Representatives in October that year. When his biographer,
Blanche d'Alpuget, asked him to name his three major achievements
between his maiden speech in Parliament in November 1980 and May
1982, on the eve of his first challenge to Hayden, she described his list
as at first glance seeming curious, even shallow, although it had more

significance in retrospect. He was pleased that he had played a role in having the Liberal minister Ian Viner moved from the Industrial Relations portfolio, he took pride in a remark by Lionel Bowen that when Hawke decided to do something in Parliament 'the Government takes fright', and he had succeeded in having his description of Fraser as 'a liar' incorporated in Hansard.

'Most importantly, while the Australian people continued to admire Hawke and stated consistently that he was their preferred political leader, Hawke was failing to impress the would-be king-makers of the Press gallery and the real king-makers: his colleagues in Parliament,' d'Alpuget wrote.[1] In July 1982, during the Labor Party's National Conference in Canberra, when the *Sydney Morning Herald*'s Peter Bowers was asked during a television discussion about Hawke's achievements in Parliament, he could only think of one. He said: 'He called Malcolm Fraser a liar and got away with it. Well, hurrah.' Bowers later recalled: 'When I saw them after the interview, Dallas kissed me, and Bill was so moved he gave me his two silent telephone numbers; unfortunately when I came to use them three weeks later, they had both been changed.'[2] Hayden's secrecy about his home telephone number and the silent line in his Brisbane office was a constant source of both irritation and amusement to political colleagues and journalists. Those who had the most recent number would protect it closely, and some were fearful of Hayden's retaliation if they revealed it. Yet often they would then discover it had been changed and they were no longer on the list. Nevertheless, as visitors to his home discovered, the telephone rang constantly.

Once Hawke was in Parliament, he had only two aims: he wanted to become leader in as short a time as possible and then defeat Fraser to become Prime Minister. There was nothing subtle about it, he simply decided to by-pass the usual process of gaining leadership by serving an apprenticeship and proving himself by performing in Parliament and in the forums of the party where policy was formed. He determined to bluff, coerce and bully the Caucus by the use of his extraordinary public popularity. His argument was simple: he could win. To many Labor parliamentarians with ambition his approach was as attractive as it was brutal. Hayden may have had the experience of twenty years in Parliament and been a successful minister and Treasurer, he may have dragged the party from its nadir of 1977, furnished it with a comprehensive range of policies, most of which Hawke supported, and he may have won enough seats from Fraser in 1980 to put the Opposition within reach of victory. But he could not guarantee that victory. Hawke's simple crusade was to convince the Caucus that he could. He was not going to win the struggle with Hayden in Parliament or the forums of the party; he was going straight to the people. As early as Christmas 1981, he was telling friends he could be Labor's leader within six months.[3]

Hayden was confronted with the problem that was later to be faced by Malcolm Fraser and his successors as Liberal leader, Andrew Peacock and John Howard: there was no real way to combat Hawke's tactics while he still enjoyed his strange rapport with the Australian electorate. The best Hayden could do was to maintain the situation as it then existed, keep the support of his Caucus colleagues who believed he would be a better Prime Minister than Hawke, and retain their confidence that he could win an election against Fraser, even though he might not win it as comfortably as Hawke might. It was to Hayden's advantage at that time, too, that Hawke was a reformed drinker. There were two clear, and to Hawke negative, schools of thought on the issue. Some who had seen him behave badly when drunk were fearful that if he became leader he might crack and go back to his old bad habits; others, who drank themselves and who had enjoyed Hawke's company when he was a drinker, now resented the fact that he now seemed bored with them. He was going home to drink tea.

Late on the night of Thursday, 18 February 1982, Hawke went to Hayden's office and they spent more than an hour together in the first lengthy conversation they had had since Hawke's election to Parliament in 1980. During the conversation Hawke referred to the opinion polls and told Hayden that his duty to the Labor Party made it impossible for him to ignore the fact that he was easily the most popular political figure in the country. Geoff Kitney assessed the meaning of the meeting in the *National Times*:

> Hawke was placing Hayden on notice that he wanted to take over the leadership. Hayden retorted that if the Caucus had shared the views reflected in the polls, Hawke would already be in the Leader's seat. But the Caucus, with its intimate understanding of them both, had maintained its preference for the present Leader. Hayden was placing Hawke on notice that he would resist any leadership bid. Few in the ALP doubt that Bill Hayden will battle with all the strength and cunning of the street fighters he saw on the copper's beat; if he goes down it will be on a bloodsoaked floor.[4]

Although he handled himself well in Hawke's presence, and, in fact, could make Hawke nervous and uncomfortable, Hayden found it impossible to come to terms with Hawke's manoeuvring and manipulation. It eroded his confidence as leader and affected his performance; it brought to the fore the defensive and suspicious elements of his nature, and some members of his staff nourished his dread and distrust of Hawke and his ambitious supporters. In May 1982, in an act of pettiness, Hayden left Hawke off an electoral strategy committee he had established; it was an empty gesture that simply drew attention to his insecurity.

The public opinion polls on which Hawke's campaign rested were a simple means of causing division in the Labor Party. Many Labor parliamentarians and party members had a much more jaundiced view of the 'capitalist press' than did Hawke. They suspected the motives of the owners of Australia's few media empires whom they believed were pushing Hawke's barrow. The sceptics in the Labor Party saw the constant headlines and speculation about Hawke — who was doing nothing of the slightest significance politically — as something of a media conspiracy that had nothing to do with its professed motive, which was to give the Labor Party effective popular leadership. These Labor Party members regarded the Hawke popularity stories as being the political equivalent of the media campaigns that drool over the details of perverse sexual exploits of clergymen under the guise of exposing and condemning them. Those who held this view saw support for Hawke as being motivated by one of two things: simply to cause conflict within the Labor Party, or to ensure that it had a far more conservative and compliant leader than Hayden.

There was division too among working journalists about the relative merits of Hawke and Hayden. The main differences were between those Peter Bowers described as 'the Melbourne sycophants' who had covered union matters and drunk and argued with Hawke, and the members of the Canberra press gallery who regarded him as, at best, an unproved political performer with a limited grasp of parliamentary procedures and a narrow range of expertise or interests.

Nobody in any of these conflicting groups could deny that public opinion polls were a powerful weapon for Hawke, but he still had a major problem to overcome that went beyond personalities and ability: in all its history the Federal Labor Party had never voted out a leader. Hawke refused to believe such tradition had relevance to him, and had convinced himself that Hayden's own aloof and uncertain character made him incapable of effectively defending himself against a sustained challenge.

Hayden's performance was significantly influenced by the pressure that Hawke was exerting on him and he veered between aggression and a retreat to isolation, to the bunker of his books and his office. 'He was awful at handling people,' said one of Hayden's own supporters. 'And he wasn't helped by members of his staff like Alan Ramsey who could alienate people without even trying.'

'The fragility of Hayden's leadership, some argue, is in his nervousness and suspicion about what his colleagues are up to,' Geoff Kitney said. 'There are fears among some, who believe Hayden would be a good Prime Minister, that he is becoming too much of a loner, a tendency which could seriously weaken his grip on the party.'[5] One of Hawke's backers, Senator Graham Richardson, said in 1988: 'Historically, it's very hard to change the Labor leadership. We [the Right] tried hard to get on side with Bill, and did not encourage Hawke too much.'[6] In fact, Hawke went through a period of doubting Richardson and the New South Wales Right, and early in 1982 berated Richardson for getting too close to Hayden. Richardson said: 'I was always of the view that Hawke should not run until he could win.'

But Hawke had one supporter, Rod Cameron, managing director of Labor's polling organisation, Australian National Opinion Polls, who was not inhibited by historic precedent or loyalties. As he saw it, he was not there to make judgments about Hawke and Hayden, he was there to tell his client, the Labor Party, what the electors thought about them. On 18 May 1982, he went to Hayden's office with the results of intensive surveys his organisation had carried out in the previous two months. He told Hayden that Australians saw him as being 'competent, smart, a good bloke ... honest and modest'. But then he added a devastating rider, telling Hayden he was also seen as 'weak, wishy-washy, a whinger, and people often just cannot understand what you are saying. They see you as carping, supercritical and never having a good word for anyone. You are not seen as a strong leader'.[7]

Cameron was not only confident that Hawke was a winner and harboured a deep-seated belief that Hayden would lose an election against Fraser, but he was also in a powerful position to influence events, and time would strengthen that position. It was a traumatic meeting for both men. Hayden was at first in a confident mood, pointing Cameron to rival poll results that showed Labor leading the Government by 4 per cent. Cameron was later reported as saying Hayden was the only leader he knew who had not been capable of coping with the sort of unfavourable news he had given him. Hayden distrusted Cameron and was critical of his ability and motives. Cameron went on to brief Neville Wran, Graham Richardson, who was then New South Wales secretary of the Labor Party, and the Victorian ALP secretary, Bob Hogg, on his research results. Hayden saw this as amounting to a campaign against him: the research provided powerful ammunition for Hawke, and he was soon made aware of it in detail. 'The truth is, we were always going to challenge; the research made it legitimate,' Richardson told Paul Kelly.[8]

Influential figures in the US Administration of President Ronald Reagan, who were angered by Hayden's aggressive attitude on a number of issues affecting American interests in Australia, played a significant role in inspiring Hawke's first unsuccessful challenge for the Labor leadership in 1982. Hayden was to suggest publicly later, when he was Hawke's Foreign Minister, that there had been an association between his stand on issues involving a key American defence installation and his eventual loss of the leadership to Hawke.

In July 1983 George Negus, a reporter for the television program '60 Minutes', questioned Hayden about a statement he had made in 1981 indicating he favoured renegotiation of the agreement between Australia and the United States for the operation of the joint defence facility at North-West Cape in Western Australia which relays messages to America's nuclear armed submarines.

The following exchange took place:

Hayden: 'When did I say that George?'

Negus: '1981.'

Hayden: 'A funny thing happened to me in February 1983.'

Negus: 'On the way to Government?'

Hayden: 'On the way to an Executive meeting. I was flensed, I think they call it in the whaling industry.'

The Australian Associated Press reporter who recorded the exchange in Washington added: 'A quick check revealed that flensing in the whaling industry means being skinned, sometimes while the whale is still alive.'[9]

Hayden had said in a speech to the Australian Institute of International Affairs on 22 June 1981, that the Australian–American alliance worked very much in favour of the USA, that Australia should have a more independent foreign policy and that it was quite wrong to 'presume that the alliance means that there is no room for disagreement and that there is no justification for striking out very much on an independent role'. Referring to renegotiation of the North-West Cape agreement, he said a Labor Government led by him would 'not be prepared to have ourselves locked in by default to a situation where a whole chain of events is unleashed which leads us into a nuclear conflict'.

Hayden came into serious public conflict with the most senior American officials in 1982, before Hawke's first unsuccessful challenge. In May 1982 George Bush, then US Vice-President, visited Australia and met Hayden, who insisted on trying to find out from him whether or not the American Central Intelligence Agency had played a role in the dismissal of the Whitlam Government. This was a piece of Labor folklore that was based on the known links between Sir John Kerr and intelligence organisations and the well-documented neurosis of the CIA about Whitlam and his Government. Bush, who had himself had a period as head of the CIA, told Hayden the agency had not been involved, but conceded, when pressed by the Labor leader, that he had not personally investigated the allegations. It was another difficult, inconclusive Hayden encounter that proved unsettling for the Americans.

In May 1982 the new Victorian Premier John Cain declared his State a nuclear-free zone and asked Fraser to tell the Americans to keep nuclear-powered or -armed ships out of Victorian ports. On 9 June in Hobart Hayden went further and said it would be 'totally undesirable for Australia or any parts of Australia to become nuclear weapon arsenals or storage or transit points'.[10] Because the Americans would not disclose whether their ships carried nuclear arms, Hayden's policy amounted to a ban on all US warships visiting Australian ports; he had gone further than Labor policy provided and found himself isolated, with support coming only from the Left. His deputy Lionel Bowen said on 14 June that it had always been Labor's policy to allow visits and it accepted that the Americans could not identify which ships carried nuclear arms.

Malcolm Fraser and the Americans exploited the breach in Labor's ranks. On 20 and 21 June 1982 there was an ANZUS council meeting in Canberra and Fraser used it to drive home his contention that Hayden's policy would wreck ANZUS, the treaty on which Australia's whole defence policy rested. On 21 June two senior US delegates to the ANZUS conference, Deputy Secretary of State Walter Stoessel and his senior adviser John Holdridge, called on Hayden in Parliament House. They made it clear to Hayden that his policy was unacceptable, that it put the alliance into question, and that they would make their views public. Holdridge was described later as having been 'aggressive, almost threatening'.[11] The Americans were as good as their word: on 22 June at a press conference Stoessel described access to ports as a critical factor in America's efforts to carry out its responsibilities under the terms of the ANZUS treaty. Five hours later, after a meeting in Sydney with a group of senior colleagues, Hayden was forced to announce that he had changed his mind.

By leaving it so late, until Stoessel had spoken publicly, Hayden made his humiliation even worse, making it apparent he had been done by the Americans, and forced to back down. To compound the disaster he insisted, against the advice of his press secretary Alan Ramsey, on accepting an invitation from the ABC program 'Nationwide' to appear that night and explain his somersault. Hayden was in a state of emotional and physical exhaustion. In the previous ten days he had attended the funerals of four young men: Geoff Jackson, a brilliant young former economic adviser to Hayden, had been killed in a freak tractor accident in northern New South Wales and Hayden had flown there and wept over the open grave during a moving ceremony; John Button's son had died in Melbourne and Bill and Dallas Hayden had stayed with the family while Button went alone to the crematorium. Then he attended the funeral of the son and nephew of a close friend in the Queensland Labor Party who had been killed in a car accident. Hayden, perhaps even more than most, has since the death of Michaela been particularly affected by the death of young people.

'Bill Hayden rarely looks good on television,' commented Kitney reviewing Hayden's performance when he attempted to explain his cartwheel on the nuclear ships issue.

> When he is tired and under stress he looks bad. His mouth droops, his eyelids get red, his nose seems longer, his pixie features accentuated, a flushed face in caricature ... Hayden looked bad and sounded worse, his wafer voice thinner than usual ... It was the worst moment for Hayden's leadership of the Labor Party. And it could not have come at a worse time ... anyone looking at Hayden back down on nuclear ships could hardly escape concluding that the odds were quickly shortening for Hawke.[12]

While Hayden's dilemma over American nuclear ships continued, Hawke moved to step up the pressure. On one of the few occasions that he was to act as his own lobbyist and numbers man, rather than leave the dirty work to his ideological supporters, ambitious sycophants and toadies, he flew in May 1982 to Sydney where he spoke to Neville Wran, Lionel Bowen, Paul Keating and Graham Richardson, as well as to John Ducker, who had retired from the State presidency of the party and had been appointed by Wran to the Public Service Board. Richardson was later to say: 'Hawkey went over the top while the rest of us were still in the trenches putting on our boots.'[13] In their private meeting, Lionel Bowen said he would continue to support Hayden, but told Hawke he did not think Hayden would win the coming election. It was a significant incentive to the challenger. Ducker also influenced Hawke by telling him that if he wanted the leadership he should get in there and fight for it. Richardson was committed to Hawke but believed more time was needed to gain the necessary support. Meanwhile, in Melbourne, members of the Victorian Centre Unity faction led by Simon Crean, Gareth Evans and Clyde Holding were meeting to plan ways of advancing Hawke's challenge.

Then, as is the way in politics, within a week a new drama erupted in the Labor Party that was to change everything. At its core were a number of ironies. Once again the issue hinged on the emotive and mysterious questions of uranium and nuclear energy. Hayden, who had taken a tough stand against the Americans bringing ships with nuclear weapons into Australian ports, now decided that Labor's policy banning the mining and export of uranium was dangerous nonsense, and that it could only be changed if he acted positively and forcefully. He determined to do so in the face of a threat from influential members of the party's Left that to do so would cost him his leadership.

Hayden was convinced that Labor would not be elected if it retained a policy that committed a Labor government to closing down, without paying compensation, the billion dollar uranium-mining industry that had been established during the term of the Fraser Government. Labor's policy had been designed to scare away foreign investors, to abort the industry. It hadn't worked. A new factor had also emerged in the years since Labor had devised its policy: one of the great mineral deposits of the world had been discovered at Roxby Downs in South Australia, and it could not be mined without also extracting the uranium that was part of the ore body. It was a find that promised substantial benefits for an isolated State which was not rich in resources. South Australian Labor politicians were convinced that it would be mined, and argued that it would be best for this to happen under safeguards established by a Labor government.

Hayden said in 1988: 'I was conscious of the fact that we could be in serious trouble in South Australia with Roxby Downs coming on. If we stopped that development Bannon's chances of winning would be nonexistent. So it was a political judgment. I could see we were going to have trade balance problems and awful problems funding the defence Budget because there were so many large expensive capital items in the pipeline. It seemed to me that if we could be sure that safeguards were effective, we should be selling uranium. It seemed to me that every problem that had been raised as a point of opposition to the sale of uranium had a response which was reassuring and satisfactory, except one, and that is disposal of waste. I have never concealed my concern about how we can safely dispose of waste. The interim arrangement I favoured was to have it securely stored until a permanent method of safe disposal was achieved. I'm a product of the early democratic socialist thinking which shows great faith in science and human intellect and the resourcefulness of people. I still believe we will get a solution to it, and in the meantime it can be stored successfully. Now that would earn us money.'

Hayden was certain, that if Labor came to power while it was committed to a policy of repudiating commitments to the uranium-mining industry made by the Fraser Government, it could only carry out the policy at the cost of bringing investment in Australia to a halt and the economy to its knees. The party's supreme policy-making body, the National Conference, was due to meet in Canberra on 5 July, but Hayden's determination to move had crystallised at a meeting of the National Executive on 7 May at which the beefy Northern Territory delegate, Bob Collins, told of a recent visit he had made to the Jabiru mining town, inhabited by working-class people dependent on uranium mining. 'Which one of you is prepared to go up there and tell these people that they have to pack up and leave?' he asked.

The New South Wales Right had long supported a change in Labor's official policy on uranium mining, and now, with Hayden in agreement, they saw the possibility of movement. Keating was impressed with Hayden's willingness to confront an issue that could not be won without huge cost and lasting acrimony. On 26 June when Hayden addressed the New South Wales State Labor Conference, Keating introduced him by saying: 'He has taken on the hard decisions that none of us like to take on, but which have to be taken if we are to win government. He is a leader of courage and determination, a man of integrity and principle.'[14] The Left acted with equal emotion but opposite intent. Tom Uren, Hayden's old confidant, a leader of the Left that had been the only group supporting him so recently when he had confronted the Americans over nuclear-armed ships, told him that he was a 'stupid bloody fool,' adding, 'We've been friends for a long time, but this goes beyond friendship'. Uren, against the tradition of the Left, which is founded on decisions being made jointly, decided to approach Hawke in an attempt to get an assurance from him that he would support the existing policy.

On the morning of 29 June, the silver-haired political guerilla Clyde Cameron spoke on the ABC's 'AM' saying '... Labor would romp home with Hawke as leader, there's no doubt about that ... If I was still in Caucus, I would have to vote for him ... We've got to face facts. The public opinion polls show that Bob Hawke now commands more support than any other politician ever registered in these public surveys.' Hawke rang Cameron at his home in Adelaide and said: 'Thanks, mate.' Hawke was interviewed that evening on 'PM', and asked about Cameron's comments. It gave him an opportunity to construct neatly a powerful equation: 'The question of the leadership of the party and the electoral welfare of the party is a matter for the Caucus.' The leadership issue, then, was not a matter of personalities; it was a matter of the electoral welfare of the party. Hawke was then asked whether he thought Caucus should take the matter up at its next meeting, and he said that there was provision for the members to do so if they wanted to. Uranium was displaced as the issue of the moment as the focus of media attention turned to Hayden's leadership.

But, unseen, there were significant undercurrents pulling leading party figures in unexpected directions. Uren was meeting with influential figures in the Victorian Left, vainly attempting to convince them to back Hawke, a man they had been in open conflict with for years, a man they detested and who fully reciprocated their sentiments. Some suspected that Uren was acting out of pique because Hayden would be neither guided nor bullied by him. At the other end of Labor's political spectrum, Richardson, gaining power as a leader of the Right and as a numbers man for Hawke, fully supported Hayden's move to change the uranium policy, but he was not going to let that divert him from his main purpose, the promotion of Hawke to the leadership. At the pre-conference meeting of Labor's National Executive in Canberra on 1 July, without a flicker of emotion playing on his pointed, fox-like features, Richardson insisted that the party secretary, Bob McMullan, read in detail Rod Cameron's latest report on his research into public attitudes to Hayden and Hawke. Paul Kelly recorded the result: '... McMullan, intensely embarrassed, read the ANOP report, not lifting his head from the document. Hayden was even more embarrassed as his deficiencies as a leader were read out to his colleagues. The coming struggle would be a pitiless contest.'[15]

The poker-faced Bob Hogg, who conceals a sharp political intelligence and a social conscience behind alert but undemonstrative dark eyes, found himself as a pivotal figure close to the centre of two vicious contests: the struggle for the leadership and the battle to change the party's policy on the mining and export of uranium. After much agonising, and exhaustive but unsuccessful attempts at conciliation and compromise, Hogg made what amounted to a brave personal political sacrifice. Having failed in an attempt to persuade Hayden to drop his proposal to modify the party's uranium policy on the grounds that it would mean, in effect, a vote on his leadership, Hogg became convinced that if Hayden was defeated Labor could not win an election. Hayden's argument, supported by the Right, was that repudiating existing uranium-mining arrangements would turn off foreign investment in Australia. Hogg realised that Fraser simply had to turn that argument on Labor, regardless of its leadership, to frighten enough electors to ensure victory. Amid the turmoil of the conference, in the frenetic atmosphere of Canberra's Lakeside Hotel, surrounded by demonstrators, drunks, political groupies, plotters, ambassadors, lobbyists and the national media, Hogg drafted a policy that sought to achieve something both Right and Left could accept, a clever and complex document allowing existing mining to continue provided there were satisfactory safeguards.

On the day the uranium debate was to take place, Wednesday, 7 July 1982, the *Bulletin* published a Morgan Gallup poll that showed Hayden's popularity rating had dropped from 38 to 31 per cent, while Fraser's had risen from 46 to 50 per cent. Hawke gave a series of television interviews in the foyer of the hotel, close to the conference room, in which he expressed concern about the poll, though he was confident Labor could win under his leadership.

In a political imitation of a traditional circus, two exciting shows proceeded simultaneously under the same roof: while Hayden was attempting to tame the lions of the Left on the uranium issue being debated on the conference floor, Hawke was preening himself before the media as the trapeze artist and magician who could carry the party on his back, in a single bound, to government. Alan Ramsey, watching Hawke's performance before the television cameras during which he said the poll results should be closely considered by members of the public and the Caucus, made an urgent report to Hayden. 'You're bleeding to death. You've got no idea of the damage being done...'[16] Hayden determined then to confront his challenger, and decided then he would lay his leadership on the line in a secret vote at a special Caucus meeting which he would call on 16 July, the Friday of the following week. But for the moment, while the uranium debate proceeded, on and off the conference floor, he kept his decision to himself.

In the emotional uranium debate Hayden used an expression that, when used later by Paul Keating, was to become part of the Australian political phrase book. Warning that the community would react against the party unless the policy of not compensating investors in the mining industry was maintained, Hayden added: 'We would almost become a banana republic in the standards of the condition of the economy.' Typically Hayden wanted to make a clear distinction between the emotional issue of uranium exports and that of the reliability and financial responsibility of a potential Labor government. It was an approach that was not popular with the more extreme opponents of the uranium industry.

Senator Peter Walsh is among Hayden supporters who regard his performance at the 1982 National Conference as his finest hour. The conference clarified Labor's capital gains tax policy so that it could not again be misrepresented by Fraser and altered the uranium policy to permit the existing industry to continue. Both these changes were opposed by powerful sections of the party and would not have occurred but for Hayden's determination and willingness to bear the personal political cost within his own party and the jeopardy in which his stand placed his leadership. If those changes had not been made Hawke would have faced a much more difficult task in the 1983 election. It would have been easy for Hayden to take the populist route within the party.

In 1988 Hayden said: 'The Left in the Labor Party are always looking for a martyr's cause, and always looking for an opportunity to rally the troops behind their position. I was never happy with our uranium policy.

I was sceptical of some of the conversions: people like Jim Cairns, for instance, who, just before we went out of office was travelling to Iran to try to make sales of uranium to the Shah, suddenly became a disciple of leaving it in the ground.'

The debate was a national demonstration of the Labor Party's strengths and weaknesses; a parade of its emotional and pragmatic elements, the drama, the love and hatred and cynicism. It all took place under the bright, hard lights of the television cameras. As the vote was taken and the Left forced a physical division — as Jack Egerton had done to Hayden years earlier when he wanted to change the laws on homosexuality — delegates were hissed or cheered by anti-uranium demonstrators as they took their positions on the Hogg amendment. It was carried by fifty-three votes to forty-six.

Hayden showed he could play the game at Hawke's level. At three o'clock on the afternoon after publication of the *Bulletin* poll, and just as Hawke was about to take the conference floor to make his major address, on industrial relations, Hayden announced that he was calling a special Caucus meeting a week later to resolve the leadership. 'I am seriously concerned that a deliberate campaign has been carried out in recent weeks to destabilise the cohesion of the Federal Parliamentary Labor Party,' Hayden's statement said. 'It has undermined the gains of this week's National Conference and is doing serious damage to the morale and credibility of the party. No leader can tolerate such insidious destabilisation of our team effort.'

One of the most intense internal upheavals in the history of the Labor Party ensued during the power struggle of the following week, with both the Left and the Right factions becoming internally divided. Tom Uren, in the end, could not hold the Left in support of Hawke. Leading Left figures including Don Grimes, Senator Nick Bolkus and Stewart West recalled the longstanding conflict between Hawke and the Left and criticised his recent tactics that had disadvantaged the party. Left-wing unions, led by the powerful Amalgamated Metal Workers' and Ship-wrights' Union and branches who saw Hayden as their ideological ally, were putting pressure on the parliamentarians to support him and reject Hawke. Lionel Bowen would not move to Hawke simply on the basis of public opinion polls. If that was to be the test, he asked a colleague, 'why not go all the way and elect Jane Fonda as leader?'

The battleground in the struggle for numbers was staked out in

Sydney. Hawke had set up headquarters in the Persian Room of the Wentworth Hotel while Hayden was operating nearby in his Chifley Square office. Paul Keating, then New South Wales president, soon became a key player in a role he had not sought. Hawke's run in 1982, he later said, was an 'ill-conceived, ill-timed, ill-thought-through, ill-advised operation'.

> We were just finishing a National Conference where Bill emerged as a winner and a bloke who defended the things we wanted defended . . . after that were we to say that it was no good, that we wanted somebody else? Bob was sort of running without talking to us, he was running without us for a while. Everything has a natural timing in politics and that was out of sync.[17]

At the start of the battle Keating told both Hawke and Hayden that he intended to back Hayden as leader provided Hayden could hold the support of the Left and his own group in the Centre and Centre Left.

Suddenly, with the return of the Left to Hayden, and Keating refusing to endorse him, Hawke was in dire trouble. Journalist Michael Gawenda returned with him to Melbourne when he retreated from Sydney without any assurances from the Right:

> . . . his mood had changed dramatically. In the car on the way to the airport he sat low in his seat, his head on his chest, his overcoat collar drawn up around his ears. It was raining and the only sound in the car was the beating of the windscreen wipers . . . all he said during the 20 minute drive to the airport was that he was tired . . .[18]

Hawke was saved from humiliation partly by the intervention of two left-wing unionists, Laurie Carmichael, a member of the Communist Party, and John Halfpenny, who had recently resigned from the Communist Party, in support of Hayden. In a national broadcast Halfpenny said: 'We feel that Bill Hayden would make a better leader of the Labor Party because he has a deeper, a more honest commitment to the Labor movement and the policies of the Labor Party.' He said he thought it was pretty common knowledge that Hawke had left the ACTU because he wanted to be Prime Minister rather than out of commitment to the Labor movement. This gave Keating, who had been under intense pressure from Richardson to save Hawke from an unmerciful drubbing, both a motive and excuse to switch to Hawke. On Wednesday, 14 July, Keating announced that the New South Wales Right would support Hayden without reservation if he won the ballot two days later, but added:

'I believe, however, that the New South Wales members will take the view that the best interests of the Labor Party, and the millions of Australians who deserve and need a Labor victory and the end of Fraserism, will be best served by Bob Hawke now becoming leader.' Keating, according to Barbara Ward, his closest adviser, had gone through hell for four days while coming to this decision; he knew that, if Hawke got the leadership, his own ambitions would be frustrated for the foreseeable future; he was not overly impressed with Hawke's ability, and he had a sense of loyalty to Hayden, with whom he had worked for ten years.[19] On the other hand he knew that some members of the Right, including Hayden's former close friend Dick Klugman, would not vote for Hayden. The Right depended for its strength on its unity. If he wanted to maintain his credentials with it he had to be part of the fight. When he went over to Hawke at the last possible moment he threw himself with vigour into the campaign, and, being Keating, expected to win.

Hawke and his supporters weren't the only ones fighting hard. Months earlier Queensland Labor MP Bob Gibbs had made a scathing attack on Hawke's friend Eddie Kornhauser who had been an applicant for a Gold Coast casino licence. Now a staff member from Hayden's office telephoned Gibbs alerting him to the fact that a Sydney journalist was working on an article reviving the allegations and the Hawke–Kornhauser connection. Gibbs obliged by contacting the journalist and offering assistance.

Hayden, arriving at Parliament House on the morning of the ballot, rugged up in an overcoat on a bleak Canberra winter's day, observed to waiting journalists: 'There are chilly winds on the plains of Philippi.' He went into a discussion of tactics with a group that included John Button and Hayden's staunchest supporters, Peter Walsh, John Dawkins, Neal Blewett, and John Kerin. There was a discussion of tactics during which Button, who had told Hayden privately that he did not think he could beat Hawke, said Hayden had to win by a convincing margin for his leadership to be valid. When the Caucus met at eleven o'clock Hayden said there would be no debate, and declared the leadership vacant. After the ballot had been taken, but before the votes had been counted, Peter Walsh turned to him and said: 'Even if it's very close, you hang on and don't let those bastards take over.' Hayden won the ballot by forty-two votes to thirty-seven for Hawke. When he returned to his office the staff cheered and ordered champagne. The Parliament House chef sent a cake with the words 'Isaiah Chapter 57, Verse 18' piped in icing on the top.

A Bible was found and the words of the verse read aloud: 'I have seen his ways, and will heal him: I will lead him also, and restore comforts unto him and his mourners.' Minutes later Hawke arrived in Hayden's office suite. It was an awkward moment. Hayden hesitated and then ushered him into his private office, closing the door. Minutes later a staff member had to buzz Hayden and inform him that Hazel Hawke had also arrived.

Hayden, Hawke and Bowen then held a joint press conference, and Hayden was asked whether he would now appoint Hawke to the electoral strategy committee. When, with a laugh, he answered 'Yes', Hawke said: 'What a hell of a way to announce it!' Hayden said: 'What a hell of a way to prove you've had to get there.' It was a frenetic little exchange, with brittle laughter covering deep divisions and difficulties for the Labor Party, whose internal conflicts and personal rivalries had been exposed.

NINETEEN

Flinders

*Was it necessary to try to take my balls
away in the process?*

Bill Hayden

IN THE WINTER of 1982, Malcolm Fraser probed the Labor Party's open wounds with merciless fascination. A Federal election was not due until the end of 1983, but Fraser had reason, apart from the opportunity offered by the conflict between Hayden and Hawke, to consider going to the polls early: he feared the world was moving towards recession. His political instinct was that Hayden would remain vulnerable to challenge from Hawke, and he feared fighting an election against Hawke more than he did against Hayden.

To clear the decks for action if an opportunity arose, Fraser used his brutal strength, built by electoral success and a dominating personality, to force an election budget on Treasury and his reluctant Treasurer, John Howard. Fraser's ability to make them act against their instincts and principles was a measure of his power and ruthlessness. One of the results was that his claim to a place in political history as a man of rigorous principle was greatly diminished: the Budget, with an expanded deficit and large personal tax cuts, contradicted all his previous economic policies and the very philosophy of Fraserism.

He then got stuck in the mud in his rush to an early election. Soon after Hayden had defeated Hawke in the July challenge a new Morgan Gallup poll showed a sharp increase in his standing as Opposition leader. Graham Richardson sent Hayden a telegram which said: 'Congratulations on the Bulletin poll. Your popularity now matches that of the National president [at that time Neville Wran]. We really did you a favour.' Hayden replied: 'I had not quite looked at the matter from this point of view, but I suppose that your motivation was to do me a big favour. However, was it necesary to try to take my balls away in the process?' The sensitive Richardson framed the exchange and displayed it on his office wall.

Hawke's July challenge established him as Hayden's successor; it also put Hayden on notice that his performance would be under constant and unsympathetic scrutiny. Any reverse would be exploited by Hawke and his ambitious lieutenants who now had a concrete measure of how few converts they needed for their cause to triumph. Some, including Richardson, officials of the Labor Party in Canberra and of the ACTU, and some business backers of Hawke, were not content to wait for the natural run of political events to determine Hayden's future; they set out to create traps and difficulties for him.

In the view of many of his supporters Hayden did not react appropriately to his victory over Hawke; he took no retaliatory measures against people who had worked against him, who included paid officers of the Labor Party, nor did he move to bring into the fold influential people like Paul Keating who had been impressed by his actions at the National Conference and ambivalent about joining the Hawke caravan, and who had ability that more than justified promotion. Hayden paid little attention either to those who still harboured doubts about Hawke's commitment to Labor policy and were also nauseated by his self-centred ambition and sense of destiny.

Richardson's pointed reference to Neville Wran's popularity in his telegram to Hayden was meant as nothing more than a minor irritant, a bit of gratuitous provocation. Richardson had now attached his fortunes firmly to Hawke's star. Even Wran had come to realise, after Hawke's impressive showing in the July Caucus leadership ballot, that he had left his own run for Canberra too late. Graham Richardson suggested to Wran that if he offered New South Wales Senator Doug McClelland a suitable job this would create a vacancy for the New South Wales Premier in the Senate. 'Thanks, but I would want to be in the first eleven,' said Wran, who realised then that the controllers of the New South Wales machine had placed their chips on a Hawke win and were going to ride with him. On 4 August 1982, Wran announced that, in a 'decision that was made easier by half a bottle of Rosemount Estate Gold Medal chardonnay' he had abandoned all plans to go to Canberra.

The Labor Party was not alone in experiencing internal difficulties at this time. The pressures that were to result in Hayden losing the leadership were intensified, and eventually given focus, by a parallel struggle in the Liberal Government. Ironically, the tactics used by Malcolm Fraser earlier in the year to secure his leadership against Andrew Peacock not only precipitated the events that led to Hayden losing the Labor leadership, but also contributed to the end of Fraser's own political career.

In his relationship with his leader, Andrew Peacock was a pale Liberal Party version of Bob Hawke. Through the early months of 1982 Fraser had suffered increasing criticism from his party rival with decreasing patience. The day after the Victorian Liberals lost the State election to John Cain on 3 April 1982, Peacock publicly criticised the party leadership. Fraser threw down the gauntlet the same day, calling a special party meeting to resolve the leadership issue.[1] Although Peacock was not known for strong views on economic or any other issues, he had managed to attract support from a group of 'dries' on the Liberal back bench virtually by default: they regarded Fraser's deputy, Phillip Lynch, as a protectionist and, as such, an ideological enemy. Fraser countered this handicap with a typical lack of sentiment by dumping Lynch, who was unable to hold the position without Fraser's support. Fraser backed John Howard who was acceptable to the 'dries' and then proceeded to thrash Peacock by fifty-four votes to twenty-seven in the party ballot. The Peacock problem was solved, but the dumping of Lynch was to have repercussions beyond the imaginings of Fraser: later in the year he got even by retiring in mid-term and forcing a by-election.

Fraser's expansionary Budget in August 1982 shamelessly appropriated Hayden's policies, giving families an average of $16.84 extra disposable income each week, where Hayden had proposed $16. But when his thoughts turned to planning an early election in the belief that 'the world was sliding towards another depression and fearing that the charismatic Hawke might soon displace Hayden whom Fraser had beaten before and was convinced he could defeat again'[2] Fraser was faced with endless frustrations. His party organisation adopted delaying tactics because its key figures wanted to avoid an election they believed Hayden would win. In the end, the organisation was able to prevent Fraser going to the polls against Hayden only because of unrelated, unexpected events: the devastating report of the Costigan Royal Commission and, later, Fraser's ill health. Costigan, who had been given a brief to inquire into criminal activities within the Victorian Ship Painters' and Dockers' Union, released his report in October 1982. It revealed tax avoidance on a massive and organised scale. Fraser, the towering puritan squatter, was outraged by Costigan's revelations and gave notice that he intended to purge the Liberal Party of the tax dodgers and fast-buck merchants that had infested it. On 27 October the party's chief executive, Tony Eggleton, Liberal Federal president Jim Forbes and the State presidents of the party reported to Fraser that they believed Hayden would win an election at that time.

On 31 October Fraser was admitted to hospital where he underwent surgery for a recurring back complaint. He had abandoned for the time being his early general election plans, but had selected 4 December, the date he had favoured for a national poll, as the day for the fateful Flinders by-election to fill the vacancy caused by the resignation of Phillip Lynch.

Within a week Bob Hawke had once again publicly paraded his naked ambition and was, as a consequence, in deep difficulty within the Labor Party. On 5 November he appeared on Michael Schildberger's midday show on ABC radio in Melbourne and discussed yet another public opinion poll which, he said, showed that the electors 'did not seem to be thoroughly approving of the performance and the style and the priorities' of the Labor Party under Hayden's leadership.

During the Schildberger interview Hawke referred to 'pretty wide-spread concern', and threw in a few of the code words that he thought would be likely to encourage Caucus colleagues to review the leadership: 'what the party may want to do or not to do is a matter for the party ... I can't and don't control my colleagues ...' His comments were widely reported, and Hayden was forced to respond publicly, saying that repeated remarks on the leadership 'would inject extraordinarily desta-bilising influences' into the Labor Party at a particularly unfortunate time — during the Flinders campaign and while there was still speculation about an early election. Even some of Hawke's most committed sup-porters realised he had stepped outside acceptable bounds, and two of those closest to him, Gareth Evans and Clyde Holding, persuaded him that a strategic retreat was necessary. Using a text they had helped

him draft, Hawke wrote to all seventy-seven members of Caucus on 8
November saying that his remarks had been misinterpreted and saying:

> I stand by absolutely the commitment I made at the joint Press conference
> on 16 July where — in answer to the question, 'Can you guarantee that
> there will be no further challenge before the next election?' — I answered,
> 'Yes'. Far from wishing in any way to destabilise the party, I will continue,
> as I was last week in South Australia and Tasmania — to campaign
> vigorously for the party.[3]

Hayden's Flinders campaign started disastrously, and did not improve.
At his first press conference, Hayden was extolling the virtues of Labor's
candidate when Laurie Oakes asked his name. Hayden had forgotten.
'You rotten bastard,' he said to Oakes. The name of the candidate, Rogan
Ward, a man accurately described by Paul Kelly as having a Prince Valiant
haircut and a build like Mickey Rooney, was one Hayden would later have
cause to remember. Ward was an aggressive real estate agent; in the last
week of the campaign *The Age* accused his firm of having been engaged
in unethical practices to inflate the price of houses. Ward had the twin
disadvantages of being unpopular and well known. He had been selected
as Labor's candidate before Lynch resigned and when it was assumed that
he would simply carry the banner for Labor in what was a safe Liberal
seat during a normal election. Labor needed a 5.5 per cent swing to win
the seat, and the fact that this was about the average swing against
governments in by-elections now made a victory critical if Hayden was
to maintain his authority. On the opening night of Labor's campaign
Hayden gave an off-the-cuff speech that was rambling and unprofessional.
The television journalists could extract no news or theme from it, and
Hayden and his staff were unable to help them in their efforts. Peter
Barron who was there in his capacity as adviser to Wran returned to
Sydney and reported to Richardson on the fiasco.

Rogan Ward and his own stumbling performance were not to be
Hayden's major problems during the Flinders campaign, however.

The restless Fraser, confined to Melbourne's Freemason's Hospital by
his sciatic back, was on a new crusade. A former West Australian premier,
Sir Charles Court, had visited him in Canberra just before he entered
hospital and had converted him to the concept of a national wage freeze,
with the savings being used for employment-creating projects. It was an
idea with immense appeal to Fraser who was still looking for an early
election strategy. He seized on Court's idea as giving him a way in which

he could be seen to be attacking the critical economic situation; there were then 650 000 unemployed and inflation was above 9 per cent. Court had convinced Fraser too of the political attractiveness of the proposal, which was represented as an appeal to the Australian ethos of mateship and idealism: here was a way in which ordinary Australians could make a minor sacrifice, giving up something which they didn't even have in the certainty that by doing so they would create jobs for the unfortunate young people who couldn't get a job. Fraser could also hold out the hope that such a small sacrifice could perhaps pin back inflation a little in the process, and even teach the greedy unions a lesson.

Court's scheme for wages to be frozen for a year fitted perfectly the mood of national uncertainty, the yearning for solutions and leadership of the time. Liberal ministers John Howard and Ian McPhee worked on giving flesh to Court's skeleton, costing its benefits and exploring ways of implementing it. McPhee visited Fraser in hospital, briefing him on details and gaining his approval. On 15 November Cabinet, under Acting Prime Minister Doug Anthony, proposed a special Premiers' Conference for 7 December to gain the support and cooperation of the States. What neither Fraser nor Court realised was that the main political effect of the exercise would be to drive a wedge between Hayden and the trade union movement and isolate Hayden further from the Labor premiers, Wran, Cain and Bannon.

As early as August, Hayden had initiated discussions with the ACTU in an attempt to achieve an accord under which there would be restraint in wage claims in return for social benefits introduced by a Hayden Labor government: employment-creation, training initiatives, better schooling, more adequate health services, tax cuts and other assistance to unionists and their families. But, at an August meeting in Melbourne between Hayden and some of his parliamentary Executive members, including Hawke, Willis and Bowen, there was an angry row between Hayden and Hawke's successor as ACTU president, Cliff Dolan. Dolan, a dour, old-fashioned union bureaucrat, would give Hayden no comfort. He made it clear to the Labor leader that neither he nor the ACTU would retreat from their insistence that wage rises should at least match inflation and that this should be achieved through automatic wage increases indexed to rises in the Consumer Price Index. This, Hayden's supporters still believe, marked the start of a conspiracy by some key ACTU figures to sabotage Hayden and ensure that Bob Hawke, one of their own and a man who understood them, became Labor's leader.

The differences were brought into sharp public focus when the Executive of the Federal parliamentary Labor Party and the ACTU Executive held separate meetings, a week apart in the countdown to the Flinders by-election, to decide how to deal with Fraser's wage freeze proposal. On 22 November Hayden announced the parliamentary party's attitude: a freeze, he said, was totally unfair and would worsen the collapse of the Australian economy that he said was then occurring. On 30 November the ACTU announced it was prepared to recommend to unions that they give serious consideration to taking part in a freeze provided certain conditions were met. The conditions were not far from those Hayden had been proposing as the basis of an accord. Now, he believed, the ACTU was offering Fraser the comfort it had denied him.

Hayden felt betrayed, but worse was to come. On 2 December, in the company of Bowen and Hawke, he met the ACTU Executive in Melbourne and flatly accused its members of a breach of faith. That, in the view of Lionel Bowen and Neville Wran, was the end of any possibility Hayden ever had of establishing a relationship with the trade union movement, and, in effect, meant his days as Labor leader were numbered. The meeting broke up without any progress being made on a joint approach to the wage freeze. The media were waiting when the participants emerged. Dolan refused to hold a press conference, but Hayden revealed to the media that the meeting had failed to reach agreement, and went on answering questions on the breach. 'Next to him Hawke smoked a cigar, blowing rings into the air, and catching the glance of journalists, rolled his eyes towards his head.'[4] The next day the Labor State premiers met the ACTU and reached agreement on a joint approach to the wage freeze. Paul Kelly reported that afterwards Wran had said to a colleague: 'I think this could be the end of Hayden. These blokes will never forgive the way he spoke to them.'[5]

Hayden had been playing in Hawke's backyard, and he had been mugged. He may have survived, however, if Labor had polled better in the Flinders by-election. The poll took place two days after the breakdown of his talks with the ACTU and the day after the ACTU agreement with the premiers. From the tally-room on the Mornington Peninsula, Alan Ramsey was overheard as he kept Hayden informed of the progress of counting by telephone: 'Bill, it's a disaster. It's just a disaster,' he said. At the close of counting it was clear Labor would get a swing of less than half of the 5.5 per cent it needed for victory. Peter Bowers drove

Ramsey through the night back up the peninsula to Melbourne. 'He never said a word. There was a desperate silence. He knew what the implications were,' Bowers recalled.[6] The following day Bowers wrote an analysis of the result for the *Sydney Morning Herald* which appeared on Monday, 6 December. Discussing the sequence of events in 1989, Bowers recalled: 'I said I didn't think there would be any immediate moves, as the country was about to go into its political dead period. I thought the Christmas–New Year holiday would be Hayden's comfort blanket, insulating him. Early in the morning, about the time the papers hit the front lawns, I got a call from Graham Richardson, in his usual blunt style: "You rotten bastard," Richo said, "you are condemning us to the Opposition benches forever. We know you love Hayden, but will you lay off it? If you keep pumping him up like that, we'll never get rid of him."'

Bowers, as political correspondent of the *Sydney Morning Herald*, exercised considerable influence in moulding public opinion. As one of the veterans of the press gallery he also shaped the opinions of other less confident commentators. 'I realised then that they were out after him, and they had to light a fire under him and give it time to get going over that Christmas–New Year period. I realised then that they were going to get him. Channel 9 used to have a Christmas show on the Sunday program and we all used to get around a rose garden and everyone was asked to make fearless forecasts, and I said I couldn't see how Hayden could survive. I still thought Hawke should do his apprenticeship, and that Hayden was the more experienced and better leader because he'd come through the fires of '75. But they took that to mean I'd dumped Hayden.'[7]

Political issues in the close community of Australian politics, and more particularly in the intimate, incestuous world of Canberra, are reduced at the practical level to issues of personality. Richardson was aware how vulnerable Hayden was at this vital aspect of the political game, how ineffectual he was in the manipulation of relationships, the exploitation of weaknesses and the fuelling of ambitions.

Hayden saw his survival as resting on his ability to develop effective and popular policies. With a small group of his trusted advisers he had embarked through December and January on developing the policy that would be the key to the party's election campaign. The central theme had been suggested by Clem Lloyd, Hayden's former private secretary who had by then taken a position at the Australian National University. In a paper presented to the party's campaign committee in September

1982, Lloyd suggested that the concept of reconstruction had a powerful appeal to Australians. Hayden was enthusiastic about the idea, and considerable party resources were being devoted to its development. Lloyd later expanded the theme, emphasising the damage that had been done to the economy during the Fraser years, and naming the program 'Recovery and Reconstruction'.

But Richardson knew that personalities and not policies were the key. He had decided that his crucial task in finishing Hayden was to erode his confidence in himself, to complete his isolation. 'I saw it as a job to do, and went out and did it,' Richardson said. 'It was a nasty job, and that means you acquire a nasty reputation; that's one part I regret. With the benefit of hindsight, I'd have to say I'd do it all again. It needed to be done: I didn't think Bill would win, and I thought Hawke would be a better Prime Minister. There were two things I worked on that were devastating blows; one was Button and the other was Peter Bowers. I worked on Bowers for months and finally heard him talking about the need for a change of leader. Button's defection didn't mean much in terms of numbers — he's never had much influence over numbers — but psychologically to Hayden it was a devastating blow. Bowers and Button were blows to Hayden's morale that he just couldn't get over. They hurt him badly: that is what they were designed to do.'[8] Richardson's aim was to break Hayden's spirit and induce him to resign. He could never be confident that, if Hayden fought, the rest of the party would be prepared to have an open battle when there was an election looming. He thus concentrated on seeking defections of those Hayden trusted.

During the uranium debate at the 1982 National Conference, John Button had asked Hayden to be given permission to vote against the changes Hayden and Hogg were advocating, although he agreed with them. His preselection as Labor's Senate candidate was to take place later that year and he feared he would not survive if he opposed the Left. Hayden granted him a special dispensation.[9]

Later Button and Hawke had a chance meeting in the lavatory of the Commonwealth offices in Sydney. As Blanche d'Alpuget records, Button volunteered to Hawke: 'Before the vote [in Hawke's first challenge] I'd told Bill that a close win wasn't enough. As soon as the vote was over, Bill said to me "are five votes enough?" and I replied "No" ... Hawke saw the exchange as of great significance.'[10] Button was a free spirit once his preselection was out of the way. Richardson, who was still New South

Wales secretary, made two trips to Canberra, the first on 14 December, to convert him to the Hawke cause. 'By the time Button committed himself, I think we were there anyway; it was a matter of trying to make sure it was not close. To make it unanimous. His importance was psychological,' Richardson said later.

Button had been Hayden's closest political confidant. Successive staff members operating the telephone in Hayden's office had been told that Button was one person who was to be put straight through, no matter what the circumstances. Hayden and Dallas had spent hours comforting Button's youngest son on the day of the funeral of his elder brother, who had died of a heroin overdose. Yet Button's loyalty had limits that were exceeded by his ambition both for himself and his party. His motives, in terms of politics, were entirely honourable; the importance of the role he saw for himself was one that he held with a burning desire that was belied by his casual, whimsical exterior. He had been in the Labor Party long enough to see whole lives and bright talents wasted and twisted in the sterility of opposition. He was an influential member of the group that had made possible reform of the Victorian branch of the Labor Party and later the coup that installed John Cain in the party's State leadership and spelt the end of Liberal hegemony in that State. Richardson played on that ego, telling Button that Hayden should have rewarded him with more important responsibilities. Richardson put forward his case with the conviction of a believer: if Labor did not win the 1983 election it was in danger of becoming politically irrelevant; another political generation that would include Button would have wasted their careers. It was not long before Button was complaining to Uren that Hayden was not consulting him and that he had got little in return for all the work he had done for him. Richardson kept in daily contact with Hawke and with Button as Christmas 1982 approached.

There is a story widely told of an incident that is said to have occurred in the members' bar at Parliament House a week after the Flinders by-election. Hayden went to the bar where a group of Labor parliamentarians, including Lionel Bowen, Ben Humphries, Gareth Evans and Senator Doug McClelland were drinking. They invited him to join them. Hayden said he wouldn't join the shout, and would pay for his own drink. Then, it is said, he borrowed 10 cents from Evans so that he would not have to break a $2 note to pay for his beer. In the wake of Flinders, with his leadership under threat, it would have been sensible politics to pay for a round, one of the members present said later. 'It's all part of his insecurity,' said another more charitably. Hawke's social ease led him into different difficulties. 'If somebody said "g'day" to him, he thought they were making a commitment to vote for him,' a colleague said.

When Parliament rose in the third week in December, Button was going to Fiji for a holiday, but, before he left, Richardson had extracted from him a commitment that he would speak to Hayden about the leadership. Once again the Hawke forces showed they were not going to let the blaze they had lit under Hayden die down for want of fuel. On Christmas Eve, before Button had had time to rub on the coconut oil, a story by Greg Hywood appeared on the front page of the *Financial Review* saying that, while in Fiji, Button would decide whether or not his group would continue to support Hayden. Button, said Hywood, was expected to fly to Queensland on his return. Richardson and his confidants in New South Wales were the only people who knew of Button's intentions.

On Christmas Day Tom Uren rang Hayden at home and told him that he should no longer trust Button. He advised Hayden to appoint Keating as shadow Treasurer. This was a complete backflip by Uren, who had virtually vetoed the same proposal to promote Keating when Hayden had made it at a dinner at Charlies restaurant in Canberra a few weeks earlier. At the dinner Uren had also told Bowen that the New South Wales Left would not accept such a move. Now Uren told Hayden the move was essential to keep his forces in balance: he was going to need support from the Right to survive against Hawke. The degree of difference in Uren's positions alerted Hayden to the seriousness of his own situation.

The phone call was one of the last of many on a matter of political importance between the two men, who had shared an ambiguous relationship for more than twenty years. There was a combination of affection and distrust on both sides, and occasions when each attempted to use the other for political advantage. One of Hayden's strongest supporters openly regarded Uren as a fool and a nuisance, but Uren on occasions was able to give support to Hayden that some of his more academically gifted followers could not deliver. Hayden and Uren often told critical little anecdotes about each other. Uren sometimes recalled an occasion when he had addressed the 1979 ALP National Conference in Adelaide, attacking ASIO and asking for restrictions on its phone-tapping powers. Hayden had defended the security services, and, in a clear reference to Uren, had said that some Labor Party members were a bit paranoid in believing their telephones were tapped. A little while later he was talking to Uren on the telephone, and said: 'Remind me to tell you something when we're not on the telephone.' Hayden tells a story about Uren ringing him to attempt to convince him to drop plans to modify the Labor Party's uranium policy. Uren, referring to discussions he had been having with rank-and-file members of the Labor Party, began by saying, 'I have been talking to the little people'. Hayden genuinely thought Uren, a keen horticulturist, had flipped and was talking to pixies at the bottom of his garden.

'Hayden spent a bitter Christmas period,' Geoff Kitney and John Hurst later wrote in the *National Times*. 'He was aware that conversations had been going on behind his back as Hawke's supporters sensed that the chance to topple Hayden was moving inexorably closer. The tension was immense and increased by the circulation of some very nasty stories about Hayden's emotional stability after a family crisis.'[11] Button flew to stay with his Victorian colleague Michael Duffy at Coolangatta on the Gold Coast and on 6 January drove to Brisbane for a critical lunch with Hayden in a restaurant across the street from Hayden's office. Hayden went to lunch believing he had lost Button's support before they met, while Button later told colleagues that it was during that lunch he became convinced that Hayden should stand aside for Hawke. Over lunch he told Hayden that he would not move against him, but Hayden correctly assumed that by giving that limited undertaking he was leaving himself the option of supporting any move against him. At the lunch Hayden told Button he was an existentialist and that he was prepared to accept responsibility for his actions. Hayden went on to describe his attitude as resembling that of Macbeth, who, when he came to fight his final battle with Macduff, never asked for mercy. Button recalled him saying, 'If I lose the election, I won't be asking anyone for mercy'.[12] 'It was quite a cheerful thing,' Hayden told a colleague later. 'He explained his position, and was quite proper about it ... and allowed me to pay for the lunch.'

Hayden determined to fight back, and flew back to Canberra on 12 January. He spent the next afternoon and evening trying to contact Paul Keating, finally establishing contact some time after eleven o'clock on the night of 13 January. He told Keating he had decided to demote Ralph Willis and that Keating was to be shadow Treasurer. When Keating told Hawke what had happened he was furious, and not sure how to turn.

'He's fucked us all. He's fucked you by giving you the job. He's fucked Ralph and he's fucked me.'[13] Hayden's move was a piece of cleverly divisive politics, but it was six months too late to protect his own position. It was, however, to have a significant impact on Australian economic management: Keating rebuffed Hawke's attempts to remove him from Treasury and restore Willis after the election, and became the most significant figure in three Hawke governments.

Malcolm Fraser returned to Canberra on 11 January 1983, the day before Hayden, and within two weeks had fixed on March for an early election. Having been frustrated by the party machine when he had wanted to call an election in early December the previous year, he determined this time to simply ignore it. The drama was now building to a climax with all the conflicting interests now aware that there was movement in the rival camps. The Hawke forces knew their task was urgent; they had to force Hayden out before Fraser called an election. Fraser knew that Hayden's days were numbered, and wanted to call the election before Hawke was installed as leader. The key to the outcome lay in the complex personality of Bill Hayden. Fraser was convinced that Hayden would only go in a way which would leave blood all over the floor, and the Labor Party so wounded that it could not mount an effective election campaign. The Hawke forces determined they would sandbag Hayden into submission. Some were prepared to force another vote and then clean up the blood afterwards; others, no kinder to Hayden, but politically more cautious, determined to hold back the Rambos in their ranks and submit Hayden to unrelenting stress and psychological pressure. Hayden, aware of new moves against him, made several phone calls to Bowen in late January. 'He was very Delphic. He never warned me. He seemed more distant than ever, and I assumed that meant he had written me off.'

The Hawke forces had a setback on 17 January when the Left, which had been under intense pressure to dump Hayden, met and decided to stick with him. But the Hawke forces had their own power base outside politics, the ACTU Executive. In early January Hayden had begun to move towards the ACTU's original position on the wage freeze, saying that while he considered it was a 'gimmick' he believed the trade union movement should try to make it work. On 18 January in a major address to the Australian Workers' Union in Sydney, Hayden went further and said that there was a need to curb wage increases to ensure that the profit share of the economy was restored to reasonable levels. The same day the ACTU announced that it was mounting a campaign against the wage freeze. Hayden was stranded once again, this time on the opposite side of the river from where he had been on the eve of the Flinders by-election when the ACTU was talking about accepting the freeze.

The pressure was stepped up the following day when the parliamentary Executive assembled in Canberra for the first meeting following the reshuffle. Mick Young raised Hayden's change of position on the wage freeze, and Hayden hit back by blaming Hawke, who he said was meant to be responsible for industrial relations and wages policy. Hawke, he said, had not condemned the freeze. Hayden also argued that support for a claim by oil workers for a substantial wage rise would play into Fraser's hands. If they began an industrial campaign which caused inconvenience and disruption Fraser would call a snap general election. Hawke put forward a motion supporting the oil workers and rejecting the freeze, and got the support of the majority of the Executive. This was the first and only open clash between the two men during an Executive meeting. Hawke was calmer and handled himself more confidently; Hayden was shrill and angry and isolated. Hayden went along with the Hawke line on the freeze and the oil workers' claim, even agreeing to issue the press announcement under his name, because he still had hopes that he could finalise agreement on a prices and incomes accord with the ACTU and launch it on 16 February. It would be the centrepiece of his election strategy. The Executive meeting instructed Hawke and Ralph Willis to step up negotiations with the ACTU on the accord, and also resolved that Hayden would separately launch his Reconstruction and Recovery policy, final details of which were to be discussed at a meeting of the National Campaign Committee in Sydney the following day.

The ACTU conspiracy now came to full flower. Graham Richardson and Mick Young had breakfast with Hawke in his suite at the Boulevard Hotel in Sydney the next morning, 20 January. They were determined that the man they were going to dump was not going to be given the opportunity to launch an economic policy that could save his leadership as well as the nation. Hawke rang ACTU president Cliff Dolan, who agreed to torpedo Hayden's plan. Dolan had an office in Sydney on one of the lower floors of Labor's head office in Sussex Street where Hayden was preparing for the campaign committee meeting on the ninth floor.

'It was a classic meeting,' Hayden said later. 'For me it was a historic determinant in influencing things. Mick Young came in and said, "Cliff Dolan wants to talk to you downstairs". I said "That's strange ... I didn't know he was in town". So I went down. He was sitting in a room by himself. There was no one else there, which I thought was strange. He told me the ACTU Executive had decided they'd not go ahead with the prices–incomes agreement, it was finished. And I thought, "Well, I know what that means ... it means they've more or less declared war on me. As far as they're concerned, I'm finished ... it's just a matter of time." ' In fact Dolan had told Hayden the unions wanted to delay any further discussions until after a special unions conference on 21 February. Hayden had got the right message though: as long as he was leader there would be no accord.

That night, in the same building, Mick Young addressed a seminar for all New South Wales 1983 Federal election candidates. After his assessment of the political scene he asked candidates if they had any questions. Jim Snow, who was contesting for the second time the seat of Eden Monaro, on the fringe of Canberra, asked: 'Yes. When are you going to change the leader?' Snow then launched into an emotional speech, breaking into tears at one point, during which he said that Hayden had done much to help him, but that he thought that without Hawke he had no chance of achieving the swing of 3 per cent he needed to win the seat. At dinner that night Young told several other candidates who had been at the seminar that a feeling similar to that expressed by Snow was universal among candidates in marginal seats and had spread through party branches across the country. Lionel Bowen was at the meeting and told colleagues later than Snow's speech had finally convinced him that Hayden had to be persuaded to step down.

Clyde Cameron, who had long believed the leadership should be changed and who had precipitated the first challenge to Hayden with his comments on radio, was again anxious to promote Hawke's cause. He rang Lionel Bowen and suggested the use of a tactic that they had last discussed when attempting to depose Gough Whitlam in favour of Hayden, the organisation of a petition to be signed quickly and secretly by a majority of Caucus. Bowen sternly warned him not to take any action, telling him that matters were under control and a better scheme was in place. He ended the conversation cryptically: 'Bill will bail if a gun is held at his head.' Bob Hawke and Mick Young independently proposed that a delegation should approach Hayden asking him to stand aside. Keating and Button talked them out of this approach, fearing that Hayden might feel they were trying to bully him, and react in his typical fashion by refusing to give ground or be stood over.

Button made another visit to Brisbane on 27 January to help launch the Queensland Senate campaign, and although he spent some hours in Hayden's company found it impossible to speak to him alone. Hayden at one stage invited him into a room at the State Parliament House but invited his biographer Denis Murphy to accompany them. The next day Button in Melbourne wrote a crucial letter in which he appealed to Hayden, as a friend rather than as an emissary for the Hawke forces, to stand down for the good of the Labor Party. His key point was that the Labor Party was desperate to win the election. He said Hayden could not win an election without the support of the ordinary members of the party and that morale among them was very bad. Button's letter was a clever blend of brutality and cajolery: he told Hayden his performance had declined considerably since he had narrowly won the July challenge; he no longer had any significant support in Caucus, the State leadership or the party organisation; and that his talk about Hamlet at their previous meeting had been bullshit. But he also told Hayden that he had the respect of even those colleagues who had difficulty working with him, and that he would retain that if he stepped aside. Many of those colleagues had deep reservations about Hawke, Button said, and he felt if Labor was to be defeated he would prefer it to happen under Hawke. As for Hayden's earlier comment that he didn't want to step down 'for a bastard like Hawke', Button pointed out that being a bastard had never been a disqualification for political leadership. By the time he read the letter Hayden had been told by a source in Canberra that Fraser was planning to call a March election.

Hayden made his decision to resign at home in Ipswich on Sunday, 30 January. It was not then irrevocable, but he resisted stirring calls to battle by the most loyal and toughest of his supporters, Peter Walsh, who urged him to fight on. Walsh later remarked that Hayden was surprised that people like Walsh, John Dawkins and Neal Blewett were prepared to stick their necks out in his defence and risk their careers against the conquering Hawke forces. Having decided to go, Hayden then purpose-fully, and without consulting anybody, began to list the conditions under which he would go. 'It was part of looking after myself,' Hayden said later of the conditions he had drafted. 'I've been round long enough to do that much. Assurance is handy, whether you're dealing with the Mafia, or the chieftains of political clans.'

On Monday morning Hayden rang Button in Melbourne and told him he wanted to discuss the matters he had raised; there were things to be settled. The funeral of former Labor Prime Minister Frank Forde was to be held at St Thomas Aquinas Church in Brisbane on Tuesday, 1 February, and Hayden suggested they meet for a private discussion afterwards. As Button knelt behind Hayden at the funeral service he was aware this was to be the crunch: Richardson had already warned him that if his techniques of persuasion failed the heavy mob were prepared to move; they were not squeamish about cracking some skulls and spilling blood.

The first phase of the three-hour negotiations in Hayden's office in the Commonwealth Centre in Ann Street in Brisbane consisted of Hayden testing Button's resolution, of putting forward his case for being retained as leader for the election that could be announced at any time. Button persuaded him that he no longer had support. Then the whole political map of Australia changed. Fraser was back in Canberra working without a compass, unaware that he would be fighting his election battle on unfamiliar ground.

'We started putting things in place,' Hayden recalls. I said: "If I'm going to step down I want some bloody guarantees. I'm not going to start with all the bloody hackwork again as a minister. If we are going to make Government, and I'm certain we will, I want to be Foreign Minister until after I get out, and I want to get out after twelve months and go to London." ' Button assured Hayden that there would be no problems about Bowen handing over the Foreign Ministry if Hawke led Labor to government.

There was an ironic interruption to the earnest negotiation. Elaine Darling, a Queensland Federal Labor MP, was on holiday on Lord Howe Island, and had heard a broadcast suggesting Hayden was in trouble. She had waited hours to get through by telephone to his office. A staff member entered Hayden's office to tell him that she was on the phone and could not hold on for long or ring back. Hayden said: 'Find out what she wants,' The staff member said: 'I know what it's about, she wants to tell you to ignore all the people who are telling you to go.' After a short silence, Hayden said: 'Put her through, and hold all other calls.'

Two other conditions Hayden imposed were to benefit others, but had not been discussed with them. He wanted the jobs of his staff members guaranteed and assurances from Hawke that his main supporters, Peter Walsh, John Dawkins and Neal Blewett, would not be victimised, and in government would be given portfolios which matched the responsibilities Hayden had given them in his shadow ministry.

It was an emotionally draining meeting for both men, and at the end, when they both shed tears, Hayden told Button he was worried about the impact it might have on his children. They parted with the understanding that Hayden would resign the following weekend. Button flew back to Melbourne that evening, stopping at Sydney airport for two hours to talk to Bowen who resented Hayden's condition that he take over the Foreign Affairs portfolio. Button played his power position to the full, calling Hawke to his fifteenth-floor office in Lonsdale Street the next morning and then telling him his great expectations were in sight of realisation. Hawke agreed without hesitation to Hayden's conditions and before they had lunch signed the guarantees that Hayden required. Labor's parliamentary Executive was to meet in Brisbane on Thursday, 3 February, and all its members, most aware that momentous events were in the air, were heading north the previous day. Button stayed over in Sydney for several hours, telephoning Hayden from the home of Jim McClelland to tell him his conditions would be met. Hayden said he would speak to him in Brisbane the following day.

On the same day a member of the staff of Lionel Bowen rang several key journalists and told them they should be in Brisbane for the Executive meeting, an event that in normal circumstances few would bother to attend, particularly while there was early election speculation boiling round Prime Minister Malcolm Fraser's office in Canberra. Bowen was giving a lunchtime speech on trade in Sydney and an ABC journalist aware of the source of the speculation about the Brisbane meeting interviewed him after the lunch. Bowen was asked if he still supported Hayden. 'I don't answer these questions. Mr Hayden is the leader,' Bowen answered. Asked if Hayden would remain as leader for the foreseeable future, Bowen answered: 'The party meets and discusses these matters. That is its privilege, not mine.' Bowen was then asked if he was certain Hayden would remain leader at the time of the next election. 'I'm not answering that,' he said.[14] The headline in the *Australian* said: 'Blow for Hayden as deputy hedges'. Hayden said later: 'The night before the meeting Bowen was on television in a way which I found rather hurtful, making comments which were quite denigrating of me. I was devastated because he knew I had given the undertaking. I suppose he was making sure I'd be locked into it. I wasn't sure that he wasn't evidencing some strong feelings that perhaps he'd had for a long time, because he was a man who would tend to allow feelings to well up over time before he unloaded them.'

Malcolm Fraser saw Bowen on television too. He knew what it meant. He geared up his plans to call an election the next day. Fraser's instincts were reinforced by a conversation with a former Whitlam Government minister that gave him a clear indication the Labor Party's climax was near, that Hayden's hours were numbered.

TWENTY

A drover's dog

I've had my little weep.

Bill Hayden

ILL HAYDEN rises early even when there is not pressing work
to do. On relaxed days at his home in Ipswich he often cooked
breakfast for the family, and a hearty meal it always was. Rissoles
with gravy was a favourite. The kitchen, described by social writer Barry
Everingham in 1980 as a 'housewife's dream', is the centre of activity in
the house; close to the front door, the sitting room, the wide corridors
that lead to the bedrooms and study, and the exit to the private area
surrounding the swimming pool. It has an ivory telephone on the broad
bench near the stove. At dawn on Thursday, 3 February 1983, Hayden
picked up that phone and was given information that set the tone for
what was going to be one of the most dramatically bizarre days in
Australia's eventful political history.

The caller was Laurie Oakes, the doyen of newsbreakers among
Australian political reporters. He told Hayden that he had very definite
information that Fraser was about to call an election. Oakes, who was
stranded in Adelaide, had already filed the story himself to be broadcast
on the 7 a.m. news in the Eastern States.

249

Hayden would not have been human if he did not reconsider his position. The Labor Party would not change leaders once an election had been called, and he was confident that Labor would win the election; the prime ministership was temptingly in reach. 'If Bill had dug his toes in that day, there is no way that there would have been a move against him once Fraser had called the election,' Mick Young said later. 'There is no way in the world we would have called the party together and had a bloodbath.'

Hayden was determined to make good on the spirit of his pledge as well as on the detailed undertakings that had been given by both sides. It was his own judgment that to do this he had to resign before Fraser called the election. Hayden has never read Paul Kelly's bestselling book *The Hawke Ascendancy*, that was officially launched by Hawke. In describing events leading to Hayden's resignation, Kelly says: 'His [Hayden's] fear was that Fraser might announce an election before he had resigned the Labor leadership, and that he would then be depicted as a coward when he did resign. So Hayden decided to bring his resignation forward; get in first and beat Fraser.'[1] That is unfair to Hayden. Given the situation as he then knew it, Hayden had the clear option of delaying his resignation until Fraser had announced the election date. There would have been no move against him: the rank and file of the Labor Party, who had been unaware of the stage the Hawke takeover had reached, would have rallied to the cause. Hayden had always been confident he could beat Fraser, and the opinion polls supported his view.

When questioned, after he had left politics, on those vital hours, Hayden shows no inclination to linger on what might have been, or to suggest he had been firmly stitched up by the Hawke forces: 'It seemed to me that the die was well and truly cast at that stage. As I recall it, there was public speculation of a high order. Suddenly I would be a sort of Lazarus of politics, coming back as a political cadaver to disadvantage the party. So I just ploughed ahead. I had no intention, given my undertaking, that I was going to retreat from it.'

As soon as he had finished speaking to Oakes, Hayden rang Button at the home of Jim McClelland in Sydney and told him he wanted to speak to him as soon as he arrived in Brisbane. Early on the same morning Fraser, who was in Canberra, contacted Tony Eggleton who was in Melbourne to talk to the Liberal Party's advertising agents, and told him the election was to be announced that day and would be held on 5 March.

Fraser started putting in train the election arrangements, which included preparing letters dissolving Parliament for signature by the Governor-General.

Button got an early plane to Brisbane. The confusion of the day, and even in describing the events later, was magnified by the fact that Queensland under the rule of Sir Joh Bjelke-Petersen refused to adopt the trendy idea of daylight saving that had been adopted by the southern States. Button arrived in Brisbane at about the same time by the local clocks as he had departed from Sydney airport. Soon after nine o'clock local time he caught the lift from the basement carpark straight to Hayden's twelfth-floor office in the Commonwealth Government building in central Brisbane, avoiding the television cameras staking out the lower floor where the Labor Party Executive meeting was to be held. Hayden, who was waiting, told him immediately that he was going to step down. Button confirmed that his conditions, including taking the responsibility for Foreign Affairs from Bowen, had been agreed, and that Hawke had signed the guarantees. Hawke arrived at 9.30 and joined Hayden and Button briefly, and they then went down separately to the conference room. At 10.15, Brisbane time, which was an hour behind Canberra, Hayden took the chair and carried on, in a surreal atmosphere, with the normal business of the Executive. Midway through the session he leant over and whispered to Bowen that he was going to stand down at the morning tea break. Button left the meeting shortly afterwards and told waiting journalists he was sure the leadership question would be discussed.

At 10.40 Hayden, Bowen and Hawke left the meeting and took the lift to a vacant office upstairs. Button followed soon afterwards. There was a brief row which began when Bowen objected to having to give up Foreign Affairs and complained about the costs he was being expected to bear. Button told him he wasn't the only one carrying a burden of cost at that point.

At 11.50 Hayden took the lift alone up to his office suite where the thirteen members of his staff waited. 'I've got something to tell you; I have decided to resign my position as leader.' He explained his reasons, and then assured those who were not public servants that they would be looked after. Turning to Ramsey he said: 'That includes you, Alan.' Ramsey said: 'It's not us we're worried about, Bill. How are you?' 'I'm okay,' said Hayden, walking into his private office, and then into the ensuite bathroom adjoining it. Animal sounds of retching and grief reverberated through the office for what seemed like minutes to the staff, some of whom were still crying three hours later. There were sounds of splashing water, and Hayden emerged and said to Ramsey who had stayed nearby: 'I've had my little weep.'

At 11.15 Brisbane time, 12.15 in Canberra, Fraser left for Yarralumla where he expected Sir Ninian Stephen to quickly sign the documents that would allow him to announce the election. He had already arranged a press conference to start three-quarters of an hour later at which he planned to announce the election, and begin his campaign.

At 11.35 Hayden returned to the Executive meeting and told the shadow ministers he was standing down. He recalled later that he attempted a nervous joke: 'I remember saying: "Every cloud has a silver lining, and I've got to say the good part of this will be that I won't have to attend any more of those excruciatingly boring Federal Executive meetings ... but what a hell of a way to get out of that task."'

Fraser, perhaps used to dealing with Sir John Kerr, had not made an appointment with the Governor-General or warned him that he was coming. Sir Ninian told the Prime Minister he would need to study his request for a double dissolution, but was unable to do so immediately, as he was entertaining the Polish Ambassador for lunch. Come back later, he advised a furious and deeply embarrassed Fraser, who had no option but to return to Parliament House to wait it out and monitor news of the drama unfolding in Brisbane. When he got no news an hour later he retreated to The Lodge for a light lunch.

Hayden had not prepared a formal resignation speech for the media: 'I wasn't proposing to speak to the press,' he told me. 'I thought it would be a case of resigning and walking out, perhaps with a couple of comments. I didn't expect the media to be alerted. I made the statement on the spur of the moment.' The media crowded into the green seats of the little basement theatrette, where Hayden sat flanked by Denis Murphy and State ALP secretary Peter Beattie. Hayden's press secretary Alan Ramsey announced that Hayden would make a brief statement, but would not answer questions. He began with a formal announcement: 'I have informed the Labor Party I will be resigning as leader of the Opposition at the next meeting of the Parliamentary Labor Party. There will be a special meeting next Tuesday to be convened at 10.30 a.m., for the purpose of electing a new leader and filling subsequent vacancies.'

Hayden's face was etched with strain and sorrow, his eyes red-rimmed, but his voice was under concentrated control: 'I didn't take this decision with any sense of joy. But it did seem to me, as a matter of responsibility to my party, that the situation confronting us was an inevitable conflict coming up in Caucus. At best I could win by only a very narrow margin ... and I do not rule out the possibility I could have won such a contest by such a margin. It would have been unconvincing to the community and would have resolved nothing. It is likely that there would have been a rather nasty brawl in Caucus, involving debate, heated ... personal perhaps ... which could have led to divisions being generated in the Caucus which would have been totally unproductive, in the process of deciding the matter.

'In all of the circumstances I had to weigh up what was in the best interests of the party. And there are some occasions where people have to be prepared to make sacrifices ... no matter how fair or unfair, right or wrong, they may think they are. One must do what one thinks is best in all the circumstances. In the circumstances as I saw them, there was only one way to resolve the problem, and that was to take the attitude which I have announced to the Shadow Cabinet today.'

Hayden then went on to coin another phrase that has found a lasting place in Australia's political vocabulary. He spoke without pause for reaction or any lightness in his voice: 'I want to say that I am not convinced the Labor Party could not win under my leadership. I believe a drover's dog could lead the Labor Party to victory the way the country is [and the way the opinion polls are showing up for the Labor Party].'[2]

Still controlled, he reflected briefly on his own feelings: 'It has given me no joy to have to do this. It has created a great deal of heartburn for me. It is not a decision I'd have preferred. As recently as Sunday I was still determined to fight the matter out. More recently it became clear to me I was guaranteeing great damage to my party and the return of the Fraser Government as the cost of my own personal hopes and aspirations.'

Then, as Lionel Bowen prepared to read a resolution of the Executive expressing appreciation of his services as leader and a formal recognition that his resignation involved considerable personal sacrifices, Hayden walked to the lift followed by jostling cameramen.

Into the middle of this drama, a little earlier, had stumbled a handsome, gangling academic Labor candidate escorting a journalist from a suburban throwaway newspaper on Brisbane's Redcliffe peninsula. The academic, Deane Wells, who has subsequently been elected to the Federal and later the Queensland State Parliament, had arranged for the reporter to have an interview with Bob Hawke, in his capacity as a shadow minister, on Labor's plans to improve employment prospects in the suburbs covered by his weekly paper. As the heavyweights of the national media thronged around the barred entrance to the conference room, the doors opened and Wells and the suburban scribe were ushered through. A shell-shocked Bob Hawke, about to become Labor leader and Prime Minister, answered in detail the questions he was asked, not one of which related to anything other than jobs on the Redcliffe peninsula.

Wells was leaving the building at 12.20 when he came across Hayden, leaning against the wall in the basement, waiting for a lift, and watched by a throng of journalists and cameramen. Hayden's press secretary Alan Ramsey was trying to usher them away: 'The press conference is over. It's all over ... please just go away,' he said.

Wells extended his hand to Hayden. 'You are quite a man, Bill,' he said. Hayden took a white handkerchief from his pocket, blew his nose and dabbed his reddened eyes.[3]

Later that day John Button, Mick Young and Bob Hawke flew out of Brisbane on a chartered plane to begin the campaign. A month later Hawke was Prime Minister, but there had been no significant changes to the policies Hayden had developed or the ministry he had selected.

TWENTY ONE

Bystander

It's a tough game, this.

Bill Hayden

A T SIX O'CLOCK on the morning of the day Bob Hawke
became Prime Minister, 5 March 1983, Bill Hayden was in the
backyard of his Ipswich home dressed in one of his old police
shirts, building a fowl house. 'My son Kirk bought some guinea fowl
chickens which are stinking the house out. Election day or no election
day, I've got to give them a new home away from our bedrooms,'
he explained.[1]

The campaign had been a time of healing for Bill Hayden, but the
process was not complete. The wrench of losing the leadership had been
compounded by the fact that he had then immediately been cast in the
role of bystander for one of the most electrifying political events of his
lifetime: Labor's revenge on Malcolm Fraser, the gutter fighter who had
destroyed the Whitlam Government. The blanket media coverage of the
contest between Hawke and Fraser was also a constant reminder to him
of Hawke's abilities on the election trail. There were also material
developments which made it clear that the union movement had denied
cooperation to him when he was Labor leader, for no legitimate reason,

which it was now providing handsomely to Hawke. Less than two days after Hawke was elected Leader, Cliff Dolan announced ACTU agreement to the Labor Party's prices and incomes policy that Hayden had been working to effect for years. The outlines of the plot, the bear-traps that had been set for him, now became clear. But he was at pains, when asked, to declare he was not dwelling on his hurt and disappointment. 'I've this facility for putting bitterness behind me because it can destroy you,'[2] he said, explaining that it was a lesson he had learnt after the dismissal of the Whitlam Government so soon after he had presented his first Budget.

But glimpses of the wounds still appeared. When, midway through the campaign, a reporter remarked on the prominence industrial relations had assumed in the contest, with Hawke portrayed as the strike-solver, Hayden said, cryptically: 'I'll just say it is significant that there has been no more talk of industrial trouble since my decision to step down.' What was he implying? the journalist asked. 'It's a tough game this,' he grunted.

Hayden had a number of difficult encounters with his colleagues during this period, the first at a meeting of Labor's national campaign committee in Sydney. 'I thought I should go down and discharge my obligations until I was out of the way,' he told me in 1988 in a painfully observant and understanding recollection of the incident. 'The meeting was in the Labor Party offices, and I walked in while it was under way. It was quite an experience. Wran was chairing it as Federal president, and Hawke was in a prominent position at the top of the table. There was only a place for me right down the end; most people didn't seem to note that I had come in, and the few who did, did so uncomfortably. At the time it stung quite a bit, but I thought later that the poor wretches were probably embarrassed; like trying to handle a bereavement — you never handle it properly; nor do you say the right things if you feel genuinely distressed for the bereaved — at least that's my experience. I don't think they were grieving over me in that sense.'

A rather sad story was written by Peter Smark who talked to Hayden in Paris in May:

> [Hayden] seems to question if it was right for him to have taken such wicked delight on the night of the first Caucus meeting after the election in marching into the guests' dining room, finding a group of Victorian Centre Unity MPs in full celebration under the tutelage of Gareth Evans, and sitting close to reduce them to proper funereal [sic] rites.[3]

On the morning of the election Hayden tried to ring Bob Hawke to wish him well, but couldn't get through: 'Bob hadn't notified me that his phone had been disconnected and I guess he was too busy in his new job to ring me.'[4] Hawke had, in fact, telephoned Hayden at his home midway through the campaign and suggested that they stage a joint meeting as a public demonstration of reconciliation; Hayden told him the exercise would look too contrived, and Hawke, who had no alternative but to accept his judgment, agreed.

For the month of the election campaign, Hayden spent most of his time campaigning in Oxley, surrounded often by slightly embarrassed sympathisers, and with practice developed a line to deal with the comment made to him frequently as he moved among the people of Ipswich. 'I'll never vote Labor again after what happened to you,' supporters would say. 'Hey, wait a minute. You'll do me out of a job,' Hayden would reply in mock alarm.

The early hours and days after his resignation were the most difficult. Journalists had started ringing Dallas before he arrived home on the day he resigned, and she said at first: 'I'm sorry, but I have nothing to say about this matter.' Journalists turned to Jenny McDonald, a staff member, still weeping hours after the event, who said: 'He was one of the most decent human beings I know.' On the following day Dallas spoke briefly to a *Courier Mail* journalist. She was composed: 'I certainly hope the Labor Party wins and I wish Bob Hawke all the best. I don't think bitterness ever gets you anywhere. I think Bill would have made a great Prime Minister — one of the best. I am proud of him and believe he is the sort of person Australia needs.' She said she believed integrity was important, and thought there was not enough of it around, adding: 'If politicians don't have it, then the community won't have it either.'[5]

'There was an air of sadness in Ipswich yesterday,' reported Brisbane's *Sunday Mail* which had conducted a series of street interviews. Len Sherman, sixty-six, of Wood End, was a typical respondent: if Bob Hawke ever went to Ipswich Len would throw all the rotten eggs he could find at him. 'I'm bitter and I won't be voting Labor this time. Bill Hayden came up from off the ground and worked his way up. I take my hat off to the man.'[6] It wasn't long, however, before Hayden was showing a bit of chirpy irreverence when the role of martyr became a little stifling. When he lodged his nomination as a candidate — with $100 borrowed from his driver when the official refused to accept a cheque — on 11 February he was asked to give a thumbs up for the cameras. After obliging, Hayden then made a couple of sharp upward thrusts of his right-hand middle finger, with the comment: 'How about that way for a few people in the Labor Party?'[7] Later, when he visited the chicken hatchery at Wulkuraka and fell over, he said: 'I suppose that's the most foul thing that's happened to me lately.'

Another minor humiliation that he took in good spirit occurred when he toured the meatworks at Dinmore, where he and Dallas had lived when they were first married. 'I was talking to the blokes on the killing line, and somebody accidentally-on-purpose bumped some freshly killed carcasses up against me and I got blood all over me,' he recalled later. Any possible symbolism was apparently lost on the meatworkers, who laughed and cheered. Hayden understood the reaction, explaining: 'They don't get much fun in that game.' Later a huge meatworker, also blood-stained, put it straight to him: 'Why did Bob Hawke double-cross you and take your job?' 'You shouldn't be so uncharitable,' said Hayden with a painful dry smile.[8]

On one of his few forays outside Queensland during the campaign, Hayden was asked on Melbourne radio about Labor's policy for Australia to become a republic. He dismissed it as a minor issue, saying such a change could only happen with the approval of the Australian people through a referendum. His further comments on air were views he had long held, had expressed publicly in comments after the dismissal and still holds: 'The big differences which would have to take place for Australia to become a republic are in terms of the Constitution and the powers of the Governor-General and the Senate. These things should proceed whether we become a republic or not because they are central to successful and stable government in this country.'[9] Although he was not given the opportunity to spell out his view on that occasion he was simply putting forward his opinion that neither the Senate nor the Head of State should have the power to frustrate the Government formed by the party with a majority in the House of Representatives. Bill and Dallas ran into Andrew Peacock at Brisbane Airport on their return from Melbourne. Hayden said: 'We discussed the possibility of me getting my hands on the little black book he is said to have compiled when he was Foreign Minister. We decided against it in deference to Dallas and to my age. My approach to Foreign Affairs might have been somewhat different if I was twenty years younger.'

On election day, 1983, Bill sat in the passenger seat while Dallas drove him round the sixty polling booths. Reporter Ric Allen rode in the back seat, and Dallas briefly reminisced: 'You know I first met Bill when he was a young police constable at Redbank and the man he stood against to win the seat was a Dr Cameron who delivered me as a baby.' She went on to talk about the support they had been receiving: 'There have been lots of phone calls and probably two sackfuls of letters sympathising with the way Bill has been treated.'[10] The remark by Dallas about the letters he had been receiving provided a private clue to the solitary activity that had provided the domestic counterpoint to Hayden's public performance: throughout the campaign, Hayden constantly dwelt on the events of the previous months and, as an almost deliberate cathartic exercise, spent much of his time writing long, introspective, thoughtful and sometimes self-pitying letters to friends and sympathisers exploring his own motives and justifying, to himself and others, his decision. The letters were dictated at home into a tape recorder and sent to his Brisbane office to be typed.[11]

The letters he wrote during the campaign are a revealing record of a man under stress who is striving to make sense of a cruel blow, who is trying to sublimate his anger and his energy. Hayden wasted little time on people in whom he had lost trust. John Menadue, who had been head of the Prime Minister's Department under Whitlam, and then had excused himself from the tactics meeting at The Lodge after being told of Whitlam's sacking, wrote to Hayden on 14 February, saying only: 'Best wishes for a continuing and successful public life.' Hayden's reply was equally curt: 'It was thoughtful of you to send me a note recently on my future.' Yet, when a schoolgirl he had not met, Linda Corfield, of Kippa-ring in Queensland, wrote to him asking about his feelings he wrote to her at length.

'Your first question is: "How do you feel about the Labor Party after your resignation?" I have as deep a commitment as I have ever had to the Labor movement. I believe it has an historic mission, and that is to bring a greater equality of opportunity for people in our community and a fairer social system then we've had in the past.

'That should not be misunderstood as a declaration that all people have to be equal whether they like it or not. They are not, in fact. Sometimes it is by choice, and that is their right and that shouldn't be interfered with. And sometimes it is through inherent inequalities. For example, a person may be a brilliant scientist or an outstanding artist. In these respects their ability must be respected at the same time as the right to be different must be protected. To respect the right to be different means that one must respect the right to be non-conforming, for example preferring an alternative lifestyle, dress and so on.'

He went on to give young Linda a broad view of his mission, and some of its excruciating complexities. 'The emphases I would give are both material and spiritual. The material things relate to the distribution of wealth in the community so that there is a greater sense of security and self-respect for those otherwise denied that entitlement. On the other hand, I believe such an undertaking must be tempered by a recognition that punishing redistributional measures are counterproductive and, in fact, can destroy initiative and industriousness in the community. The spiritual things relate to ... quality of life ... for example what we do to help the creative arts as an expression of the aspirations and an interpretation of the condition of our societies. It relates to matters such as an enshrinement of the rights of humankind — perhaps through a Bill of Human Rights — and certainly through a fierce and unyielding defence of the basic rights of people within the community, especially in civil liberties. It refers to such things as the environment, and there I contemplate not just conservation of various areas like the south-west of Tasmania, but also the improvement of the areas in which we live so that aesthetically there is a quality about such areas that inspires and ennobles the people.'

Linda's last request was for his prediction about the result of the coming election. 'As I see the situation right now, I believe we are going to win, and I expect to win handsomely,' he answered.

His most open and agonisingly analytical letter was written to Neal Blewett on 28 February, in which he said plainly that it was his judgment that if he had not given in to Hawke's challenge the Labor Party would have been shattered.

'Dear Neal,

You were kind enough to write to me after the awful experiences of recent times. Dallas and I appreciated that greatly. It wasn't an easy decision, and you better than most would understand it.'

A clear sense of the way in which Hayden was brooding on his past at this time was the fact that he then recalled a remark he had made himself some years earlier, just as he had done in a letter to his old schoolteacher Ron Baynes, written about the same time. 'You may recall,' Hayden wrote to Blewett, 'that a long time ago I mentioned to you I never wanted to face an Arthur Calwell situation.' Calwell as Labor leader in the sixties had been consumed with jealousy and bitterness towards his deputy and then successor, Whitlam, and inflicted great damage on the party by staying on in smouldering vengeance.

'When I said it,' Hayden continued, 'I wasn't quite sure whether I would be able to muster enough courage to make the sort of decision I was implying, should the event ever arise. Well, I sincerely hope I didn't get to the Arthur Calwell situation. On the other hand, I had recognised I'd reached a situation which was impossible unless I was prepared to tear the party apart. I am quite convinced that there were others who were prepared to do that if I wasn't prepared to be reasonable. Perhaps some day I would speak to you, although I am not sure that I will speak to anyone about all of the circumstances that arose in this period, and which I am aware of, and explain to you the sort of impasse that I saw us arriving at. Impasse is really the wrong term, for what was arising where, if I didn't give, the party would be shattered.'

Hayden also reflected, as he had in several other letters, on earlier days: 'I was well aware of all of the tricks of the trade. I've been there a long time and I went through all the very bitter and nasty things in the immediate post-Split period of the mid and late 1950s. I had been active in the party at the time of the Split in Queensland. I had seen how the tough hardheads operated in that period. Strangely enough, in that general period I had been impressed by the toughness, the unyielding bellicosity of the various factions when the bust-up took place. I had always believed that I would fight to the last ditch, and that that was the mark of courage should that sort of ultimate challenge eventually start to catch up with me.'

There were a very few people in the Labor Party, though they included John Button, who were aware that one of the Hayden children had been in an extremely distressed emotional state over the Christmas period, adding to the torment in the family. Hayden made an oblique reference to the situation in his letter to Blewett, in which he also said he was aware of the plotting against him: 'One of the strangest things I had to adjust to as I sat down and rationally watched what was happening over Christmas — and it was the most extraordinary Christmas; I would never hope to see anything faintly like it ever again, for I knew almost every step that was unfolding from well before the Christmas period started — was to recognise that the easier decision of the two was to keep fighting. In a way I suspect that most people wouldn't understand that, because I find most people who were friends of mine thought I should have kept fighting. I did too. I am now convinced that was an atavistic response.'

He then went on to make one of his very rare references to his father, casting him in a much more favourable, and quite different, light than he had in the past when he had made references to his drinking, a suspected shady past, and the claim that his father's politics had prevented him joining the Labor Party. His letter to Blewett continued: 'There are some things that are much more important than self-interest, however it is described, and coming from a fairly radical political family — my father was an old IWW in the American Merchant Marine and my mother bitterly Irish Republican — they none the less had an overriding belief that, for all its shortcomings, the Labor Party stood for some invaluable values and objectives, and that to subjugate that to personal ambition would be despicable. The last thing I would ever want to do would be to try to moralise about these sorts of things, but I hope in the ultimate, at least on this occasion, I was able to live up to that standard that my family background has always heavily invested in and which no doubt had conditioned me, but with mature reflection and rational consideration, had endorsed quite independently anyway.' The loneliness of his position as he perceived it then was reflected in his closing lines: 'I really haven't mentioned these sorts of things to anyone else because I doubt that there would be many others, if any, who would understand what I am talking about.'

At his home in Ipswich as the afternoon of Hawke's triumphant election day wore on, and reporter Ric Allen left Ipswich, the Haydens were heading for the local soft-drink factory. Bob Hawke and his family and entourage had taken a set of suites at the Lakeside International Hotel in Canberra to prepare for their victorious descent on the tally-room. 'My campaign manager Kev Hooper has looked after the beer and Dallas and I have been instructed to order the soft drinks. He's a good campaign manager that Hooper, you know, and possibly more trustworthy than other people I've met in politics,' was Hayden's parting remark to Allen. At the party they watched as Malcolm Fraser brushed aside a tear as he faced the television cameras, and Hayden later said he had felt pity and respect for him. 'All through the campaign he was like a harness horse that could never get its gait straight,' he said. 'He had a moment of greatness in the way he handled his declaration of defeat and announced he was standing down as leader.'[12]

Late on the night of the election, at Hayden's party in Ipswich, a guest entered with a freshly printed newspaper poster announcing Hawke's win and yelled: 'Hold it up Bill.'[13]

'No. Bob can hold that up,' he said.

The Queen's Man

TWENTY TWO

The caravan
moves on

By *the time he gets home he will have the
biggest collection of King Tuts in Australia.*

Niki Savva Australian 27 January 1984

AYDEN went to the Foreign Affairs portfolio as a caretaker: his horizon was fixed by the deal he had set in concrete with Hawke before resigning the leadership: after a year or so, at a time of his own choosing, he would go to London as Australia's High Commissioner.

He had decided on that course of action for two reasons. First, he doubted whether he could work under Hawke, a man he did not trust, and, on recent experience, had no reason to trust. The second motive was the old Hayden story: he wanted some security of employment for himself and a position that he believed his family would see as confirming that he had risen for ever above his origins.

Hayden had doubts, too, about whether Hawke, given the instability of his past, would be able to cope with the prime ministership, and he never again wanted to be an Opposition candidate fighting an election. Hayden at that time did not seriously entertain illusions that he would be recalled to the leadership if Hawke failed. He had recognised that, although he was younger than Hawke, his time had passed; the wrenching transfer of allegiances that had been part of the leadership change could not be reversed. The operation had been irreversible; some wounds would never heal properly and would remain forever raw.

The acrimony of the leadership change did not evaporate when Caucus gathered victorious in Canberra to elect the Hawke ministry. Hayden was, for many, the spectre at the feast, the dampener on celebrations, a walking reminder of the nastiness that had been involved in gaining government. Hayden said later: 'I thought that, by the time we got into the voting, old scores could have been forgotten, but there were several people who took the opportunity of voting against me. But, in politics, people have long memories. Fred Daly says: "Don't get angry, get even," and I can't say I have been totally immune to that either, so I can't complain.'

In accordance with his intention to remain only briefly in the position, an intention that was not known publicly or to his officials, Hayden did not make dramatic changes to his department and left Peter Henderson, a son-in-law of former Liberal Prime Minister, Sir Robert Menzies, in its senior position. This was to increase the bitterness and confusion a year later when he had decided to stay on as Foreign Minister, and sacked Henderson.

There were suspicions among Hayden's critics, and colleagues led by Lionel Bowen, that his insistence on taking the Foreign Affairs portfolio was another demonstration of self-indulgence; that he was in it for the perks, the endless VIP-class overseas travel, all on the public purse. This explanation, in fact, falls short of the truth. He had conceded defeat to Hawke and wanted to give him room to get on with his job. Despite his treatment by many of his colleagues he still believed as passionately that Labor had a social mission to repair the divisions in Australian society that had been caused by Whitlam's dismissal and Fraser's governments, and he believed that in any domestic or economic portfolio he would be in constant conflict over policy with Hawke and his closest right-wing supporters.

Hayden was in bare feet and a pair of shorts sitting at a table beside his secluded backyard swimming pool, drinking a glass of coke that Dallas had just brought out, when he described to me the moment when he had decided not to become Australia's High Commissioner in Britain: 'I was sitting here during that most beautiful blue and gold weather that we can have in Queensland, it was lovely and balmy, and I thought to myself, I just couldn't live through a grey northern hemisphere winter in London. Not one, let alone five. I just couldn't do it. There is only one country I want to be in: there is, quite literally, nothing that equals the sense of lift, almost spiritual lift, you feel as you are coming into Sydney airport in the early morning after you have been away overseas for a while.'

There had been an expectation, particularly by Hawke supporters, that ideological differences between Hayden and the Prime Minister would destabilise the Government, but this never, even in private, became a serious problem. Recalling the early days, one minister who was not particularly sympathetic to Hawke or Keating told me recently: 'On his visits to Australia Bill would try hard to find differences with Keating in Cabinet discussions on economic policy, but with time he became one of his closest supporters. There was little difference in their approach.' Another minister, who was a strong Hayden supporter, said that in his early interventions into economic debates in Cabinet Hayden had 'not been particularly constructive or consistent'.

Taking the Foreign Affairs portfolio did not, of course, remove Hayden from the need to work under the influence of Hawke, who had his own set of emotional passions in international affairs. Hawke and his family had been threatened with death both for his commitment to Israel and for his opposition to apartheid, and he had wept in Parliament over the plight of Jews in Russia. The Prime Minister's love of Israel and his willingness to fight for it had, as Blanche d'Alpuget recorded, caused 'problems which veered close to wrecking his life and career'.[1] Hawke hated and distrusted the Russians who, he believed, had treated him treacherously in 1979 during one of the most complex and traumatic series of events in his life. He believed he had negotiated in Moscow an agreement that exit visas would be granted for many heroic Russian Jewish refuseniks with whom he had formed close emotional bonds; the supposed agreement was announced prematurely and celebrated across the world. Hawke was devastated when the Russians reneged, and during a drinking bout that followed told a friend he was considering killing himself.

Hawke had also played a significant role within the Australian and international trade union movement to establish firm sanctions against South Africa and bans on Springbok tours in his crusade against apartheid. Hawke was an admirer of the United States and considered President Reagan's Secretary of State, George Schultz, a close friend.

Within weeks of Hayden taking the job Hawke also warned him that he was not to disturb Australia's relationship with Indonesia,[2] a caution that did not prevent Hayden writing a private note on a confidential departmental document in December 1984 that said: 'There is no doubt about it, the Indonesians are erratic hostile people to deal with, with an added sententiousness which makes them difficult neighbours.'[3]

Hawke was not a man who was going to allow Hayden free rein as Foreign Minister, even if his own wish was to heal the breach between them. Hayden fully shared Hawke's views on apartheid and bans on sporting contacts with South Africa, but, consistent with the position he had adopted on Afghanistan, he had doubts about the effectiveness of trade embargoes unless they were universally applied.[4] He had for nearly twenty years spoken out against Russian violations of human rights and use of armed might to subjugate reform movements in its satellite countries, but did not share Hawke's emotional animus: 'They [the Russians] have got to be watched. But that is not a justification for the obsessiveness that comes up in some quarters which leads to, in my view, silly initiatives or proposals in foreign policy,' Hayden told an interviewer two weeks before Hawke became Prime Minister. It was a direct, snide, and quite justified tilt at Hawke's attitude to the Soviet Union.[5]

In the same interview he expressed the view that Australia should, in the interests of both countries, preserve a reasonable independence from America: 'Within the ANZUS alliance, and acknowledging that we are neither neutralist nor non-aligned — we are part of the association of Western nations — nonetheless I believe there is room for Australia to be more assertive and independent in the views it puts on a range of matters: it would be respected much more. I don't think Australia under conservative governments has been impressive by running along tooting behind America — allowing America to make all the decisions and take all the responsibility.'[6]

The critical area where there seemed most potential for an irreconcilable breakdown between Hawke and Hayden was over Israel. Hayden as Labor leader had in 1980 insisted on going to the Middle East for a meeting with the head of the Palestinian Liberation Organisation, Yasser Arafat, mainly because Hawke's close friend Isi Leibler, president of the Executive Council of Australian Jewry, had put pressure on him to cancel the visit. After a personal conversation with Hayden, Paul Kelly said Hayden's 'experience as a Queensland cop had left him with a deep sense of defiance when intimidated'; he had interpreted Leibler's actions as an act of intimidation and only then decided to go ahead with his visit. It was an act that cost him and the Labor Party electoral and financial support.[7]

Despite the handicaps of their relationship and Australia's relative insignificance in the international community, Hayden and Hawke achieved an effective, if wary, working relationship in running Australia's foreign relations: in the end both made a positive contribution though in other circumstances they might have achieved more memorable results.

By the time he became Foreign Minister, Hayden was at the conservative end of the spectrum of Labor Party thinking on foreign policy, but he was more in touch with the concerns of most of its rank-and-file members and a substantial section of Cabinet on sensitive issues than Hawke was. Hayden saw holding the Labor Party together on foreign policy as one of his major aims and was aware of the very strong feelings which many of its members held on key issues. 'The Labor Party is an emotional party; that is one of the attractive things about it, because it really cares. It can get carried away with that emotion at times. I remember one day, I was sick with the flu before the 1977 conference, and we had a meeting of the Queensland ALP's foreign affairs and defence committee in Brisbane. Billie Watts, who is old-style Left (if I can say that — I find her a very attractive person), was getting carried away, and going for the Yanks. I got very impatient, and said: 'For Christ's sake, Billie, you're just engaging in emotional anti-Americanism.'

Ms Watts, a handsome woman with straight hair drawn back severely, wasn't going to be bluffed. Hayden recalls: 'She flared and said: "There's something wrong if I can't engage in emotional feelings in the Labor Party. We have very strong emotions."

'I thought: "Jesus, you've said it all." It was one of the great insights I had always been aware of, but had never articulated in my own mind, and, when I thought about it I realised that I could handle the party a lot better if I recognised and respected it. But to handle that, and at the same time handle the Indonesians was not bloody easy.'

Hayden was a man trained for most of his life to repress emotion: his mother placed emphasis on keeping up appearances and concealing the reality of her situation from the outside world; when she had been a barmaid the neighbours thought she had been a nurse, when she was cleaning floors they thought she worked in an office; his father's unpredictable reactions and age did not encourage shows of feeling. The police force reinforced his training in bottling up his emotions and showing an unmoved exterior to the outside world. In politics his softer, caring side was largely expressed through hard work for social change. His anger, kept under tight control under provocation most of the time, would spill over in bitterness or erupt with volcanic force when it could no longer be contained.

Peter Smark, writing after breakfast with Hayden at the Plaza-Athenee Hotel in Paris in May 1983, during the Foreign Minister's first overseas trip as minister, gave Hayden's version of his first official meeting with departmental representatives:

I was in a rather peevish state of mind. It was before the election [and after he had stood down as leader] and someone came over representing Foreign Affairs. Out of perversity and provocativeness, and because I objected to the affected English accent, I asked: 'By the way, what trips are coming up this year?'

He said he was so glad I had asked that question because they were all wondering in the department whether, should I become minister, I would be a travelling minister or whether I would maximise my time at home to get on top of the administration.

I said: 'Listen, I'm going to be a travelling Minister. I'm going to be everywhere. I'm going to North America, I want to go right through Europe. I haven't touched base in Africa yet. And there's Mauritius.'

A week after the election I turned up at the department and there was a big thick volume of briefing notes. The first one was labelled 'Obligatory trips,' the next one was 'Trips overseas desirable and justified.' In the second lot was a notation that a trip to Mauritius could well be justified because of its increasing strategic significance in the Indian Ocean.[8]

Hayden regarded that as a great joke, and Smark, a wily and vastly experienced international journalist, predicted that he would play merry hell with the department: 'To those who thought the Mauritius ploy had worked, try again,' he suggested.[9] They did: more than forty separate Hayden overseas trips later, there were doubts among commentators about the justification for many of his excursions to exotic places, and even friends wondered whether Hayden hadn't, in fact, been seduced by the endless travels on the department's magic carpet. One of his former senior economic advisers who remained in occasional contact with him suggested: 'What I think happened was that he became bored. Foreign Affairs is a bullshit portfolio, and Bill is not very interested in bullshit.'[10] Hayden did not, himself, regard the portfolio in quite those terms, but certainly did not think it gave him great power to change the world, or to have much influence over the lives of Australians.

A particular candour sometimes arises between experienced Australian journalists and politicians who know each other well when they meet overseas, on neutral ground, far from home. Both Peter Smark in Paris and John Edwards in New York provided a vivid picture of Hayden's state of mind about his own condition and his attitudes to Hawke at the time each of them had breakfast with him on opposite sides of the world. Smark in May 1983, on Hayden's first visit to Europe as minister:

> At breakfast in the Plaza-Athenee Hotel, the visitor eats with two people. Both have the gritty integrity which are so pre-eminently Hayden qualities. For more than an hour they spar for position, the loyal party man and the man. In the end it's the man you want to embrace and comfort. Labor assassinated a good man when it killed Bill Hayden, and the party knows it. His walking ghost is an uncomfortable reminder, and he has started to take pleasure in it, which makes irresponsible people like journalists cheer in a most reprehensible way. His survival in any political form is distinctly untidy, and there are those of us who like a little untidiness in our politics ... [His] face bears witness to the scar tissue on his back ... You look at his face again, and he manages at once to be impish and yet still stricken ... but the humour lines are deepening once more. Healing is under way.
>
> Dallas defines the role of supportive wife. Hayden calls her 'remarkable' and 'a constant source of strength.'
>
> Her importance in his life is evident when they are together ... Lazarus walks because female hands anointed the stricken limbs.[11]

Edwards sat with him at breakfast in New York six months later in October 1983:

> Hayden was talkative and amusing in his nervous, uneasy way. His breakfast was ruined by an interview, he said: it was a lousy breakfast anyway ... mine was OK? Too bad ... all the worse ... he was sorry to hear it.
>
> Hayden today — most of the time — is more or less reconciled to Hawke ... His attitude to Hawke is almost paternal. Hayden has more ministerial experience than Hawke and a better idea of the kinds of situations in which Caucus or Cabinet can contradict the leadership. Hayden and Hawke have no fundamental dispute about uranium, for example, but Hayden has a greater sensitivity to the implacable mood of important elements of the party and how tough it would be to defeat them.

Edwards noticed a marked change in Hayden's appearance:

He has put on a comfortable bit of weight. He dresses in Foreign Minister style, with dark pinstripe suit, monogrammed shirt, black brogues and subtle tie. He smells very nice and expensive. These are some of the external signs of frequent travel. The suit and shirts were run up in Hong Kong, the shoes are from Italy; the Raban aftershave and Roger Gallet eau de toilet were duty-free in one of the dozens of airports through which he has moved since taking on this job. Hayden likes the change: he likes to keep people surprised and off balance.[13]

About this time a former staff member who was an active member of the Queensland ALP talked with him at a meeting and came away complaining: 'He's become a silvertail.'

Before he became Foreign Minister, Hayden's eccentric dress sense was a regular source of amusement in Canberra and despair to his female staff. Louise Holgate would regularly don dark glasses when he wore one particularly loudly checked suit; once, when he strode to the dispatch box in an all-white outfit, an Opposition backbencher called out: 'Three chocolate-coated ice creams please.' Mick Young joked that when Sam the Hong Kong tailor had added Hayden's name to his list of prominent patrons he had lost half his customers. Hayden never threw anything away. Two members of his staff once planned to break into his Canberra unit and burn half his suits. When mild uproar greeted his appearance in the mid-eighties in a checked suit with flaring lapels, he looked surprised: 'Nobody laughed when I wore it in here in 1973,' he said.

Edwards was, in October 1983, optimistic about Hayden's future performance: 'Given his intelligence and experience, the excitement and interest he creates around him, Bill Hayden could be one of Australia's great Foreign Ministers.'[13] Hayden did not fulfil his expectations, as Edwards made clear in a stinging article less than two years later.[14]

Hayden, discussing his years as Foreign Minister with me soon after his retirement, said the first objective of the job, as he saw it, was to exercise a greater degree of national independence in Australian foreign policy than had generally been seen in the past. 'The Whitlam period was a big breakthrough,' he said. 'Peacock, in fairness to him, kept that sort of Australianism going. There was a tendency for Fraser, however, to want to lurch into Cold War rhetoric and attitudes and, publicly, appear as a sort of American satellite. Privately the evidence will probably come out that he was pretty tough with the Americans. I thought his attitude was unhealthy, and, in any case it was not something that would be borne by the Labor Party. At the same time I was sensible enough to realise we had to keep a good relationship with the Americans: they're an extraordinarily powerful country, and they are quite capable of taking reprisals which aren't announced but can show up in trade accounts and various other ways.'

The Americans, in fact, opposed one of Hayden's early, most memorable and controversial initiatives, which, ironically, Hawke had set in motion: an attempt to mediate a solution to Vietnam's occupation of Kampuchea. Vietnam had sent in its troops to end the murderous regime of Pol Pot's Khmer Rouge and had installed a government headed by Heng Samrin. Hayden's long-running effort to bring about a negotiated withdrawal by the Vietnamese was carried out in the face of opposition from a surprising coalition comprising China and the ASEAN nations as well as the United States. The Kampuchean resistance, which included elements of the genocidal Pol Pot regime, depended on the supply of Chinese arms, secure bases in Thailand and food supplied by America.

'There are those who say the big number on Vietnam and Kampuchea was an effort by me to show the Left that we were active, and to buy them off with that at the cost of East Timor,' Hayden said in 1988. 'The funny thing with that is that I was frightened of the Vietnam exercise; I thought it could blow up on us. Hawke got me in and made the proposal, and I remember saying: "Listen, Bob, this is not an industrial dispute we're getting involved in. It's a very bloody sensitive area." And he said: "Aw, not much difference ... just a bigger canvas." I've got to say it was worth taking on, although we didn't get all that far. Hawke's instincts were right. I found as time went by that Hawke wasn't just interested in political opportunism, he really did want to see Australia play a helpful role if Australia could.'

Hayden remains convinced that, although Australia is unlikely to receive credit, its initiative did contribute to progress in resolution of the situation in Kampuchea: 'I am satisfied that we made the opportunity for Indonesia, which was the dialogue country with Vietnam on behalf of the ASEAN countries, to move more surely and often, and more easily, because we were the sort of lightning rod deflecting the sparks which were coming out. In 1983 at my first post-ASEAN conference in Bangkok I came under a bit of pressure when I said: "A military solution won't work in Vietnam, it has to be a political one. If you think you can win with a military formula, the Vietnamese will stay in Kampuchea till the fires of Hell freeze over." There was thunder round the place. We were seen as interlopers upsetting what was nicely organised there, the way they were running things. In 1986 at the Manila post-ASEAN conference, in public session, what does my beaming friend Mochtar [the Indonesian Foreign Minister] say, with the media there: "A military solution won't work. They will stay there forever. It has to be political."

'The first time we were there the room was sizzling with blue smoke, and lightning flashes were running round the walls: yet here we are three years later, and because we had gone in there and I had copped quite a lot, I believe we created the opportunity for Indonesia to move forward more surely and with less opposition, because we were being concentrated on.

'But I think we've played our part and when the history is weighed up we won't get much more than a footnote, if we get that much, but it is probably going to be recognised that Hawke's original inspiration, his original gut-level feeling, was right, in ways which he couldn't possibly have apprehended. Vietnam was his idea. We talked about it and decided to give it a run. The good thing about it was he backed me all the way.'

Hayden feels his initial relations with the Americans started out badly and ended up quite reasonable. 'I remember saying to George Schultz [Reagan's Secretary of State] a couple of years ago that my political nature and values were radical. "We're not under any illusion about that Bill, you're quite radical," he answered. It was an insight into how they saw me. I said: "I'd like the Left at home to hear this, they would be falling apart in hilarity." '

Despite his almost light-hearted reference to the attitude of key figures in the American administration towards him, Hayden has clear and painful memories over the way they had forced him into a humiliating backdown over the nuclear ships issue when he was party leader. The powerful men had always preferred Hawke, and continued to use that relationship to limit Hayden's options.

Hayden, by nature circumspect in his personal relationships, carried that wariness into his conduct of foreign relations. 'I was always cautious with the Americans, and with any country I dealt with where our interests were at stake. You don't throw yourself into the arms of another power, because they have their national interests to look after too.' Another of Hayden's early clashes with the Americans, which began after the United States started competing with subsidised agricultural exports in Australia's traditional markets and reducing Australian access to its domestic market, led to high-level complaints to Hawke and to Hayden being left without the support of a single other minister. Hayden publicly suggested that American defence establishments on Australian soil, long opposed by the Left, should be subject to review in the light of the economic effects United States agricultural policies were having on Australia. He recalls: 'When the trade stuff started to blow up I flew a kite outside Parliament about the joint facilities. I did it carefully. My view was, and is, that all bargaining chips are up for negotiation or for leverage if you are being treated unfairly. Others [in the Government] did not like it at all: in fact, I was alone on that.'

Hayden raised the bases issue again several times during his period as Foreign Minister; once, in Geneva, he suggested that Australia would have to look at the agreement carefully if America didn't start getting serious about discussing arms control with Russia. Each time he mentioned the issue there would be a flurry of phone calls between Hawke and Schultz and a face-saving public explanation. But Hayden's view of the Americans, or at least his admiration of some of their policy makers, came, in time, to be very close to that of Hawke: 'In the end I came to have an enormous respect for their senior military people: their intellectual capacity, their intellectual balance, and their intellectual and personal discipline in assessing East–West relations and talking about options available to them and saying why certain options weren't tenable because of the loss of life that would be involved. I came to respect the awesome responsibilities they had.

'My attitudes in some important respects changed about the Americans. As one of the great powers of the world and one of the two superpowers, they are often going to be put in very difficult situations, making judgments as to what they should best do as between competing interests of allies on the implications arising from a particular issue. That's just got to be recognised and respected. They don't like the word hegemony, but I said it to them in Washington this year: their strategic and commercial hegemony, as much as I can see, has been a benign one and whatever way you look at the world there are going to be spheres of power, interest and influence coming from great powers. It has always been this way in modern history, and you are not going to get rid of it, no matter how much you might moralise. If you try to retreat from it you are probably going to be more vulnerable to the pressures and influences of great powers who are not as benign as you would wish. When I look around at the alternatives to the Americans, I prefer the Americans every time. They'll sometimes do things in a clumsy way, and sometimes some of their agencies will behave in a less than desirable way, but essentially I think their intentions are well-meaning. That doesn't mean we throw ourselves under their umbrella.'

As with America, Hawke and Hayden came to share a much closer view on Israel, with both moderating their positions in the light of experiences and events. In his third term of government Hawke came under severe, albeit private, criticism from hardline but influential Zionists. Hayden says: 'Hawke has been magnificent on the Middle East. First of all I got a policy up where I thought I might have trouble with him because of his emotional commitment. He can separate himself from that emotionalism. I have seen it happen a lot: he's made a number of statements which were pretty powerful. If I had made them all Hell would have broken out. He made them and got away with them because of that relationship he has with the Jewish people; therefore his role is much more significant than mine. I had to be fairly careful. Hawke warned Israel's leaders that demography would destroy them if they didn't wake up: he's talked about the legitimate rights of the Palestinians, in the Great Synagogue in Sydney.'

Hayden has expressed his ambivalence about Israel's policies towards the Palestinians directly to members of the Israeli government: 'I'm seen as having very deep sympathies with the Palestinian people, and I certainly have. I have enormous sympathy for them. I understand their problem, as would anyone who has an Irish background where the issue of land and sovereign territory has been something that has been discussed a lot in the family with feeling and bitterness. My mother was uncompromisingly hostile towards the English over what she saw as the occupation of Ireland. But for the same reason I can understand the Palestinians, and the Jews should be able to. I said this in my 1984 speech in Israel.

'I think I was the first Foreign Minister to go into the refugee camps and I did that on each occasion I've been there. They [the Israeli authorities] handled it badly, and stationed a lot of troops on the roofs.

The Israeli soldiers were very young, about Kirk's age, and I felt sorry for them.'

Hayden had been involved in the peace movement before he entered Parliament and for idealistic as well as political reasons did not want to see it isolated from the Labor Government. As Foreign Minister he was responsible for Australia playing an active role in international arms control and disarmament debates. 'It is said that Australians can't do anything in this field. That is to advocate a sort of sanctity of futility, a retreat into nothing; it never appealed to me,' Hayden says. He became Foreign Minister in Reagan's first term as President when tension between the superpowers was extreme. 'Relations between East and West were awful in the early eighties; rhetoric about evil empires and god-lessness and so on was terrifying. That's why people poured out onto the streets in their hundreds of thousands to protest. I remember talking to Bob Hawke in his office soon after the 1983 election. It was just after Palm Sunday when that huge crowd spontaneously turned out, and I said: "Bob we better watch this. We've got to move to make sure we control the argument about arms control and disarmament; our party's committed to it, we believe in it, it's important ... and if we don't, others will take the leadership by default."

'If leaders don't move early to give the right sort of leadership, and moral leadership, and make sure they are holding the reins, then the troops will take over. It's a very democratic party, particularly when you're in opposition. In Government the parliamentary party dominates the party, more now than before. But in opposition, the extra-parliamentary party reasserts its authority, and that's a very tricky area, tricky times. It's much harder to be a leader of the Opposition than the Prime Minister in that sense. But even in government it seemed to me something like this could become a problem, and lead to fissures and fragmentation within the party. I said: "The reason it's happening is a reaction against this bloody rhetoric between East and West, between Brezhnev and Reagan."

'Anyway, I put a number of propositions to Bob to show that we were willing to take the leadership, and one of them was an Ambassador for Disarmament. He thought it was a bit gimmicky, and that's not an unreasonable sort of reaction first off. Then at Question Time one day I got a question on the issue, and he whispered to me, while I was standing at the dispatch box answering the question: "Announce an Ambassador for Disarmament", so he'd obviously thought about it.

'We pursued the nuclear-free zone in the South Pacific, and we took up a whole range of initiatives. Things like that are important to the party. The Government wasn't selling out on principles the party believed in. There would be enough conflict over some issues anyway, because in government your responsibilities are much broader, and the seeming simplicity and purity of issues at party conferences gets clouded and confused and complex when you are in government because you are dealing with other countries.'

Hayden also raised human rights issues wherever he travelled.

'I even raised human rights with the Americans in respect of capital punishment under their legal system,' he recalls.

'When I raised the issue in Tibet one of the diplomats with us expelled a great stream of air and said, "God. No." But the Chinese took it. You obviously don't take everything on by the tusks, but it is important to let people know you care about these things. You don't do a lot by yourself, particularly a country our size; but, collectively, countries can do a fair bit over time. Sometimes it takes a long time; but look at the Soviet Union now. I raised human rights in Central America with Duarte in El Salvador and even with d'Aubuisson [the leader of the ultra-right-wing ARENA in El Salvador]. I told him I had seen stories that he was leader of the death squads and asked what did he have to say about that. He denied it, of course. The record for Australia has been pretty good.'

At the start of his term as Foreign Minister, Hayden had quoted Bertold Brecht to the diplomatic correspondent Niki Savva, to explain the approach he intended to take, saying: 'You can't navigate by hugging the coastline all the time. Occasionally you have to go into the open sea.'[15] Hayden's navigational skills once he embarked upon the trackless oceans were subject to some thoughtful criticism that was not purely political, and there were some common themes. 'Hayden looks at foreign policy fundamentally as an aspect of domestic politics, so the issues he pursues make more sense to his Labor Party audience than to foreign governments,' John Edwards wrote in the *Bulletin* on 26 March 1985. This, of course, is a criticism that can be applied to all countries, and in fact governments would not survive unless they operated in this way. Edwards said that there was not the remotest chance that either of the superpowers would agree to the comprehensive test ban treaty Australia was vigorously advocating. The conflict arising from Vietnam's presence in Kampuchea, which set it at odds with China, Thailand, the other ASEAN countries and the United States would continue, not because of a misunderstanding, but because the interests of the protagonists were irreconcilable.

Hayden's own reflections do not dispute the thrust of those observations but suggest they are based on the premise which he had rejected: if Australia was not to have decisive influence it would be better to do nothing. Edwards ended his critique on a note of regret:

Hayden is well aware of the constraints of Australian foreign policy. If pressed, he would probably say that the cost of taking symbolic positions is not very great and that keeps the party happy. But the cost is greater than this — the cost Australia pays is to have the energies and intelligence of one of its most experienced politicians preoccupied with grand-sounding but empty posturing, instead of the careful administration of things over which he has influence.

Hayden did not have the option of returning to a domestic portfolio where he could be a careful bookkeeper, or any desire to do so under Hawke. He did neglect foreign relations in Australia's closest area of immediate influence, the South Pacific. His interest was in the main game, and he had been given private assurances by very senior Russian authorities that the Soviet Union had no interest in establishing strategic footholds in any of the small independent nations in Australia's region. He was contemptuous of what he regarded, with some justification, as the ludicrously old-fashioned attitude that the island nations could be used by an invasion force as stepping stones to Australia.

Despite the private urging of Gough Whitlam he maintained a view that Australia should make what contributions it felt appropriate to these tiny island countries on a bilateral basis, rather than through international agencies.

Whether an alternative policy could have had better results is debatable; the fact is that, at the end of Hayden's term as Foreign Minister, Australia's immediate international neighbourhood was dotted with countries ruled by unstable regimes with their people living in pathetic social conditions marked by high infant mortality and low literacy rates.

In his critical review of Hayden's performance as Foreign Minister, Edwards referred to one of the more messy minor incidents of Hayden's term. In doing so Edwards endorsed a reported assessment of Hayden by America's Assistant Secretary for East Asian and Pacific Affairs, Paul Wolfowitz, as being one of the most incisive of analyses of his style:

'Hayden was ambiguous and unpredictable, Wolfowitz said, and seemed to enjoy the uncertainty this created in other people's minds.' Wolfowitz has been described by the respected and veteran Australian foreign correspondent Peter Hastings as an 'eager beaver' even in the context of the shrill Cold War rhetoric of the first Reagan administration, a headless coalition unified only by the self-righteous anti-Soviet blustering of its feuding elements. Washington discovered only in 1985, when a senior Russian agent, Oleg Gordievsky, defected to Britain, that all KGB stations in Western capitals had been on full alert from early 1981 to the end of 1983, believing the US was preparing to attack the Soviet Union.[16]

In Washington in October 1983, Hastings, who was at the time foreign editor of the *Sydney Morning Herald*, had an off-the-record interview with Wolfowitz during which the American made 'several pungent comments on some of Mr Hayden's alleged foreign policy views'. Without putting too fine a point on it, Wolfowitz was painting Hayden as a Communist sympathiser who was disrupting relations between the anti-Communist nations in the Pacific. 'On my return to Australia,' Hastings later wrote, 'I warned Mr Hayden in a personal letter of these comments ...' As Hastings quite properly remarked, he had not published the confidential material, and an American journalist in a similar position might well think it proper to tell George Schultz what Australians in high office were saying about him behind his back. But the warning became public as a result of actions by Hayden, and the whole incident led to more recriminations and uncertainty in American minds. Hayden worsened the situation by directing his department to take up with the Americans, through their embassy in Canberra, some of the issues raised in the private letter Hastings had written.

The right-wing Australian journalist and commentator Peter Samuel, in the *Australian* on 5 January 1984, under the heading 'Relations with US strained "due to Hayden",' said the Americans were furious because Hayden or his department had strongly endorsed Hastings. 'Why, they [the Americans] asked, would a close friend and adviser of Mr Hayden cause such trouble?' Hayden categorically denied that either he or his department had made representations on Hastings' behalf to the United States authorities that resulted in him getting the confidential briefing by Wolfowitz. After Samuel's article appeared Hayden replied in a letter that placed Hastings in a dilemma by leaving to him the option of responding on his own behalf to suggestions he had broken the rules.

Hastings did so calmly, revealing the fact of the briefing but not its substance; within hours, Wolfowitz was on the phone from Washington accusing him of a scandalous breach of faith. At the end of his own letter to the editor of the *Australian*, Hastings said: 'For my own part I regard Mr Samuel's description of strained Australian–US relations as highly unlikely, and his statement that the US Government mistrusts Mr Hayden as equally improbable.'[17] This incident, blown out of proportion as it was by the fact that a number of significant commentators were directly involved, was also clear evidence that as a result of his personal and idiosyncratic style, Hayden was under close observation by an international audience.

Part of Hayden's constant audience was made up of representatives of the Australian media. Peter Bowers said: 'Foreign Affairs was never a real challenge to him; I think he did it well enough, you know, and he developed a style, and even a bit of panache, in a way. Frankly, I found him the most interesting person to ever travel with abroad, because things were always happening from a news point of view. And if there were people he couldn't see for one reason or another, like Yasser Arafat's brother, who he couldn't see for diplomatic reasons, he'd line it up for the media to go and see, or Walid Jumblatt, the Druze leader and one of the more skilled players in Beirut. We all found ourselves sitting on a marble floor in Damascus one night with "Wally" Jumblatt. He's a great long streak of a bloke and he was bent, sort of doubled up ... rattling his worry beads on the marble floor, for two hours while we discussed the Lebanon and the Middle East conflict. Bill couldn't see him but he arranged it for us. Jumblatt offered to take us down the next day from Damascus to Beirut, but we all found we had pressing duties elsewhere. When we were leaving that night and went to get back in our taxis, all these cloaked Arabs had taken over the cab and had all their bloody weaponry all over the place ... AK 47s everywhere.'[18] Hayden tried to visit Beirut in January 1984 and had arranged meetings with Jumblatt, the Lebanese president Gemayel who was later assassinated, and the head of the Shi'ite grouping Nabih Berri. Niki Savva of the *Australian* reported from Cyprus on 19 January that the visit had been cancelled for security reasons against the wishes of Hayden who wanted to make a personal appraisal of the situation in Lebanon.

The caravan moved on: a week later Ms Savva was reporting from Luxor on the Nile under the heading 'Hayden goes head-hunting in

Egypt' that, while collecting heads was run-of-the-mill work for any politician, Bill Hayden had taken to it with a vengeance: 'Mr Hayden gave the Egyptian economy a decided fillip when he played tourist among the ancient ruins of Luxor. He showed a strong preference for the carved heads of the ancient pharoahs and their queens. By the time he gets home he will have the largest collection of King Tuts in Australia.' Hayden, who was visiting the Australian contingent of the Sinai peace-keeping force, also visited the tombs of Ramses XI and Tutankhamen at the same time as a group of women from Adelaide who recognised him. The guide then pointed him out to others as Australia's Prime Minister. 'Mr Hayden said nothing to correct him; this was put down to his partial deafness,' said Ms Savva.[19]

TWENTY THREE

No need
to be liked

*There is a suggestion that I suffer from some
inferiority complex.*

Bill Hayden

V IEWS WITHIN the Foreign Affairs Department about Hayden
were mixed and generally critical, although some officials
welcomed the shake-up he had given its hierarchy and the
challenge he had made to some of the assumptions on which the
department had previously operated. In November 1983 the head of the
department, Peter Henderson, sent a memorandum to heads of Australia's
overseas missions warning them that a major characteristic of Hayden's
style was his rigorous judgment of specific issues against his perception
of Australia's national interest.

'This concept is defined in hard-edged terms: it does not give much
weight to any imprecise need to be "liked" by any other country or group
of countries,' Henderson wrote.[1]

The gist of Henderson's message was that the sensitivities of other
countries to Australian policies were not grounds for those policies not
to be pursued. This was to be Australia's foreign policy framework as
constructed by Bill Hayden, the ex-copper from Queensland who
wouldn't be pushed around by anybody, and the politician who had once

said he would never be Labor's leader because of his abrasive personality and his willingness to take up unpopular causes when he knew them to be right.

'He wants precise details of a country's objections [to any unpopular Australian policies] and a thorough explanation of why it is in our interest that we should react to them,' Henderson told the top diplomats. 'We are serving a very practically minded government. There can be no assumption that the government will go along with policy proposals simply because of past practice, a certain disposition to move in certain directions, or, even less, because of pressure from other governments.' Henderson advised officials that Hayden expected firmly argued advice, irrespective of whether it favoured his known or suspected preconceptions, and did not wish his views to be anticipated by his department. 'It is not for the department to develop a cast-iron recommendation on any issue, but to offer Mr Hayden a range of options and to provide the analytical and factual background on which he may base his decisions.'[2]

The uncertainty principle introduced by Hayden was not to the taste of some of the shell-backed veterans of Foreign Affairs, and was also the subject of quite legitimate and well-based criticism. One of the most extraordinary public attacks on him came from a minor but long-serving diplomat named James Cumes, who, when refused an extension of his overseas service by Hayden, resigned and wrote a book entitled *A Bunch of Amateurs*, lamenting how badly Australia was governed. The book opens with a description of a meeting. Cumes does not identify the location or the participants, but makes it obvious that he and Hayden met in the Australian Government offices in Ann Street in Brisbane. The building houses the Queensland outpost of the Foreign Affairs Department and the Brisbane offices of some Federal politicians of all parties including, at the time of the meeting described, Senator Lady Florence Bjelke-Petersen. Cumes was possibly not aware that it was also where Hayden had shed his tears the day he handed over the leadership of the Labor Party to Bob Hawke.

Cumes was coming to the end of his term as Australia's Ambassador to The Hague at the time of the meeting, and wanted his overseas service extended. His description of their meeting begins: 'The office has the temporary air of a holiday home — a place lived in only a few times a year. A shortish, middle aged man, oppressed by time, hurries through the outer office, pushes open a door to semi-circumnavigate a large, empty table and sits himself on a chair on the far side. Seated, he glares defiantly.'

Cumes then describes himself as a rather taller man following in Hayden's wake and taking a seat in a visitor's chair. The description continues:

> Minister: (looking resentful) You know, don't you, that I'm seeing you at the greatest inconvenience?
> Ambassador: I'm sorry to hear that, Minister, I didn't want to inconvenience you.
> Minister: (sounding put-upon) Well, you have. Another thing. I don't like this business of going to the Prime Minister.
> Ambassador: I didn't speak to the Prime Minister ...
> Minister: Someone did. He told me I had to see you.
> Ambassador: He wouldn't have meant it like that ...
> Minister: How would you know? (petulantly) I would have seen you anyway.

The dialogue continues, suggesting that Cumes is the very model of an excellent diplomat, while Hayden is bored, uninterested and out of his depth.

> Ambassador: Would you like me to start or would you like to ask me some questions?
> Minister: (impatiently) You asked to see me, didn't you? I didn't ask to see you.
> Ambassador: Thank you Minister. Well, then, the main issues confronting us are ... He talks [and this is Cumes describing himself in a less than modest account of his own performance] in a crisp, well-disciplined style for some 10 to 15 minutes about political, economic, strategic and other relations with his country of accreditation and with the region at large.

Cumes then goes on to describe Hayden's understandable reaction:

> The Minister's attention wanders. His eyes glaze. He stifles a yawn.
> Ambassador: How do you see the Embassy, Minister? Do you think it is carrying out its functions properly — working along the right lines — doing the job you want it to do?
> Minister: (He seems rather startled by the question) Eh? Oh, yes .... The right job? (He seems to be asking himself what is the right job for an embassy.) Yes ... I think so. So far as I know ...[3]

Cumes's account of the meeting, with his parenthetical interpretations of Hayden's thoughts and mood, continues in similar vein, with Cumes eventually asking for another overseas posting at the end of his present term, and Hayden agreeing to let him know. Hayden was, in fact, saying: 'Don't call us, we'll call you.' Cumes, on the basis of his brief acquaintanceship, also analyses Hayden's character:

> Hayden, perhaps because of what he conceives to be his modest social and intellectual — 'deprived' — background, is shy of many people with whom he must deal and lacks deep confidence in himself. He seems to assume on first meeting that any fellow Australian started life less poor and 'deprived' than he did ... His native shyness and lack of assurance about his intellectual gifts and cultural background bedevil his relationships with some people. For example, a European minister who attended a conference with him reported later that Hayden 'did not like diplomats'. This applies to his own diplomats, with many of whom his relations can be nervous and from whose impedimenta he tends to distance himself. A curious feature of his visit to The Hague in 1984 was his flat refusal of all invitations to the Australian Residence, a fine house acquired by a former Labor administration and inherited by Hayden's government. [Cumes happened to be living in the house at the time Hayden refused the invitation.] He angrily countermanded an instruction to an embassy driver even to pass by it so that, if he wouldn't enter its portals, at least he could see it from the outside. 'No' he snapped heatedly. He wanted none of it.[4]

Cumes says Hayden was less brash and aggressive than many Australian ministers abroad who, he suggests, have a tendency to use coarse language and tell racy stories. He concedes, too, that Hayden was able to discuss issues intelligently and even allows that he gave the impression of being generally on the ball.

After he had been minister for a year, Hayden decided to remove Henderson as head of his department. Hayden called Henderson, a tall quietly spoken man, to his office on 8 May 1984, and told him that he was not satisfied with his performance and particularly the lack of information about foreign political situations in the briefing notes he was getting from the department. Hayden told Henderson that the fact that he was married to Heather, the daughter of Sir Robert Menzies, had not been a consideration in his decision, a remark that led Henderson to say later: 'The fact the Hayden felt it necessary to assure me that his wish to move me out had nothing to do with Sir Robert led me to think that it had everything to do with it.'[5]

Hayden refused Henderson's offer to stay on if he could take the plum position as Ambassador to the United States; Hayden merely offered some lesser diplomatic postings which Henderson refused. He then became, after John Stone, the second person to be forced to retire, with compensation, under a new section of the Public Service Act.[6] Henderson's disappointment at his dismissal was increased by the fact that Hayden had not made his dissatisfaction plain earlier; the complaint and the sacking came at the same time. Cumes commented: ' ... whatever Hayden's motives and rationalisations, his behaviour lacked style and maturity. He comes through in the affair as a brooding, devious man who suddenly pounces on his unsuspecting victim with unforgiving zeal.'[7]

Cumes's book caused a short-lived but vigorous controversy and provoked Hayden into making a lengthy statement to Parliament, sections of which were quite revealing about Hayden himself, and in particular about how intensely suspicious he could be about the motives underlying unwanted offers of hospitality. Revealing also was the fact that he felt it necessary to devote most of the statement to demonstrating that Cumes had been a hopeless failure as a diplomat, and had been judged as such by his colleagues, both his superiors and those who had worked under him.

Hayden, who spoke at the end of a debate on defence, led into his attack by saying that diplomacy must always be held up to critical scrutiny.

> The practice of foreign affairs and the concerns of defence policy intersect at a number of points. The most critical and, of course, finally important point is when diplomacy breaks down and the defence machine has to take over; that means war and that represents the ultimate failure of diplomacy ... this reminds me that the conduct of foreign policy, the diplomacy behind it, the way in which policy is developed, should therefore always be held up to critical scrutiny.[8]

He said there was no lack of appropriate critical scrutiny in Australia, but he thought he should place a number of matters on the record which would help people to get a balanced assessment, particularly of the adequacy and objectivity of Cumes. But, before doing so, Hayden defended Malcolm Fraser who had been, in Hayden's words, 'made to look something of an oaf' as well as ill-informed and inadequately briefed, in a section of the book that had been published in a weekend newspaper.

Hayden then said he had been advised very firmly by Henderson that Cumes was lazy and incompetent and should not be offered another overseas job. When Cumes returned to Australia, Henderson, true to the assessment he had given Hayden, refused to provide him with a job in

the department and he had left, 'a bitter man'. He referred to reports on
Cumes by three department heads going back to 1957 which Hayden
summed up by saying:

> What the record shows is simply this: Dr Cumes, for all of the pretensions
> he was engaged in, was indeed a personally vain and pretentious man, was
> a bully to the staff who worked under him at a series of missions, was
> incapable of good labour management of those individuals, was lazy and
> uninvolved and was very much a failure.

Hayden said he had quoted from the official record, and not his
own sentiments, to show there was absolutely no evidence indicating
that Cumes was qualified to be passing severely personally critical
judgments on people, including Fraser, who had given good service to
Australia. Then he went on to expose some of his own sensitivity
and vulnerability:

> I also attract commentary of rather a severe nature. I offer no assessment,
> however, of the justice or otherwise of that. For all I know, it may well
> be a view of me which is shared by many people, so I do not intend to
> explore reactions on that ... There is a suggestion that I suffer from some
> inferiority complex. I certainly do, and I think that is fairly evident not just
> as far as I am concerned, but as far as anybody is concerned. No one who
> was self-confident and who had any commonsense would have spent as
> much time in this Parliament as I have ... the evidence produced was that
> I did not want to go to his home and that I objected very strongly when
> the car driver sought to take me there. The story is a little different. I
> resisted strongly Cumes's ingratiating efforts, nauseating as they were, to
> try to involve me socially at his home and with himself. I knew what his
> motive was, it was to try to establish some sort of rapport as a prelude to
> slapping onto me a demand to extend his appointment ... I objected
> strongly, and resisted the proposition that I come to his home because I did
> not want to get drawn into this obvious and clumsy tactic he had adopted.

There is an element there of the essential, suspicious Hayden, with all
his awkwardness in personal relationships.

Cumes's jaundiced view of Hayden extended to rubbishing the
effectiveness of his tireless and sometimes tiresome work habits:

> Hayden mostly just sat lugubriously turning over telegrams and other
> papers dealing not with his visit to The Netherlands but with other
> politically more exciting parts of 'his' world, including especially Australia.
> Hayden seems to be more oppressed by his duties — to be working closer
> to the margin of his capacities — than some other ministers.[9]

Journalist John Hamilton, who spent a day with Hayden travelling from Ipswich to Brisbane and then Sydney, gives a description of the process:

Once aboard the TAA Airbus, Bill Hayden begins work, even before takeoff. His private secretary, Michael Costello, begins to feed him yellow files from a locked black attache case. 'He insists on reading all the cables from our embassies overseas instead of reading summaries. In Canberra the cables come in three times a day. When he is overseas he gets copies of all the cables forwarded to him via a secure telex.' There are files stamped secret. 'Other agencies also supply reports,' says Costello, 'but Bill often asks for the raw material, looks at it and makes his own assessment. He is very demanding. The economic analyst comes out all the time. He is always asking questions.'[10]

Hamilton observes Hayden annotating the cables, the reports from ambassadors and the departmental submissions.

I take a side peek at one document, a draft speech prepared for him to deliver overseas. The Hayden comment is a bit like a schoolmaster delivering judgment on a bad essay: 'This is very disappointing,' he has scrawled, 'I would have thought the following points would have been covered ...' and there they are, down the margin of the page. Later he tells me: 'The volume of paper work is terrific. I took a speed reading course once, which helps a lot. But you've got to keep on top of it otherwise it would swamp you. I get a lot done aboard aircraft. At the weekend I took one of those Qantas bags full of documents home with me from Canberra. I managed to clean up most of it on the way down to Launceston and back on Saturday ... I could make this less of a job, but I don't think I can be Foreign Minister by running a correspondence course. You've got to go out and meet people.'

John Edwards detailed the anatomy of the development of another Hayden overseas speech, to the United Nations General Assembly in October 1983:

... it was prepared in outline according to his guidelines by his department and by his personal staff in Canberra with some policy material from his disarmament ambassador Richard Butler and some prose polish in an introduction by former speechwriter Ken Randall. Hayden wrote a section claiming that economic prosperity is a prerequisite of peace and democracy in the Third World. In New York the speech was filled out by the Australian UN mission with policy material and its introduction partially rewritten to excise what the mission regarded as a sanctimonious and unhelpful demand that the UN pull its socks up. Hayden regarded the product of all this as a typical Foreign Affairs anodyne, so he and his staff rewrote the speech again. The complete copies were ready just in time to catch their Australian deadlines. As one might expect from this rundown of its creation, the speech itself was dreadful.[11]

Hayden's crisp annotations on Foreign Affairs documents became a matter of public record and controversy after he had resigned from the job before becoming Governor-General; more than 10 000 pages were leaked, Hayden believes from the department rather than his personal office, to Brian Toohey, editor of the independent magazine *The Eye*. The Government took legal action to suppress and recover the documents but was frustrated when Toohey gave an assurance that they had been destroyed.

Hayden referred in the annotations to the Indonesians as erratic and hostile people, and to the behaviour of the Malaysian Foreign Minister, Ghazalie Shafie, as 'oafish'. He was no kinder to the Japanese; commenting on a briefing paper prepared by his department for Prime Minister Bob Hawke who was to visit North Asia early in 1984, Hayden first said the document needed to be savagely pruned to about one-third of its present length, and then added: 'I think we can be a bit more direct. The fact is the Japanese soft-soap the ASEANs but are keenly interested in Indo-China in their hypocritical self-effacing way, and are flat out to get whatever advantages they can for their future benefit — let's say this, but more elegantly than I have.'[12] According to *The Eye*, Hayden also 'threw in an intriguing morsel about Israel being the source of captured Palestinian arms going to the genocidal Pol Pot forces — not a point R.J.L. Hawke was likely to make a conversational centrepiece in his official talks.' Hayden reacted sharply to a suggestion by the Australian Ambassador to Peking, Hugh Dunn, that Australia respond favourably to Chinese attempts to 'change the image of the Pol Pot group, and to reconstruct the three factions into a truly single entity'. In a note in the margin of the accompanying departmental letter of 10 January 1984, he wrote simply: 'Crikey, No!'

There was something disturbing about Hayden's exhausting attempt to be a one-man Foreign Affairs Department, bombarding his unfortunate underlings with a blizzard of memorandums. Many of his comments were perceptive and refreshing in their frankness — he told it the way he saw it; yet he reveals a distinct tendency to see the world in terms of racial stereotypes. He was commenting, usually, on the broad trends of a country's policy aims, rather than on individuals, but there were some suspect and at least subconsciously racial overtones.

There were clear dangers, too, in his work style: while he remained on his constant world-circling roundabout he would not delegate responsibility, or set priorities. He insisted on reading everything he could lay his hands on, which resulted in everything getting what amounted at times to a superficial once-over. Bogged down in petty detail, and dogmatic in his opinions, there seemed little time for proper reflection or the establishment of fresh and imaginative goals. Henderson made it clear that it was dangerous to attempt to advise him directly: he was likely to take the opposite line. His responses were subjective, and often depended on the source of the advice. All these attributes are common to some degree among effective and successful politicians. In Hayden's case, during periods of his term as Foreign Minister they appear to have been taken to extremes: the department was not to be trusted, nor the Office of National Assessments which had been established by Fraser and which coordinated intelligence relevant to Australian decisions involving other countries. Least of all to be trusted were the countries with which Australia was dealing. It was a treacherous world out there.

When, in April 1984, the Government of Papua New Guinea threatened to expel an Indonesian military attaché after a border infringement by an Indonesian aircraft, there was conflicting advice to Hayden on whether Australia should become involved. Hayden dictated a three-page memorandum to his department in the course of which, in the words of Toohey, Hayden 'foresaw an ever deepening crisis in which all the principals, except him, lacked maturity':

> I think the Papua New Guineans have behaved very foolishly in this matter, but my suspicion is that Australian domestic sympathy will be with them. My worry is that the Papua New Guineans are likely to be faced down in their rather clumsy bluff, and that, given their limited maturity and experience in such matters, might proceed with more bluster and bluff, getting deeper and deeper into a quagmire of confusion and incompetence. My belief is that we would find it extremely difficult to remain a spectator of such developments. It may be that the Indonesians respond with restraint and let the Papua New Guineans down lightly. I doubt that will happen. First, I do not believe they have sufficient maturity to do that, and especially when their military are making a play for a more influential role in their domestic politics. I would like to draw your attention to a recent Office of National Assessments document (which has more credibility for me than some other ONA assessments I have seen in recent times) which signalled to me that Foreign Minister Mochtar's position is eroding and that General Murdani appears to be promoting himself internally. I know the department has totally discounted the scenario I put forward some time ago about the potential for problems with Indonesia in respect of PNG which could

be associated with Murdani's ambitions. Frankly I find no reason for discarding those possible considerations and these factors add to my anxiousness in this matter.

Another document indicated that Hayden had been concerned to protect Prime Minister Bob Hawke's relationship with the Americans, even at the expense of potential political refugees in El Salvador whom even the Australian Security Intelligence Organisation had described as non-violent types. Members of their families had been tortured and executed, and their own lives were in peril from the horrendous murder squads established by the founder and *éminence grise* of the Arena Party, Roberto d'Aubuisson, who Hayden himself had challenged with abuses of human rights in a face-to-face meeting.

The Eye said:

> Bill found he sometimes had to explain the subtleties to ministerial colleagues. He wrote his own record of conversation after having to give Immigration Minister Stewart West a lesson in the diplomatic pitfalls in saving lives. West outlined to him on 3 June 1983, a proposal to take some refugees from some 600 political detainees about to be released in El Salvador. [Hayden wrote:] 'He [West] said they would undoubtedly be the victims of right wing "death squads", that ASIO had given an assessment of these people as non-guerilla, non-violent types. I pointed out to him that the situation was somewhat more complex. The US was strongly opposing this initiative from Australia ... and I didn't want PM Hawke to arrive in America to find he had his "ears pinned back" by the Americans, especially in circumstances that were leaked to the media. A second matter concerned the ability of the Americans to create difficulties for us within our own region, viz the ASEAN countries, at a time when we had some rather delicate tasks ahead of us.'

Hayden's torrent of notes to his department extended to detailed planning of his movements and appointments, and on the eve of a conference with ASEAN Foreign Ministers he warned Australian officials making his arrangements: 'I do not wish to tear around the hotel corridors like an overheated greyhound.' He was devastating in his reply to a departmental minute sent to him on 12 December 1983, which raised the possibility that Iran might retaliate against Australian exports if an Immigration Department proposal to allow twenty-seven anti-Khomeini students into Australia was accepted. Hayden wrote: 'On balance I think Iranian human beings have to be considered above slabs of hotel beef.'

The Toohey revelations had one interesting effect on Hayden's future plans; although arrangements had not been formalised, he intended to visit the ASEAN countries before being sworn in as Governor-General. When his scathing remarks about some of the leading figures there were published, he decided such a tour would be controversial and counter-productive. He decided to travel further afield.

In a discussion at his Ipswich home during which he reflected on his period as Foreign Minister, Hayden referred to how his attitude to the United States had changed over the five years, and then, soon afterwards, made the observation that some of the more attractive ideas for resettle-ment as part of a solution to the conflict between the Israelis and Palestinians were coming from Jews. He paused, gave a wry smile, and said: 'So, you can see ... when you start putting all these things together ... it was time for me to get out of politics. I was getting too fair minded: once you can see both sides of the argument, you're finished.'

TWENTY FOUR

The hazards
of the future

*Well, the old chap came from South
Brisbane without much hope, that's the
family background, and look where he
ended up.*

Bill Hayden

'I 'M TERRIFIED of the thought of sitting out here at home having
a few Scotches each night, probably a bit earlier each night than
the month before,' Hayden remarked to a journalist at his home
in Ipswich in February 1987.[1] This was a solitary man, bored with his
job and concerned about his future, who was already, secretly, planning
his bid to be Australia's Head of State. As early as 1984 he had indicated
an interest in the position to Hawke. At that time it was, at best, a
remote political possibility: the Governor-General of the day, Sir Ninian
Stephen, still had four years of his term to complete. But Hayden had
put his name down. He was at the head of the queue, and Hawke
owed him.

Hayden was always an ambitious man, and while an element of that
drive was to achieve something of benefit for his country and his fellow
Australians, his ambition had also been fuelled by concern for the future
economic security of himself and his family. His savings went into
investments in property, safe shelter against the hazards of the future. But
his insecurity did not seem to lessen as he accumulated assets that, by the

standards of average Australians, amounted to considerable wealth: his assets; the house in Brassall, an apartment in Sydney and a home unit in Canberra, when combined with his superannuation rights, were worth more than a million dollars at the time he was worried about developing into a lonely drinker. Nor did his financial concern lessen as his electorate became secure. As a minister in the Whitlam Government he had opposed salary rises for parliamentarians, yet as Opposition leader he had supported them, and according to one of the Hawke Government ministers he had, while Foreign Minister, strongly opposed proposals to reform the system of travelling allowances. According to this source, Hayden had stated plainly that he could not afford to maintain the mortgage payments on his three properties if the system were changed so that ministers, while away from home, did not get a generous fixed allowance, but were simply reimbursed for their outlays.

There were other elements in Hayden's professed fear of the solitary Scotch. He had confessed privately that he was concerned about his inability to maintain friendships, that he had become estranged from many people he had once been close to. Appointment to Yarralumla as Governor-General would not put any restraint on drinking; in fact his own experience with Sir John Kerr suggested rather the reverse. It is popularly accepted among old Canberra hands that when Viscount Dunrossil passed away peacefully in his sleep while in office at Yarralumla on 3 February 1961, he left a half-finished can of Victoria Bitter on his bedside table. Yarralumla was not a place that inhibited drinking, but its occupancy guaranteed that one would never need to drink alone. At one stage of his life, according to political colleagues, Hayden harboured a fear that he might follow his father's descent into alcoholism. By the time he was Labor leader and later as Foreign Minister he was an extremely moderate drinker and inclined to be sententious about drinkers among his political colleagues.

There were several considerations that Hayden weighed before reviving his push for the vice-regal job. He had, a decade earlier, thought of a career as a barrister. The crush of events had prevented him completing his legal studies, and increasing deafness now ruled out such a course. Some of his fellow ministers believed that, with his experience in foreign affairs and economics, he would have no difficulty finding prestigious and well-rewarded positions in private industry or commerce. Hayden had, though, been on the public payroll since he left school. He had no taste for business, and unlike Hawke was uncomfortable in the presence of business people. Hayden had very narrowly missed out on the one position that would have ensured his place in history; but in Parliament House, as well as portraits of prime ministers, there are also those of all Australia's governors-general. It is the next best.

Hayden was tired of the same arguments and problems being thrashed out in Cabinet. After twenty-seven years in Parliament there was nothing new for him. There was another worry: 'It is important in politics to know when your time has peaked and not stay around after it, after your time has gone,' he told me in 1989 shortly before taking up the job. 'Calwell made the big mistake of staying after his time was long gone, and that had a big influence on me. Menzies came in to the House and said: "I won't be here tomorrow," and he wasn't. When the time to get out comes, you have got to get out. There was another factor. My values were formed during the Great Depression, amid influences about "them and us", about socialism and democracy, about the Brave New World that would come out of the struggle; that's where my values came from. There's a new generation that hasn't heard about the Great Depression. They know nothing about the insecurity that came with it, the suffering, the anguish that continued for many families well into the Second World War and even after; the great legacy of bitterness and distrust about the unfairness of the system. Things are much different now. I have often found in Cabinet that I would go away tired and depressed at the end of the day. I started to think about it and ask, "What's wrong? Why am I like this?" In the Whitlam days, I'd be passionate about arguing issues, and now I wasn't passionate about them, because I knew I wouldn't win anyway. Sometimes I had been through it before and I knew it was history repeating itself ... foolishly or wisely. That's when I really realised it was a generational thing.'

'It was time to move on, to move on productively ... and this was a worthwhile place to go to. We have to have a Governor-General ... the Constitution provides that. People who oppose the Governor-General's role because they are republicans, apart from getting everything confused, are really implying, because they haven't thought their way through it, that they'd rather have someone running the thing who was very deeply committed to it, and would justify in certain circumstances using the extraordinary powers available for a governor-general. Powers such as those Kerr used. I don't think that's smart. Politicians, and I include the

British politicians who have held the position, have, I think, been more adept at handling the role and the community than the non-politicians.'

Early in 1988 Hayden telephoned Graham Richardson and invited him to his office in Parliament House where he told him he wanted to be Governor-General. He told Richardson that it would be a good thing for someone with his background, who came from humble origins, to be doing the job. Richardson sensed an insecurity about Hayden, a concern about what people thought about him and how they had assessed his career, and also got the impression that Hayden had had enough of politics and felt that he should devote more time directly to Dallas. Hayden asked Richardson to support him and to make that support clear to Hawke. Richardson immediately agreed; he was very surprised that Hayden wanted the job but believed him eminently well qualified. Richardson's conversation with Hawke lasted only a few minutes. Hayden had already spoken to the Prime Minister and Richardson got the impression that Hawke was pleased to have an opportunity to make amends to Hayden.

'To understand why he wanted the position, you have to understand the guilt he feels towards Dallas and the family,' said a staff member who knew the Haydens well. From midway through 1985, Dallas had been suffering from depression possibly associated with the menopause. It is probable that a combination of factors united to make her feel more desperate around the time of Christmas 1986. The Haydens discovered on return from an overseas trip that Siggy, their faithful German Shepherd dog which had been left in a boarding kennel, had been put down on veterinary advice without their knowledge. They had bought the dog after Dallas was attacked by a youth in her home in September 1976, and it had followed her protectively round the house and yard for a decade. A few days later Kirk, the Hayden's only son, had a car accident in Canberra. Within a week Mrs Hayden was stopped by a store security person outside Waltons store in Sydney with some cosmetics worth about $100 that she had not paid for. Bill Hayden wrote to the New South Wales Police Commissioner John Avery and gave him details of his wife's state of health. Avery spoke to her doctor and psychiatrist before forming the opinion that the police would not be able to prove guilty knowledge and that a case against her would not succeed. Avery found the police officer who had been called had not recommended prosecution. Although senior police reject many appeals for lenience in similar circumstances,

Avery had taken a similar course in nine other comparable cases in the previous nine months, and said he believed there was 'an element of tragedy' involved in the case of Mrs Hayden. The fact that the charges had not been proceeded with was leaked to the media, and there was a brief, almost furtive, campaign of vengeful whispering. Typical of the media reaction was the editorial of the Brisbane *Sunday Sun* on 25 January 1987, which said: 'Those who wish to mow down tall poppies, those who wish to return to Victorian values and those who feel cheated for any reason, should think again. The decision [by Avery] was the only one possible and it was correct.'

The Haydens knew, however, that the incident would be publicly canvassed and the debate rekindled if they proposed to move to Yarralumla. Some people who had been close to them felt that it was an extraordinary move by Bill Hayden, when deciding that he should devote more time to Dallas, to seek the leading ceremonial office in the nation, one that is under constant scrutiny, where the names of visitors and dinner guests are published daily. Although they would have more time together it would not be in the conditions of relaxed privacy that they had enjoyed gardening together in Ipswich.

The public management of the announcement was soon beyond Hayden's control; a senior member of Cabinet leaked to Alan Ramsey of the *Sydney Morning Herald* the fact that the appointment was under consideration. Few members of the Centre Left faction of the parliamentary Labor Party had ever seen Hayden as angry as he was at an after-dinner meeting in a Senate committee room soon after the speculation began. The meeting, which was also attended by John Button, was to consider a division within the faction over the appointment of Bob Hogg as national secretary of the party. Hayden said someone present in the room had been spreading rumours about him becoming Governor-General. 'I don't have any time for the person I hold responsible,' Hayden said. 'He's playing the sort of games he has played before. I would prefer he spoke to me directly instead of playing these sort of backdoor games.' Hayden never attended another Centre Left meeting.

The first political public reference to Dallas came from a predictable source, the bullet-headed leader of the National Party, Ian Sinclair. He had a hide like a rhinoceros and a few scores to settle: Hayden had shown him little mercy when Sinclair was involved in a family scandal of his own. In Parliament on 5 April 1984, Hayden had said:

The Leader of the National Party has established his price. He displayed that he is prepared to rob his father, down to the last brass farthing from his father's grave ... the Leader of the National Party, well known for his virtuoso appearances before the criminal courts and Royal Commissions of Inquiry into improper conduct.[2]

Sinclair raised the issue obliquely by saying that the role of the Governor-General was a dual job which required an effective team. 'I am saying Mrs Hayden and Mr Hayden would not be capable of fulfilling the responsibilities of the job,' he said on 11 July 1988, and when pressed to clarify his statement, added: 'If you don't know the how and the why, I suggest that 90 per cent of other Australians would know exactly what I am talking about.' Nobody had any doubt; all media reports recalled the shoplifting incident.[3] Liberal leader John Howard rang Sinclair and let it be known he was appalled and extremely annoyed. Treasurer Paul Keating, asked to comment on Sinclair's remarks, said: 'Well, he is a pretty low form of political life, and he demonstrates that every six months.' Malcolm Fraser said: 'I think the attack on Mrs Hayden was totally and absolutely unforgiveable ... it was just beyond the pale.'

The Haydens had been on an official visit to China and Tibet when Sinclair spoke. When they returned, by agreement with Hawke, Hayden decided to test public feeling on the issue of him taking the job and the reaction to Sinclair's involving Dallas in the debate, and, as a means of achieving this, agreed to a lengthy interview with Paul Lyneham on the ABC's '7.30 Report'. It was an unusually, embarrassingly open display of his feelings, and it mollified many of his enemies while making some of his supporters cringe. Lyneham opened the interview by asking Hayden if it was correct that the vice-regal job was his for the taking. Hayden said there were other things to consider, and, when asked what they were, replied: 'My wife, my family, they must come first. My obligations to people in the Labor Party, particularly my own electorate who have been such stalwarts of mine as volunteer workers, to the party generally and I guess to the community.

Lyneham: Presumably though, you are not making yourself available to discuss this publicly because you find the idea basically repugnant?

Hayden: Oh, increasingly I find it an idea with many attractions ... it is a role which has considerable public prestige and respect. If you allow for my background from infancy ... South Brisbane where we never saw a Governor-General and rarely saw a politician ... let alone ever expected that someone from that area would gain such a respected office. The more I look at it the more I find it a very interesting role. For my family's point of view I think it, if I were to decide to take it, some small reward for the extraordinary sustained sacrifices they have put up with over the many years I've been in public life ...

Lyneham: You do feel a bit guilty don't you about the burden your family has had to carry over the years?

Hayden: Oh it's a very selfish life, much more selfish than most ... I spent about half of it away from home ...

Lyneham: You've been away at some very crucial and tragic times.

Hayden: Yes, yes, of course.'

Later in the interview Lyneham said: 'Now you mentioned your wife, how important do you see the role of the vice-regal consort — is that the word, consort?'

Hayden answered: 'Companion. My wife has been a very constant companion of mine ... an undeviating supporter of mine ... Dallas has been an extraordinary successful person in doing that, a great companion, charm, if I can say so, and grace in what she's done, and done it well.

Lyneham: Now Mr Sinclair's reference to her, you have described that as hurtful, but you must have expected that someone would raise it.

Hayden: But of course.

Lyneham: Did it give you, or her, any misgivings about considering the idea further?

Hayden: No. It gave some pain but not misgivings. At the time the incident occurred which has been referred to, we received an extraordinary flood of mail ... nearly all the letters from women, in fact there were only two exceptions, were supportive and understanding. I think we men don't properly understand women at certain difficult periods in their life, the menopause is one of them. Sometimes child-bearing is one, from the letters we got. I read an article in the *Sydney Morning Herald* early this year by Beatrice Faust; and even after all these years of married life I was surprised at how little I understood women. I think we men have to try to understand a woman much better, understand crises they go through, the sort of support they need. You see, living with each other day by day, things change, but, because they change moderately each day we don't realise that over a period a big change has taken place.

Lyneham: Like suddenly realising your kids have grown?

303

Hayden: My kids have grown up but the menopause is for many women quite an awful thing.

Lyneham: Do the Australian people, do you think, have the right to have that incident involving Dallas discussed openly and frankly, or is it none of their business?

Hayden: Oh, no. No, it happened ... and when it happened it was fully publicised, the details were in the media, they have been in the media much more in recent weeks than they have before. This is an open society, much as we might find it painful and discomforting. One of the great strengths, on the other hand, is the openness of the society: we don't try to slide something in through the back door without being candid about it, or impose things on people: they make their own decision. I think, overwhelmingly the Australian public are very understanding: it's a very liberal society.'

And so it proved to be: Sinclair's intervention, in fact, guaranteed that Hayden would take the job. There was brief debate about whether or not a potential Governor-General should so openly have raised the issue of his wife's menopause on television, but, possibly because Australian men found this too delicate a subject to discuss, it soon lapsed. Sinclair was ostracised by all but a tiny section of the Opposition. By challenging Hayden's suitability for the position on the minor and all but forgotten incident involving Dallas, he compromised those who would have opposed it on other, and perhaps more persuasive, grounds. A more telling criticism of Hayden's major television appearance came from those who regarded his apparent attitude — that he and his family were owed such a position as a reward for his constant travel — as another example of self-centred indulgence. He wasn't subtle about it: asked by Lyneham what he thought was attractive about the job, Hayden said: 'It is an office of public respect and public esteem. It has its importance. I suppose, if I'm indulging myself in my selfishness, it would allow, I hope my wife, and, more particularly, our children — and, maybe one day, if I can be old-fashioned and say, if our children will settle down to their respon-sibilities and provide us with grandchildren — the opportunity for them to say: "Well, the old chap came from South Brisbane without much hope (that's the family background) and look where he ended up." That may be a small reward for them, if I decided to do it.'

Hayden was at great pains to deny he was or had been a republican, although the Opposition had been able to collect numbers of statements he had made that were critical of the office, particularly his assertion that 'the Governor-General should be put in his proper place as a ceremonial figure on leave from *The Merry Widow*'. Hayden conceded to Lyneham that some of his statements about the job had been very mocking and cynical, but explained that, in the past, he had tended to have a 'self-mocking attitude' and that the statements had been influenced by the 'atmospherics' of the times, particularly after Kerr's action of 1975. He said that it had been important to hold the Labor Party together, 'reassuring it and yet holding ourselves within the system in a constructive way, and moving ahead to try to get away from the poisoning that many people experienced in that period'.

The favourable public reaction to Hayden's performance on the '7.30 Report', and fear that public speculation raging on for months would be damaging to the Government, and the Haydens, without achieving anything, prompted Hawke to telescope the timetable. On the night of Wednesday, 17 August 1988, Hayden attended his last Cabinet meeting and said his corporate goodbye to the Government. 'Strangely, it was an awkward affair, a stilted, almost uncomfortable farewell,' wrote Alan Ramsey, his former press secretary.

> All the right things were said by Hawke and Hayden. But the atmosphere, the mood, seemed wrong. There was little camaraderie, apparently. No obvious sense of the ties that were being cut, the contemporary Labor history, peaks and troughs that Bill Hayden was taking away with him after almost 27 years, five of the most grinding of them as its leader. Hayden has always been a loner. In the end, typically, he just went out the door by himself, almost self-consciously saying goodbye, his hand shaken by just two or three colleagues who left the Cabinet table to do so, among them Peter Walsh, his drinking mate and closest friend in Government ... the departure was curiously subdued. This is mostly a hard-headed, unsentimental Government. It behaved accordingly.[4]

There was to be one more damaging controversy when the extravagance of his spending on an overseas trip in October 1988, as a prelude to taking up the position, was revealed. The man who was reportedly reluctant to break a $2 note of his own to buy a drink had no such inhibitions with public money. Documents from the department of the Prime Minister and Cabinet to an estimates committee showed he had spent $1335 on lunch for six in New York. In New York, where his only official engagement had been a meeting with the president of Fiji, he had hired a Cadillac limousine for four days at a cost of $4959, while the total bill for the seven days in the city staying at the Helmsley Palace Hotel amounted to almost $20 000. Then there was four nights at the Savoy in London at $1038 a night, and a telephone bill there of $1895. The total cost of the trip which lasted just three weeks was $61 659. Protocol prevented Hayden publicly defending himself, and no members of the Government came to his assistance. It was a distasteful episode that marred his farewell to politics and his transition to the position of Governor-General. The trip was cut short in sad circumstances when the Haydens returned to Australia to attend the funeral of Jill Blewett, wife of his former close associate Neal Blewett, the Minister for Social Security.

Hayden returned to Ipswich where he and Dallas spent the remaining months before moving to Yarralumla working daily on landscaping their large garden with brick paths, planting a miniature rainforest and building rustic steps to the front door with railway sleepers. Hayden also spent time in his workshop where he made a stand out of polished blackbean and cedar on which to mount a bronze head he had bought in Asia. Every room in the Hayden house contains artefacts, carvings, paintings, carpets, metal and earthenware pots and other items they have collected on their travels to every corner of the world. There are carpets from Kashmir, stone carvings from Africa, Chinese screens decorated with ivory figures, temple dogs from Burma, a carved wooden figure with a giant penis from New Guinea. In the garden are stone Japanese lanterns, pottery lions and large Fijian figures carved from tree ferns that were given to him by the owner of a hotel after he had admired them. Hayden began the eclectic collection long before he became Foreign Minister, but that job gave him unlimited opportunity to scour the bazaars of the world. He is sensitive about criticism of the collection by some of the journalists who travelled with him, but, while some of the pieces are of the obvious souvenir genre, it contains some very fine, interesting and valuable pieces.

At his home in Ipswich, as he sat in bare feet and a pair of shorts, interrupting reluctantly the physical labour he enjoys, I said to Hayden that many people in the Labor Party found it hard to work out why he wanted to be Governor-General. His instant reaction was to criticise his critics. It seemed to him that there was a body of people who had attempted to appropriate him to their causes. Those people had become angry when they found he did not agree with them; a recent example had occurred when he supported Education Minister John Dawkins in opposing free university education, characterised by Hayden as a very selfish policy which redistributed money to the middle class away from the working class.

'Now, I've been constantly invoked as a republican since I've taken the job; but I've never been a republican. I come from a family which was anti-ruling class, but they were as much anti-capitalist ruling class in this country as they were anti-royalist. There was, of course, on my father's side, and more pronounced on my mother's side, the Irish thing. But, I have always argued, particularly after 1975, people who rushed off arguing the case for a republic have mistaken the shadows for the substance. The power of the Governor-General exercised in 1975 was the problem: if we had a republic, or the system the way it is, or something in between, without a change in that power of the Governor-General, then the problem remains. Now, it's not going to be fixed by having an elected president or a republic, because, once you have a person elected they have public support; and once they have public support they have power they can draw on, public power. There will be a tussle between the elected president and the democratic houses of Parliament: he would be as much a democratically elected representative as they, and it would be a struggle over who is going to have power, and it could be a very nasty one. I just don't think people think their way through this.'

Hayden also made clear his view that he took immense satisfaction in the office as measuring the distance he had travelled: 'In terms of capping what has largely been a working lifetime in prominent public office by this ... largely ceremonial office, I admit, but nonetheless important and prestigious public office ... this is something of which one can say, "well, there is the final achievement". You have seen the house where we grew up in South Brisbane; it's a big step if you start measuring the size of the tread on the staircase from the bottom end of the dead-end part of Mabel Street. When we lived there it was a dirt street, we didn't have bitumen for a long time. I can remember the sewerage being put through when I was very, very small. From that to ending up as the number one figure in the ceremonial ratings of the country is something the kids can feel proud of.'

Despite the trauma of 1975, Hayden had, in fact, shown that he placed importance on the role of the Governor-General in the Australian system and was unwilling deliberately to weaken it. In one of the first significant speeches he made as Labor leader, on 28 February 1978, he even suggested that he may have held a lingering suspicion that Kerr had acted properly in November 1975. Hayden pointed out in 1978 that, until that time, he had not personally criticised Kerr. The breaking point came when Malcolm Fraser appointed Kerr as Australia's Ambassador to UNESCO. In initiating a debate on the appointment, Hayden said:

> It is a further demonstration of the degree by which the high office of Governor-General has been abused by the former incumbent for personal gain and manipulated by the Prime Minister for political advantage. The matter of Sir John Kerr's actions in November 1975 has been an issue of the most divisive political debate in the Australian community. More recently his acquiescence to the Prime Minister's request for an unnecessary election a full year before it was due similarly created widespread controversy. This latest appointment can do nothing but confirm the views of those who believe Sir John acted with gross impropriety in each case. The dimension that is added to the debate is that he did so — certainly in the most recent instance — for his 30 pieces of silver.[5]

But Hayden said he made these accusations with regret:

> I ask members to recall one fact: since November 1975 until the present they will find no record of my having said anything tough or anything personal about the previous Governor-General [Kerr] and the sacking of the Labor Government in 1975, except to express concern that he had not allowed Supply to run out before he took his precipitate action. Any reservations that I may have harboured in the deepest part of my heart about the action he took have been completely destroyed by his behaviour and that of the Prime Minister in recent times.

In his speech in February 1978, Hayden referred to a principle Kerr had set down firmly in a speech in India in February 1975, and which, in Hayden's view, he had been prepared to bury just as determinedly in late 1977. Kerr's words, quoted by Hayden, were:

> Parliament should not be dissolved early simply to help a party leader or a party solve their own difficulties. The country should not be forced to an early election merely to help leaders solve internal party questions, but only when it is necessary to deal with a situation which Parliament itself cannot solve. The decision to dissolve Parliament in mid-term is one of the matters which the Constitution leaves to the Governor-General to decide on his own.[6]

Given Australian political history, it would be surprising if Hayden were not, at some stage of his term in office, confronted with the need to make a public act of judgment on a request by the Prime Minister to dissolve Parliament for an early election.

In the same speech Hayden set down a principle that will determine his own future. After criticising Fraser for resorting to political jobbery, Hayden said:

> I shall move on because Sir John Kerr the person is not important ... What has happened in his case though implies at least that there will be rewards for tractable Governors-General. Those who are prepared to toe the line can expect that the future will not end with the termination of their periods of service as Governor-General. If they toe the line that is laid down they can expect further plums, further considerations, further comfort and accommodation.

He finished his speech by asking: 'Will governments — more precisely, will Prime Ministers — in future make Governors-General tractable by holding out the promise of plums, rewards if you prefer to be vulgar, for those who toe the line?'

Hayden was sworn in as Governor-General in an eight-minute formal ceremony that took place in the Senate chamber of the new Parliament House in Canberra beginning at three o'clock on the afternoon of 16 February 1989. There was some controversy over the fact that Hayden chose to make an affirmation, rather than swear an oath on the Bible. Prime Minister Hawke had declared the ceremony an Event of National Importance and it was telecast live by the Australian Broadcasting Corporation. Hayden stumbled slightly over the words as he read the Affirmation of Allegiance: 'I, William George Hayden, do solemnly and sincerely affirm and declare that I will be faithful and bear true allegiance to Her Majesty Queen Elizabeth the Second, Her heirs and successors according to law.' That night there was a restrained celebration at Government House to which he had invited some of his former staff members and his children.

On Good Friday, 24 March 1989, Bill and Dallas, who were then staying at Admiralty House, the Governor-General's official Sydney residence on the foreshore of the harbour opposite the Opera House, attended Mass at St Mary's Cathedral. Hayden's staff had contacted officials at the cathedral and seats were reserved for them, two staff members and security officers. There was no official reason for the visit, and Clem Lloyd, contacted as a friend of the Haydens, said, 'I couldn't offer any explanation why he was there'. He was not aware of any new interest on their part in religion. Within a month Hayden had informed the Scouts that he could not become head of their movement because he was unable to take their oath which required swearing a belief in God. Scouting officials welcomed his announcement which aborted a controversy that was being generated by some of their more crusty traditional members.

The speculation about Hayden's relationship with higher powers was taken up by a publication called *Nexus* which describes itself as the New Times magazine and which reported in its Autumn 1989 issue: 'The home town of Bill Hayden was visited by an eerie omen the month he was sworn in as Governor-General ... Ipswich was deluged by a violent downpour of squirming sardines.' It went on to say that police had verified reports that small live fish had fallen from the sky. The magazine did not take the omens too seriously, printing the report under the heading: 'The Fish John West rejects'.

Hayden confided to the Brisbane *Courier Mail*'s Glenn Stanaway at the end of April that he was spending some of his time in Government House studying philosophy to gain a better understanding of his inner self. He was planning also to change most of the paintings at Government House and to introduce modern and abstract works into the staid formal collection.[7] Hayden had previously told friends that he was uneasy about fully indulging his tastes in art at Government House because the gloomy, despairing works he favoured tended to make guests uncomfortable and uneasy.

Stanaway, the son of Jack Stanaway, a respected Queensland journalist of Hayden's generation who has worked on the staffs of leading Labor figures including Mick Young and Tom Burns, asked the natural question that comes immediately to those who have had an association with Hayden over the years: 'So what inspired a one-time republican to want to become the Queen's top man in Canberra?' Hayden by now has a well-machined response: 'I thought it would offer a new set of challenges, considerable intellectual stimulation and the opportunity for more involvement in our society with different and interesting people. I also believe it's a job I can do as well as anyone else who has held the job and better than some.' In Stanaway's words, Hayden, sipping coffee with a dash of lemon, became 'slightly testy' when it was suggested that, given his active political background, he would soon become bored.

That's so wrong. There are so many delightful things. I find people treat you very differently — it's attractive. People don't see you as a competitor or a threat as if you're an active politician. They talk more openly and candidly.

They regard you as one of them. I hadn't realised as a working politician even friends would tend to pitch their discussions with you within some mental boundaries. Now they talk openly about a range of matters. Mind you, I keep clear of political discussion.

The almost absurd and inherent contradiction in Hayden's position — after having spent half his life in politics — was neatly satirised by Clyde Cameron who, in April 1989, sent him a copy of a speech he was delivering to senior union representatives at the Clyde Cameron College suggesting there were dangers that those who would benefit from privatisation may be tempted to influence Labor leaders by making campaign donations. Cameron drew to Hayden's attention a section of the speech which said:

> In all the 31 years I was a member of the Labor Caucus, only one Leader ever offered members the right to see details of all donations made to the Leaders' Campaign Fund, commonly known as the 'slush fund'. That Leader was Bill Hayden ... he handed me all the documents and left the room while I made a minute examination of all receipts and payments from the slush fund.

Cameron in his covering note advised Hayden not to read the rest of the speech because it contained politics.

Hayden told Stanaway that it was deeply ingrained in him that social justice was the most important and worthwhile cause that could be pursued. He had recently visited a group of supporting mothers, many of whom had been bashed by their male partners, and had been deeply moved:

> [They] were delightful — all mature-aged women, extremely articulate, running self-awareness classes and helping women to understand their problems, to articulate their case for social justice. They weren't bitter about husbands or companions who'd deserted them. They even sought to understand, but not be uncritical. They had experienced wife-beating. If you'd asked me before I got there I would have expected bitterness, yet together they were working out healthy ways of responding to their experiences.[8]

Hayden said that at Government House, after only two months in the job, he had started writing about his earlier experiences and this had reactivated his interest in metaphysics and philosophy. 'Because of my background I tend to invest a very big commitment in the exercise of free will. But as I started reading metaphysics which I haven't read for many years, I must say that determinism — another school of metaphysics and philosophy — also has a very big role in my life. I might be called a soft-determinist. I enjoy getting into that area. I will be following these things up. They aren't indulgences — they are related to life, and the way we lead life. The determinist school simply argues that there are things over which we can't exercise free will because of circumstances, environmental experiences, conditioning. Now, some of us are able to exercise a greater deal of free will than others because we've been more fortunate in experiences we've had in life and the opportunities which have opened to us have shown how we can exercise free will. The freedom school is one of accepting ultimate responsibility for your acts, which is something I guess most of us have to do, rather than blame others.'

There was something sad and excessively self-effacing about Hayden's answer when he was asked to list his most rewarding achievements; but the deserted mothers were still in his mind: 'You get to my age and think, where have I been and what have I done? The great moments that seemed almost Olympian, they seem to have shrunk into the landscape — it's hard to see them. You wonder how meaningful life has been. Then, like dealing with those supporting mothers who did not realise I initiated the supporting mothers' program, others come after you and build on what you have built. So it gives me pleasure as I come to terms with my life to know I was part of social evolutionary developments which are still going on. Instead of seeing a high-water mark somewhere, there's a smudge where a small ripple ran through. That's better than nothing.'

Hayden's reflections, in April 1989, on how he had been moved by his meeting with supporting mothers who had been the victims of violence, his sad assessment of his achievements as representing a smudge where a small ripple ran through, and his enjoyment at rediscovering pleasure in studying metaphysics and philosophy reminded me sharply of a spontaneous remark that had been made to me about him when I was working on this book. Before he had accepted the position as Australia's Head of State, I was discussing Hayden with Anne Warner, then the only Labor Party woman holding a seat in the Queensland Parliament. As a member of the Socialist Left faction she had had her share of disagreements with him. In 1988, she said: 'He's a progressive, a political practitioner and an intellectual ... so, of course, he's going to be a tortured soul.'

Endnotes

Much of the material in this book is derived from interviews with Bill Hayden and others. I conducted interviews with Hayden at his home in Ipswich in 1988 and 1989 and in Canberra in 1988; throughout the book there is extensive quotation from these interviews. Interviews with other politicians, with journalists or with staff members are acknowledged in the notes, as is information gained from such people more informally. Some former staff members and others who gave information have wished to remain anonymous.

Books listed in the bibliography are cited in the notes by short title only.

Chapter 1

1   Peter Bowers *Sydney Morning Herald (SMH)* 17 February 1988.

2   Early in 1972 it seemed likely that the Australian Labor Party would, under the leadership of Gough Whitlam, come to power at the election to be held later that year. Labor had spent more than two decades in the political wilderness. John Edwards, then working for the *Australian Financial Review (AFR)*, began writing a series of profiles of members of the Opposition who would be likely to play an important part in a Labor government. His article on Hayden, published in the *AFR* on 29 June 1972, stands as the most revealing and perceptive article to have been written about Hayden. But Hayden kept secrets from Edwards. In 1989 I obtained a copy of a letter dated 10 February 1972 that Hayden had written to Edwards while he was working on that article. The quotation is from that letter.

3   Bill Hayden's impression from early family memories has been that his mother's first husband had drowned in a dam on an outback station. When I obtained the death certificate of Cornelius Claude

Quinn, male, thirty-one years, shearer, who had died of asphyxia by drowning (accidental), I suspected there was a mistake in the transcription. On the line that required an answer to the question 'when died and where' the certificate says: 31 January 1926 Con Hole, Boulia Road, Winton. Many western Queensland towns have deep and permanent waterholes that do not dry out even in extended drought, and in them survive the largest and most prized Australian freshwater fish, the Murray cod. These places are commonly known as the 'Cod Hole'. Bill Glasson, Minister for Land Management in Queensland in 1989, who represents the area, has told me that the Con Hole where Quinn drowned is a popular, though remote, recreation area that is treacherous in flood. I have it on his authority that A.B. 'Banjo' Paterson camped near there on his way from Elersly to Dagworth station on the night before he wrote 'Waltzing Matilda', Australia's unofficial national anthem which ends with a drowning.

4   Murphy *Hayden* p.3.
5   A.B. Paterson (ed.) *Old Bush Songs* Sydney: Angus & Robertson, 8th edn, 1932. Another version called 'Two Professional Hums' was collected by Warren Fahey in Broken Hill and published in *Eureka: the songs that made Australia famous* Hackney, SA: Omnibus Press, 1984.
6   C.G. Law 'Sugar Bag Days: the 1930s Depression in Brisbane' in *Brisbane Retrospect: eight aspects of Brisbane history* Brisbane: Library Board of Queensland, 1978, p.50.
7   Fitzgerald *From 1915 to the Early 1980s* pp.167–68.
8   Betty Surmon, interview with author, 1988.
9   Janet Hawley, *Courier Mail* 9 October 1980.
10 Edwards, *AFR* 29 June 1972.

Chapter 2

1   *Bulletin* 26 March 1977.
2   Hawley, *Courier Mail* 9 October 1980.
3   Gary O'Neil, interview with author, 1988.
4   Hawley, *Courier Mail* 9 October 1980.
5   Telegram in possession of Sir James Killen.
6   Copy of letter held by author.
7   Don Cameron, interview with author, 1988.
8   Natalie Funnell, interview with author, 1988.
9   Edwards, *AFR* 29 June 1972.

10 Hawley, *Courier Mail* 9 October 1980.
11 Chris Bennett, interview with author, 1988.

Chapter 3

1 *Australian Penthouse* September 1980, p.35.
2 Betty Surmon, interview with author, 1988.
3 Ed Casey, interview with author, 1988.
4 *Australian Penthouse* September 1980.
5 Ted Loane, interview with author, 1988.
6 Norm Gulbransen, interview with author, 1988.
7 *Trend* February 1970, pp.21–23.
8 ibid. p.23.

Chapter 4

1 Hayden to Edwards, 10 February 1972.
2 Murphy *Hayden* p.7.
3 ibid.
4 Murray *The Split* p.307.
5 For a concise account of the turbulent history of factionalism and disputation in the Queensland ALP see Swan in Parkin and Warhust *Machine Politics* esp. p.103.
6 See Whitlam and Stubbs *Nest of Traitors*.
7 Edwards, *AFR* 29 June 1972.
8 Sally Loane, *The Age* 13 August 1988.
9 See Murphy *Hayden* p.9.
10 Edwards, *AFR* 29 June 1972.
11 Murphy *Hayden* p.10.
12 See ibid. pp.10–12.
13 12 March 1977.
14 Murphy *Hayden* p.1.

Chapter 5

1 *Queensland Times* 14 December 1961.
2 Peter Bowers, interview with author, 1988.
3 Edwards, *AFR* 29 June 1972.
4 *Commonwealth Parliamentary Debates* House of Representatives *(CPD)* 1 March 1962, pp.423–27. The quotations in the following pages are from this speech.

5 Edwards *AFR* 29 June 1972.
6 Murphy *Hayden* p.1.
7 Tom Uren, interview with author, 1988.
8 *National Times* 16 August 1977.
9 *CPD* 10 October 1962, p.1337.
10 Denis Murphy 'Bill Hayden — a profile' *Labor Forum* 1, 3, 1978, p.20.
11 Edwards, *AFR* 29 June 1972.
12 Killen *Inside Australian Politics* p.51.
13 Freudenberg *A Certain Grandeur* pp.19–21.
14 Wayne Swan, interview with author, 1988.
15 2 December 1963.
16 Murphy *Hayden* pp.20–21 and interviews with staff.
17 Hayden to Edwards, 10 February 1972.
18 *CPD* 17 March 1966, p.371.
19 Murphy *Hayden* p.23.
20 ibid. p.25.

Chapter 6

1 Freudenberg *A Certain Grandeur* p.24.
2 ibid. p.34.
3 Peter Bowers, discussion with author, 1966.
4 Gough Whitlam, interview with author, 1989.
5 *Canberra Times* 26 March 1966.
6 *CPD* 19 August 1965, pp.268–72. Several quotations from this speech follow.
7 See Freudenberg *A Certain Grandeur* pp.51–53.
8 For a person of Jessie Street's connections — she was wife of one Chief Justice of New South Wales, and mother of another — it was unusual to take an active interest in what was then a very lonely cause.
9 Murphy *Hayden* p.28.
10 Sally Loane, *The Age* 13 August 1988.

Chapter 7

1 Edwards, *AFR* 29 June 1972.
2 Tom Uren, interview with author, 1988.
3 Murphy *Hayden* p.31.
4 Edwards, *AFR* 29 June 1972.

5   *CPD* 22 February 1967, p.72.
6   *National Times* July 4–10 1982.

Chapter 8

1   Clyde Cameron, interview with author, 1988.
2   *Canberra Times* 17 March 1977.
3   See Oakes *Whitlam PM* pp.13–46.
4   *Australian Penthouse* September 1980, p.38.
5   *CPD* 17 March 1966, p.371.
6   *CPD* 8 May 1968, pp.1210–13.
7   *CPD* 9 October 1968, pp.1735–38.
8   *CPD* 20 March 1969, pp.776–80.
9   John Stubbs *The Hidden People: poverty in Australia* Melbourne: Cheshire/Lansdowne, 1966.
10 Eric Walsh, interview with author, 1989.
11 Murphy *Hayden* pp.44–45.
12 'I was a recipient of the statements and sometimes an observer during their preparation.'

Chapter 9

1   Freudenberg *A Certain Grandeur* p.102.
2   ibid. p.105.
3   Retold by Clyde Cameron to author, 1988.
4   Clyde Cameron to author. The story had been told to him by Hayden, who confirmed it in a later interview with the author.
5   This is one of the Queensland ALP's best remembered incidents. This version is a combination of the recollections of Tom Burns, Jack Stanaway and Norm Harradine.
6   Murphy *Hayden* p.39.
7   Edwards, *AFR* 29 June 1972.
8   *The Age* 13 April 1971.
9   Caucus Minutes July 1972.
10 *CPD* 12 March 1970, pp.365–68.
11 Edwards, *AFR* 29 June 1972.
12 National Superannuation Scheme, Outline of Proposals, 3 March 1972 at conference arranged by Pensioners Reform Campaign Committee, Melbourne.
13 Fabian newsletter, July–August 1972, p.9.

14   ibid. p.8.
15   ibid.
16   Edwards, *AFR* 29 June 1972.

Chapter 10

1   Murphy *Hayden* p.68.
2   Whitlam *The Whitlam Government* p.341.
3   ibid. p.329.
4   Murphy *Hayden* p.69.
5   *Courier Mail* 5 December 1972.
6   ibid.
7   *SMH* 6 July 1973.
8   'This Day Tonight' 6 August 1973.
9   *Canberra Times* 28 November 1979.
10   Murphy *Hayden* p.72.
11   *CPD* 13 March 1974, pp.2853–55.
12   Lunn *Johannes Bjelke-Petersen* p.106.
13   *Australian Penthouse* September 1980, p.40.
14   ibid.
15   Freudenberg *A Certain Grandeur* p.289.
16   Bill Hayden, Arthur Calwell Memorial Lecture, Monash University, 22 September 1975.
17   Freudenberg *A Certain Grandeur* p.296.
18   Murphy *Hayden* p.83.
19   Whitlam *The Whitlam Government* p.349.

Chapter 11

1   Confidential interviews with a number of those present. Subsequent information on meetings of the economics committee comes from the same source.
2   See Hughes in Patience and Head *From Whitlam to Fraser* p.12.
3   Sydney *Sun* 28 July 1974.
4   Clyde Cameron, interview with author, 1988.
5   d'Alpuget *Robert J. Hawke* p.212.
6   Cumes *A Bunch of Amateurs* p.16.
7   ibid.
8   *Queensland Times* 7 March 1987.
9   Murphy *Hayden* p.101.

10 Copy made available to author.
11 Hughes in *From Whitlam to Fraser* p.24.
12 Oakes *Crash Through or Crash* p.114.
13 Interviews with observers and participants, including Hayden and Whitlam.

Chapter 12

1 Lloyd and Clark *Kerr's King Hit!* p.118.
2 ibid. p.128.
3 Norm Harriden, interview with author, 1988.
4 Gay Raby, interview with author, 1988.
5 Cairns *Oil in Troubled Waters* pp.102–3.
6 Norm Harriden, interview with author, 1988.
7 *Australian* 16 August 1975.
8 Di Fingelton, interview with author, 1988.
9 Freudenberg *A Certain Grandeur* pp.17–18.
10 Di Fingelton, interview with author, 1988, and other staff members.
11 Murphy *Hayden* p.130.
12 Copy of memo held by author.
13 Gay Raby, interview with author, 1988. FAS is, of course, bureaucrat-speak for first assistant secretary, VDRs for variable deposit ratios, SDRs special drawing rights, and PPS for principal private secretary. (RS: ratshit.)
14 Douglas was the originator of a fringe economic and political doctrine known as Douglas Credit, based on a belief in lavish spending on credit. Social credit philosophies had a strong following in Oxley in the early 1960s and according to Denis Murphy one of the basic reasons Hayden had studied economics was to be able to refute their arguments (*Hayden* p.17).
15 Hayden's Budget planned for growth in outlays of 22.9 per cent compared with estimated growth in wages of 22 per cent and an estimated 25.2 per cent increase in tax receipts, to yield a forecast domestic deficit of $2068 million. Hughes in Patience and Head *From Whitlam to Fraser* p.31.

Chapter 13

1 Oakes *Crash Through or Crash* p.174.
2 ibid. p.186.

3   McClelland *Stirring the Possum* pp.170–71.
4   Gay Raby, interview with author, 1988.
5   Cohen *The Life of the Party* p.56.
6   Whitlam *The Truth of the Matter* p.xi.
7   Letter held by Clyde Cameron.
8   Elizabeth Johnston, *Australian* 8 March 1983.
9   Norm Harriden, interview with author, 1988.

Chapter 14

1   Graham Freudenberg, interview with author, 1988.
2   d'Alpuget *Robert J. Hawke* p.291.
3   Murphy *Hayden* p.152.
4   *SMH* 14 January 1976.
5   ibid.
6   *Courier Mail* 15 January 1976.
7   ibid.
8   Dallas Hayden, interview with author, 1989.
9   d'Alpuget *Robert J. Hawke* p.296.

Chapter 15

1   Freudenberg *A Certain Grandeur* p.415.
2   Oakes *Crash Through or Crash* p.294.
3   Murphy *Hayden* p.152.
4   Caucus Minutes 7 April 1976.
5   Documents in possession of Sir James Killen, made available to author.
6   Murphy *Hayden* p.153.
7   George Munster, *Nation Review* 29 September–5 October 1977.
8   Peter Samuels and Jacqueline Rees, *Bulletin* 26 March 1977.
9   Murphy *Hayden* p.156.
10 *Courier Mail* 13 July 1976.
11 Murphy *Hayden* p.186.
12 Gough Whitlam, interview with author, 1989.
13 *Bulletin* 26 March 1977.
14 McClelland *Stirring the Possum* p.163.
15 Sydney *Sun* 18 March 1977.
16 Cohen *After the Party*. The following quotations are from pp.148–50.
17 McClelland *Stirring the Possum* p.193.
18 Laurie Oakes, *Sun Pictorial* 9 July 1977.

Chapter 16

1 Mick Young, interview with author, 1988.
2 *Australian* 31 May 1977.
3 ibid.
4 Michelle Grattan, *The Age* 14 January 1978.
5 Caucus Minutes 2 February 1978.
6 Graham Richardson, interview with author, 1988.
7 Kelly *The Hawke Ascendancy* p.79.
8 *SMH* 9 May 1978.
9 Michelle Grattan, *The Age* 16 May 1978.
10 Note held by Sir James Killen and made available to author.
11 *National Times* 6 May 1978.
12 Caucus Minutes 14 August 1978.
13 Kim Swan, interview with author, 1988.
14 *Bulletin* 13 March 1979, p.56.
15 Gay Raby, interview with author, 1988.
16 Michael Sexton, interview with author, 1988.
17 Dick Klugman, interview with author, 1988.
18 Peter Walsh, interview with author, 1988.
19 d'Alpuget *Robert J. Hawke* p.374.
20 ibid.
21 Graham Richardson, interview with author, 1988.
22 Kelly *The Hawke Ascendancy* pp.81–82.
23 *National Times* 28 July 1979.

Chapter 17

1 Craig McGregor, *SMH* 31 December 1979.
2 Graham Richardson, interview with author, 1988.
3 Steketee and Cockburn *Wran* p.256.
4 ibid.
5 ibid.
6 ibid. p.257.
7 ibid. p.258.
8 Kelly *The Hawke Ascendancy* p.84.
9 Ayres *Malcolm Fraser* p.666.
10 Caucus Minutes 10 February 1980.
11 Ayres *Malcolm Fraser* p.367.

12 ibid. p.369.
13 Swan in Parkin and Warhurst *Machine Politics* p.115.
14 ibid. p.118.
15 *Australian* 1 August 1978.
16 *Courier Mail* 12 July 1978.
17 *Australian* 1 August 1978.
18 Swan in *Machine Politics* p.120.
19 ibid. p.121.
20 Max Jessop, *Australian* 1 March 1979.
21 Swan in *Machine Politics* p.123.
22 *National Times* 24 February–1 March 1980.
23 Mick Young, interview with author, 1988.
24 *Australian* 5 April 1980.
25 Swan in *Machine Politics* p.124.
26 *Courier Mail* 3 July 1981.
27 Kelly *The Hawke Ascendancy* p.81.

Chapter 18

1 d'Alpuget *Robert J. Hawke* p.400.
2 Peter Bowers, interview with author, 1988.
3 d'Alpuget *Robert J. Hawke* p.401.
4 Geoff Kitney, *National Times* 4–10 July 1982.
5 ibid.
6 Graham Richardson, interview with author, 1988.
7 Kelly *The Hawke Ascendancy* p.173.
8 ibid. p.175.
9 *The Courier Mail* July 1983.
10 *SMH* 10 June 1982.
11 Kelly *The Hawke Ascendancy* p.185.
12 *National Times* 4–10 July 1982.
13 Kelly *The Hawke Ascendancy* p.190.
14 ibid. p.195.
15 ibid. p.202.
16 ibid. p.206.
17 Carew *Keating* p.63.
18 The *Age* 17 July 1982.
19 See Carew *Keating* p.63–64.

Chapter 19

1   *SMH* 5 April 1982.
2   Ayers *Malcolm Fraser* p.425.
3   *Australian* 8 November 1982.
4   Kelly *The Hawke Ascendancy* p.316.
5   ibid. p.317.
6   Peter Bowers, interview with author, 1988.
7   ibid.
8   Graham Richardson, interview with author, 1988.
9   Kelly *The Hawke Ascendancy* p.206-7.
10 d'Alpuget *Robert J. Hawke* p.404.
11 *National Times* 13-18 March 1983.
12 Kelly *The Hawke Ascendancy* p.346-47.
13 Carow *Keating* p.66.
14 *Australian* 3 February 1983.

Chapter 20

1   Kelly *The Hawke Ascendancy* p.383.
2   *Australian* 4 February 1983. The sentence in square brackets is not
    in the *Australian* but is in the *Courier Mail* of the same date and in
    Kelly pp.388-89.
3   Deane Wells, interview with author, 1989.

Chapter 21

1   Ric Allen, *Sunday Mail* 6 March 1983.
2   ibid.
3   *Advertiser* 11 May 1983.
4   *Sunday Mail* 6 March 1983.
5   *Courier Mail* 4 February 1983.
6   *Sunday Mail* 6 February 1983.
7   *Courier Mail* 12 February 1983.
8   Peter Hamer, Brisbane *Telegraph* 23 February 1983.
9   Paul Lynch, *Australian* 16 February 1983.
10 Ric Allen, *Sunday Mail* 6 March 1983.
11 Copies held by author.
12 Elizabeth Johnston, *Australian* 8 March 1983.
13 ibid.

Chapter 22

1   d'Alpuget *Robert J. Hawke* p.248.
2   John Edwards, *Bulletin* 25 October 1983.
3   Brian Toohey, *The Eye* September 1988.
4   *Australian* 25 February 1983.
5   ibid.
6   ibid.
7   Kelly *The Hawke Ascendancy* pp.77–78.
8   Peter Smark, *Advertiser* 11 May 1983.
9   ibid.
10 Gay Raby, interview with author, 1988.
11 Peter Smark, *Advertiser* 11 May 1983.
12 John Edwards, *Bulletin* 25 October 1983.
13 ibid.
14 *Bulletin* 26 March 1985.
15 Niki Savva, *Courier Mail* 27 June 1983.
16 *New Yorker* 2 January 1989.
17 *Australian* 8 January 1984.
18 Peter Bowers, interview with author, 1988.
19 *Australian* 27 January 1984.

Chapter 23

1   *Courier Mail* 27 November 1983.
2   ibid.
3   Cumes *A Bunch of Amateurs* pp.vi, vii, viii.
4   ibid. p.25.
5   *Courier Mail* 5 September 1986.
6   *Australian* 30 January 1985.
7   Cumes *A Bunch of Amateurs* p.115.
8   *CPD* 23 March 1988 p.1237.
9   Cumes *A Bunch of Amateurs* p.22.
10 John Hamilton, *Courier Mail* 4 August 1984.
11 *Bulletin* 25 October 1983.
12 Brian Toohey, *The Eye* September 1988. The quotations that follow are from this source.

Chapter 24

1   *Queensland Times* 23 February 1987.
2   *CPD* 5 April 1984.
3   *Australian* 12 July 1988.
4   Alan Ramsey, *SMH* 20 August 1988.
5   *CPD* 28 February 1978, pp.207–9.
6   ibid.
7   Glenn Stanaway, *Courier Mail* 24 April 1989.
8   ibid.

Bibliography

Ayres, Philip J. *Malcolm Fraser: a biography* Melbourne: Heinemann, 1987

Blazey, Peter and Andrew Campbell *The Political Dice Men* Vic.: Outback Press, 1974

Cairns, Jim *Oil in Troubled Waters* Melbourne: Widescope, 1976

Carew, Edna *Keating: a biography* Sydney: Allen & Unwin, 1988

Chalmers, Rob and Jenny Hutchison *Inside Canberra: a guide to Australian Federal politics* Melbourne: Currey O'Neil, rev. edn, 1983

Cohen, Barry *The Life of the Party: political anecdotes* Penguin Australia, 1987

—— *After the Party: political anecdotes* Penguin Australia, 1988

Cumes, J.A. *A Bunch of Amateurs* Melbourne: Sun Books/Macmillan, 1988

d'Alpuget, Blanche *Robert J. Hawke: a biography* Melbourne: Penguin Australia/Schwartz Publishing Group, 1984

Dunstan, Don *Felicia: the political memoirs of Don Dunstan* Melbourne: Macmillan, 1981

Fitzgerald, Ross *From 1915 to the early 1980s: a history of Queensland* St Lucia: University of Queensland Press, 1984

Fitzgerald, Ross and Harold Thornton *Labor in Queensland: from the 1880s to 1988* St Lucia: University of Queensland Press, 1989

Freudenberg, Graham *A Certain Grandeur: Gough Whitlam in politics* Melbourne: Sun Books, 1978

Hughes, Barry 'The Economy' in Allan Patience and Brian Head (eds) *From Whitlam to Fraser: reform and reaction in Australian politics* Melbourne: Oxford University Press, 1979

Hurst, John *Hawke: the definitive biography* Sydney: Angus & Robertson, 1979

Kelly, Paul *The Hawke Ascendancy* Sydney: Angus & Robertson, 1984

Killen, James *Killen: inside Australian politics* Sydney: Methuen Haynes, 1985

Lloyd, Clem and Andrew Clark *Kerr's King Hit!* Melbourne: Cassell, 1976

Lloyd, C.J. and G.S. Reid *Out of the Wilderness: the return of Labor* Melbourne: Cassell, 1974

Lunn, Hugh *Johannes Bjelke-Petersen: a political biography* St Lucia: University of Queensland Press, 2nd edn, 1984

McClelland, James *Stirring the Possum: a political autobiography* Penguin Australia, 1989

McGregor, Craig *Time of Testing: the Bob Hawke victory* Penguin Australia, 1983

Murphy, Denis *Hayden: a political biography* Sydney: Angus & Robertson, 1980

Murray, Robert *The Split: Australian Labor in the fifties* Melbourne: F.W. Cheshire, 1970

Oakes, Laurie *Crash Through or Crash: the unmaking of a prime minister* Drummond Vic., 1976

—— *Whitlam PM: a biography* Sydney: Angus & Robertson, 1973

Oakes, Laurie and David Solomon *The Making of an Australian Prime Minister* Melbourne: Cheshire, 1973

Steketee, Michael and Milton Cockburn *Wran: an unauthorised biography* Sydney: Allen & Unwin, 1986

Swan, Wayne 'Queensland: Labor's graveyard?' in Andrew Parkin and John Warhurst (eds) *Machine Politics in the Australian Labor Party* Sydney: Allen & Unwin, 1983

Toohey, Brian and Marian Wilkinson *The Book of Leaks: exposés in defence of the public's right to know* Sydney: Angus & Robertson, 1987

Walter, James *The Leader: a political biography of Gough Whitlam* St Lucia: University of Queensland Press, 1980

Whitlam, Gough *The Truth of the Matter* Penguin Australia, 1979

—— *The Whitlam Government, 1972–1975* Penguin Australia, 1985

Whitlam, Nicholas and John Stubbs *Nest of Traitors: the Petrov Affair* Brisbane: Jacaranda Press, 1984